Table of Contents

Chapter 1: The Early Life and Inspirations of Nagai
Chapter 2: The Coming of the Europeans
Chapter 3: At the Nagasaki Medical College
Chapter 4: The Impact of *Pensées*
Chapter 5: The Suffering Christians
Chapter 6: The Bells of Nagasaki in Urakami
Chapter 7: Beyond This Peaceful Scene
Chapter 8: Obsession with X-Ray Technology
Chapter 9: "Please Come Back, I Will Be Praying for You"
Chapter 10: The Summons
Chapter 11: "Father... I Don't Even Know Why I Came"
Chapter 12: "I've Argued with My Father—He's Sure I'm Lost"
Chapter 13: The Graceful Wife
Chapter 14: "But What Peace? What Justice?"
Chapter 15: "One Day, This Place Might Not Exist"
Chapter 16: "No Need for That, Nagai-kun—You've Carried More Than Anyone Could Ask"
Chapter 17: Midori—A Woman Who Never Faltered
Chapter 18: *Fat Man*—The 4.5-Ton Atomic Bomb
Chapter 19: "I'm Seeing Hell! Hell!"
Chapter 20: When Night Fell on August 10
Chapter 21: "But Midori—What Had Become of Her?"
Chapter 22: The Potsdam Proclamation
Chapter 23: "I See Something of God's Greater Plan"
Chapter 24: *Nyokodō* (The Hut of Love)
Chapter 25: The Little Girl Kayano
Chapter 26: His Death (The Fall of the Iroko)
Chapter 27: Funeral and Legacy

Chapter 1

The Early Life and Inspirations of Nagai

Takashi Nagai was born in the peaceful, scenic region of Shimane Prefecture, nestled along the Sea of Japan. It's a place known for its rugged mountains and long, sweeping coastline—where icy winds from Siberia roll in during winter, covering the valleys in thick snow. You can easily imagine why early travelers from China and Korea might have passed through this remote corner of Japan, hoping to find new beginnings in a distant land. The terrain is wild and tough, but also breathtaking—rich, volcanic soil feeding thick forests that make the land feel vibrant and full of life. It's the kind of place that seems to breathe with the rhythms of nature, shaped over ages by powerful forces.

Japan's story, geologically speaking, began millions of years ago when it still lay beneath the ocean. Earthquakes, volcanic eruptions, and shifting glaciers slowly pushed the land up from the depths. Over time, these dramatic changes carved out the deep valleys and rich plains that define the islands today. Humans have lived here for thousands of years, and around the same time the Roman Empire rose in the West, Japan was experiencing its own cultural awakening. As early Japanese societies formed their own ways of life—governance, spirituality, and traditions—a powerful clan eventually established control, laying the foundation for Japan's first capital in what is now Nara Prefecture.

Before writing ever existed, the Japanese people kept their history and beliefs alive through stories passed down by word of mouth. Many of these tales were rooted in Shinto, their native spiritual tradition. One of the most sacred sites in this belief system, the Izumo Shrine, stands in Shimane. It's deeply tied to ancient myths—stories of gods, monsters, and legendary heroes that still echo through Japanese culture today.

Growing up surrounded by these legends, young Takashi Nagai would have absorbed them like air. They weren't just stories; they were part of the world around him. These myths helped shape his view of life, instilling a deep respect for his culture and a quiet pride in being Japanese.

In the quiet hills south of Izumo, just beyond the small town of Mitoya, there's a little village that seems almost frozen in time. Tucked between gently rolling mountains, this village is home to a few old-style houses—some still standing with thick, thatched roofs made from miscanthus reeds, a grass once widely used across rural Japan. These roofs weren't just for looks—they were smartly designed to keep the homes cool in summer and warm during the bitter winters. And they had a natural charm, blending effortlessly with the landscape around them. But as Japan modernized and the cost of maintaining these roofs went up, fewer people kept the tradition alive. Many of the old houses were either left to crumble or replaced by modern buildings.

One of these traditional homes, though, has been lovingly preserved. It once belonged to Takashi Nagai and is now cared for by his cousin, Saburo Yasuda. The house still stands just as it did when Nagai was a boy—a living memory of the past, and a sign of the deep respect the Nagai family holds for their roots.

Not far from the house lies a small, peaceful cemetery where Nagai's parents and grandparents are buried. Their graves are marked not with the usual carved stones seen in Buddhist cemeteries, but with simple, uncut stones. This choice reflects the Shinto view that the divine is found in nature—in its most raw and untouched form. There's something deeply moving about these natural markers. They don't call attention to themselves, but instead blend into the earth around them. They quietly say that the land remembers—that the soil holds the stories, the lives, and the spirits of those who came before.

The Nagai family carried a legacy of honor rooted in both traditional medicine and samurai heritage. Takashi's grandfather, Fumitaka Nagai, was a village doctor who practiced *kampo yaku*—an ancient form of Chinese herbal medicine handed down through generations. The local farmers held him in high regard, relying on his deep knowledge of herbs and natural treatments to care for their ailments. In the village of Tai, where he worked, people began calling it "the well in the rice fields"—a place where healing flowed as freely as the water from the wells. Fumitaka's work wasn't just about medicine; it reflected a deep respect for nature and its quiet, restorative power—values that shaped not only his practice but the heart of the whole community.

There's something timeless about the bond between the people of Shimane and the land they live on. It's a way of life grounded in simplicity, humility, and wisdom—an unspoken understanding that nature isn't just a resource, but something sacred. From the wild beauty of the countryside to the unadorned graves of Takashi's ancestors and the healing art of *kampo yaku*, everything seems to speak the same quiet truth: life, in its purest form, deserves reverence. This was the world Takashi Nagai was born into—a legacy of simplicity and respect that would guide him as he faced the trials and tragedies that awaited him later in life. His childhood, surrounded by folk tales, gods, and a tight-knit community, became the roots of the remarkable man he would one day become.

Takashi's father, Noboru, was a different story altogether. Though his name meant "calm," his early years were anything but. Wild and rebellious, young Noboru was expelled from not one or two, but six different schools. It must have broken Fumitaka's heart, yet he never gave up on his son. Instead of forcing him back into another rigid classroom, he tried a new path—bringing in a private tutor, hoping that one-on-one lessons might succeed where the school system had failed. But even the tutor, without the structure and support of a formal setting, eventually gave in to Noboru's lack of interest.

Through it all, Fumitaka remained steady. He didn't raise his voice or lose hope. Deep down, he knew that some lessons couldn't be learned from books or lectures. So, as a last attempt to guide his son, he sent Noboru to work on a nearby farm. Fumitaka believed the land had its own way of teaching—through sweat, patience, and the rhythm of the seasons. Maybe the earth could reach his son in ways he couldn't.

It was out there in the fields, under the open sky and among the rugged hills, that something began to change in Noboru. The daily work—planting rice, climbing the slopes to tend trees rooted in difficult soil—slowly grounded him. Nature, with its quiet discipline, started to settle his restless spirit. He began to notice things he'd never cared about before: the way the clouds moved across the sky, how the dirt clung to his fingers, the silent strength of the mountains surrounding him. Even the sudden bursts of rain, wild and uninvited, stirred something gentle inside him. His once wild defiance started to fade, like snow softening under the touch of spring. He wasn't completely transformed, but something steady and purposeful began to take shape in his heart.

At twenty, Noboru made a bold decision. He packed up a few belongings and left home without telling a soul. He was weighed down by the shame of his past and driven by the desire to redeem himself. He wanted to rebuild his life—not for glory, but to prove himself worthy of the faith his father had never stopped showing him. It was his own version of the prodigal son's return, a quiet journey of redemption.

Eventually, Noboru found work with a doctor who practiced modern Western medicine. Eager to help, he threw himself into any task: running errands, hauling water, preparing medicine, and assisting with patients. The doctor, noticing his energy and sincerity, let him study from his medical books in the evenings. For someone who once clashed with education, Noboru now couldn't get enough of it. He studied deep into the night, fighting off sleep with pure will. To keep himself awake, he tied a rope from the ceiling to his chin so that if he started to nod off, it would jerk him awake. That's how determined he had become. What once seemed like a burden had turned into his path forward.

Years of relentless labor had not only built Noboru's body but strengthened his mind. What once seemed like scattered thoughts and a restless spirit had given way to deep focus and clarity. He found himself absorbing difficult medical concepts with surprising ease. His transformation was not accidental—it was anchored in the quiet discipline of his samurai lineage, a heritage that taught perseverance, honor, and inner strength.

What began as an impossible journey—an unruly boy's struggle to find his place—had turned into a calling. Noboru devoted himself to the art of healing. He wasn't just memorizing facts; he was preparing to fight suffering with precision and compassion, one patient at a time.

By the age of twenty-five, he was ready. After years of late-night study, self-sacrifice, and tireless determination, he sat for the national medical examinations under the Meiji government. He passed with distinction. The year was 1904. When he returned home, he was no longer the rebellious son who had once walked away in silence—he was now Dr. Noboru, a man shaped by discipline, pain, and quiet resolve.

His father, Fumitaka, received him with the grace that had always defined him. There were no grand words, no dramatic embraces—just the kind of stillness that speaks more than speeches ever could. Fumitaka had never lost faith in his son. Each morning, long before the sun rose, he would go to the garden and kneel in silent prayer—not asking for success or fame, but simply that his son would one day find his way home. Not just back to the house, but back to the values that had always guided their family: honor, duty, and service.

Noboru's transformation was not the product of punishment or traditional education. It was shaped by the steady love of a patient father, the humbling work of the land, and a personal commitment to change. His story reminds us that true growth doesn't always come through loud moments. Sometimes, it arrives quietly—through sweat, silence, and second chances.

When it came time for marriage, Noboru followed the same tradition that had shaped much of his life. In Japan, arranged marriages (*omiai kekkon*) are often misunderstood in the West. Many assume they are cold or impersonal, but in truth, they are thoughtful and deeply intentional. Families seek the guidance of a *nakōdo*, or matchmaker, not just to unite two individuals, but to bring together values, heritage, character, and potential.

The process begins with a formal meeting, a *miai*, where both individuals decide—freely and respectfully—if they wish to continue. From there, the relationship blossoms step by step, with clarity and intention. Unlike many love marriages (*ren'ai kekkon*), which start with emotion and face challenges later, arranged marriages often grow from mutual respect and shared values, leading to surprisingly strong and lasting bonds.

Through this tradition, Noboru was introduced to Tsune—a woman whose name, meaning "constant," perfectly captured her personality. She came from a distinguished samurai family and carried herself with quiet confidence and strength. The matchmaker had chosen wisely. Noboru, now a respected physician, had found his equal—not just in intellect, but in spirit.

Tsune's strength, though soft-spoken, had already been tested in extraordinary ways. As a young woman, she experienced a terrifying break-in. One night, she was startled awake by the presence of a thief in her room. He threatened her with a knife, pressing his hand over her mouth. But even in the face of danger, Tsune remained calm.

She gestured that she wouldn't resist and politely requested to use the bathroom before handing over any money. The thief, deceived by her composure, allowed it. Behind the bathroom door, she acted swiftly—smearing lipstick on her fingertips and marking the money she had hidden. Then she returned, handed the marked bills to the intruder, and watched him flee into the night.

The next day, her detailed description guided the police straight to him. The red stains on the money sealed his fate. Her quick thinking and steady nerves became a family legend—a quiet tale of courage passed down through generations.

In Tsune, Noboru found not just a wife, but a partner—someone who shared his values, his strength, and his resilience. Together, they represented two lives once tested by hardship, now united by purpose.

When Noboru and Tsune were married, it was not just the union of two individuals—it was a moment of deep pride and quiet fulfillment for Noboru's father, Fumitaka. A devout herbalist and follower of Taisha Shinto, Fumitaka had long lived by the rhythms of nature and tradition. Seeing his son marry a woman of strength and honor felt like a prayer answered after many years of patient hope.

Their wedding followed the sacred customs of the Shinto faith. In a solemn ceremony beneath the watchful gaze of the *yaoyorozu no kami*—the "eight million gods" believed to guide and guard human life—Noboru and Tsune exchanged three cups of sake. This symbolic act of unity before the priest and the divine spirits sealed their bond, not only in tradition but in heart and spirit. It was a day of reverence, not extravagance, where faith, family, and ancestry converged.

Soon after their marriage, Tsune became pregnant, and the family's joy grew. But her labor would soon test her strength in ways no one could have foreseen. Noboru was away on a medical house call when her pains worsened, and the attending doctor became alarmed. The birth was not progressing—Tsune's body fought to deliver a child whose head would not descend.

Her face was pale with sweat, her body trembling from the intensity of the pain, yet her spirit did not falter. As the doctor hesitated, weighed down by the possibility of a grim intervention, he quietly said, "We may need to crush the baby's skull to save you."

Even through the searing agony, Tsune's voice was clear—fragile, but unwavering:
"No. Don't harm my baby."

Moments later, as if in response to her resolve, the silence was broken by the strong, defiant cry of a newborn. Noboru arrived just in time to hear it—his son had been born. Healthy. Whole. Alive.

The baby's head, large and round, would later become a running joke in the family—especially when he struggled to find hats that fit. But in that moment, it was a symbol of survival, of his mother's unshakable love, and of the quiet miracle they had all witnessed.

The naming of the child was a sacred moment for Fumitaka. His eyes welled with tears as he looked at the boy, the continuation of everything he had lived and hoped for. They named him **Takashi**, a name meaning *"noble"*—a name that carried within it a legacy of strength, honor, and promise.

Shortly after, the family held the *miyamairi*—a ceremonial visit to the shrine to give thanks and formally introduce the newborn to the gods. It was a moment of pure joy for Fumitaka. He had spent his life honoring the old ways, guided by Confucian values of family, respect, and lineage. For years, he had silently grieved the time when Noboru had strayed from those values. But now, standing in the shrine with his grandson in his arms, he felt the circle of life had gently, and beautifully, closed.

Not long after the shrine visit, Fumitaka passed away.

He was only sixty-one, but he died peacefully, with a heart full of contentment. He had lived a life of duty and quiet sacrifice—and in the end, he had seen the family line restored, the ancestral values renewed, and his legacy passed on.

It was 1910. The end of his life marked not just the passing of a man, but the closing of an era. Yet in Takashi's cry, in

Tsune's strength, and in Noboru's dedication, a new chapter had begun—one rooted in the past, but reaching boldly into the future.

Noboru was deeply shaken by the unexpected loss of his father. Grief, like a heavy mist, enveloped him, and in the stillness of his sorrow, he sought solace in honoring his father's memory with the utmost reverence. He immersed himself in the time-honored Shinto rites, following them with painstaking devotion, as though the very act of ritual could somehow bridge the space between life and death.

The priests arrived in their ceremonial white robes, their presence both solemn and otherworldly. Their tall black hats, reminiscent of those worn by nobility in the ancient Imperial courts of Japan, stood as a silent tribute to the long lineage of tradition they upheld. As the ceremony began, the mournful strains of wooden flutes rose into the air—melancholic, yet beautiful. Their haunting melody seemed to reach across the centuries, as if calling from another time, from an era when the land of Yamato was untamed, and the skies were alive with the song of wild birds that had long since disappeared.

In that moment, surrounded by the music and the sacred rituals, Noboru felt a profound connection to his ancestors. The passing of his father had somehow bridged the gap between the present and the distant past. It was as if the very act of mourning had opened a doorway to a world that had once been, a world that still lingered in the echoes of the flute's song and in the hallowed ground beneath his feet.

Noboru realized, with a clarity that took him by surprise, that life—no matter how fleeting—was but a single thread in a vast, unbroken tapestry. The cycle of existence, stretching beyond the lives of individuals, was woven into the soul of the land itself. His father's death was not an end, but a continuation of a much larger story—one that spanned generations, cultures, and centuries, forever intertwined with the history of his people.

Chapter 2

Coming of Europeans

In the mid-1500s, the shores of Japan were visited by European traders, who brought with them a wave of new goods, ideas, and technologies. This exchange sparked a sense of wonder and curiosity among the Japanese people, as the outside world beckoned with promises of advancement and knowledge. It was the dawn of a new chapter—one where distant lands, once only imagined, were now within reach.

Yet, by the early 1600s, a shift in Japan's leadership brought a harsh new reality. The Tokugawa shogunate, growing increasingly wary of the foreign influence that was beginning to seep into the country, took drastic measures to protect Japan from the growing power of Western nations. With fears of colonization and the exploitation that had ravaged other parts of the world, the shogunate closed Japan off from the rest of humanity. Europeans were barred from setting foot on Japanese soil, and any foreigner caught attempting to do so faced the ultimate punishment. Similarly, Japanese citizens who ventured abroad and sought to return home were condemned to die. This policy of seclusion was not merely a defensive tactic—it was a desperate act of preservation, an attempt to shield Japan from the fate that had befallen nations like India and the Philippines, carved up by European imperial powers.

For nearly two centuries, Japan stood in silence, observing the unfolding of world events from a distance, insulated from the waves of change that swept through the rest of the globe. But in 1839, when the Opium War erupted between China and Britain, the calm was shattered. From the sidelines, Japan watched as China—once a proud and mighty empire—succumbed to the force of Western military power. The humiliating treaties and territorial concessions forced upon China were a brutal wake-up call. The message was clear: if Japan did not change its ways, it, too, could fall victim to the same fate of foreign dominance.

Then, in 1853, a moment of reckoning arrived. American Commodore Matthew Perry sailed into Japanese waters with a fleet of steamships, their black hulls cutting through the sea like symbols of an unrelenting future. Perry's message was simple, stark, and undeniable: open your ports to the world, or face the consequences. Caught off guard and powerless in the face of such overwhelming force, the Tokugawa shogunate had no choice but to yield. In the small fishing village of Yokohama, under pressure and duress, the shogunate signed a treaty that would forever alter the course of Japan's history. The ink on the paper marked the end of Japan's centuries-long isolation and the beginning of a new era—one that would force the nation to confront the modern world and its place within it.

At first, Japan struggled to reconcile with its new reality. The arrival of the West—bringing with it foreign technologies, ideas, and demands—shattered centuries of isolation. For a nation rooted in tradition, the sudden upheaval felt like a violent storm, tossing them out of the safe harbor of their past. Yet, Japan quickly realized that resistance would only leave them vulnerable to the same fate as China. There was no turning back. With unwavering resolve and determination, the Japanese embarked on a monumental transformation. Factories emerged, cities flourished at an astonishing pace, and railways and steamships revolutionized the way they moved and connected. The government took bold action, making education mandatory for children and founding universities to cultivate scientific knowledge. The aim was clear: to close the gap with the West and ensure Japan's place in the modern world.

Amid this transformation, the samurai—once the revered elite with exclusive rights to bear swords—found their roles evolving. Many joined the military, others assumed leadership positions in the government, or moved into the rapidly growing private sector. In just a few short decades, Japan had reinvented itself.

By 1894, only four decades after Commodore Perry's fateful arrival, Japan stood as a formidable power. The country launched a successful war against China, seizing control of Korea. But their ambitions didn't end there. A decade later, Japan faced off against the colossal Russian Empire, and in a stunning turn of events, Japan emerged victorious. The Russian fleet was obliterated by the Japanese navy, and for the first time in centuries, Japan dictated the terms of peace. This moment, when a nation once isolated and backward defeated a major European power, sent shockwaves through the Western world. Japan's emergence as a global force was undeniable.

Looking back, Japan's remarkable transformation from a secluded feudal society to a modern imperial power in just a few decades is a testament to the resilience, innovation, and adaptability of its people. What began as a defensive reaction to foreign influence became a powerful wave of modernization, allowing Japan not only to survive the pressures of the outside world but to rise above them, asserting itself on the global stage with newfound confidence.

Driven by a fierce sense of national pride, the Japanese rallied behind the Meiji government's ambitious goal: to transform their nation into an industrial powerhouse, on par with the Western giants. Among those who answered the call were Dr. Noboru Nagai and his wife, Tsune. Their mission was not for personal gain, but for service. With no desire for wealth or fame, they set out to the remote valleys around Mitoya, bringing Western medical practices to the isolated communities that had never seen such modern care.

Their life in the countryside, however, was far from comfortable. Financially, they were modest, working among impoverished tenant farmers who suffered under the grip of wealthy landowners. But the Nagais never asked for payment from those who couldn't afford it. Their goal was clear: to serve, to heal, and to give, no matter the personal cost.

The winters in Shimane were harsh, the snow so deep it seemed to smother the land, testing the resolve of the people who lived there. For Dr. Nagai, these frigid nights brought their own challenges. When an urgent call came, Tsune was always there, preparing him for the bitter cold. She layered his clothes and wrapped straw rope around his boots to protect him as he ventured into the snow, his steps muffled in the stillness of the night. She watched him disappear into the darkness, her heart heavy with concern, yet filled with quiet trust that he would return.

When his familiar voice echoed through the frozen air, Tsune would rush outside with a lantern, guiding him back to the warmth of home. After brushing off the snow and removing his boots, she would help him relax in the steaming bath of o-furo, the warmth soothing his tired body. She would then serve him a simple, yet comforting drink of sake with a cracked egg—a ritual, born of love and care, to restore his strength and bring him peace after the long night's work.

Tsune was more than just the doctor's supportive wife; she was his steadfast partner, his right hand in the clinic. From the very beginning, she embraced her role as his assistant with grace and dedication, becoming indispensable to his work. Together, they navigated the complexities of their medical practice, with Tsune standing by her husband's side, sharing in both the challenges and triumphs. Their eldest son, Takashi, grew up in an atmosphere charged with intellectual energy and quiet devotion. He watched his parents study side by side, absorbing knowledge from their shared textbooks—many of them old German medical illustrations—and witnessing his father patiently teach his mother the intricacies of anatomy. The joy they found in learning, in growing together, left a deep and lasting imprint on Takashi. To him, education was not a chore but an essential, joyful part of life—much like sharing a meal or telling a story.

Years later, as a medical researcher in Nagasaki, Takashi would reflect on those formative years in the family home, recalling it fondly as his "thatched-roof university." For him, the lessons learned within those humble walls were as valuable as any academic institution.

The Nagai children were raised with values rooted in Japan's warrior traditions, lessons that were woven into the fabric of their everyday lives. One lesson that Takashi cherished most was embodied in three simple characters: "firefly," "snow," and "success." These symbols told the story of a poor student who, unable to afford candles, studied by the light of fireflies and the moonlight reflected off the snow—a powerful lesson in perseverance, resourcefulness, and the relentless pursuit of knowledge. Takashi often recalled how his parents taught him that the lack of money was no excuse for the lack of effort in learning.

Another story that resonated deeply with the Nagais was that of a lioness who cast her cubs down a steep slope, only nurturing those who managed to climb back up. To the Nagais, this story became a symbol of resilience and strength—a reminder that true success was earned through determination and self-reliance. Tsune, in particular, never pressured her children to study, instead fostering an environment in their home where curiosity and a love of learning could thrive. She encouraged them to explore, to ask questions, and to find joy in discovery. However, when it came to discipline, Tsune's expectations were clear. She welcomed the playful teasing and laughter of her children, but never tolerated disrespect. One winter's day, Takashi made the mistake of speaking back to her. Without hesitation, Tsune stripped him of his warm clothes, carried him out to the veranda, and unceremoniously tossed him into a deep pile of snow. In that simple, icy moment, she reinforced the lesson that strength and respect went hand in hand.

There is an old Japanese saying: "If you love your child, send them on a journey." The meaning is clear—overprotecting a child stunts their growth. In 1920, at the age of twelve, Takashi left his rural home to take the entrance exams for a respected school in the city of Matsue. He passed, and with that success, he bid farewell to the simple pleasures of his childhood—the winding stream, the distant hills, the quiet evenings spent with family. The journey ahead would be one of growth and change, but the lessons learned in the Nagai household would remain with him, guiding him every step of the way.

Takashi's move to Matsue marked a turning point in his life—a stark contrast to the serene rhythms of rural life that had shaped his early years. Suddenly, he found himself immersed in the energy and excitement of the city, a place alive with discovery and boundless possibility. His new home near the ancient moat of Matsue Castle—once the residence of the enigmatic Lafcadio Hearn—became a symbol of transformation, of knowledge that could bridge worlds. Takashi's relatives often spoke of Hearn's remarkable journey: how a foreigner had come to Japan, learned its language, embraced its culture, and then shared his insights with the outside world. It was a story that ignited something within Takashi. Perhaps, he thought, he too could one day follow a similar path—using knowledge to bridge cultures, to contribute to something greater than himself.

Despite the excitement of his new surroundings, Takashi couldn't shake the deep sense of longing for the simplicity of home—the quiet hills, the familiar faces, and the slower, more peaceful pace of life. Yet, he did not dwell on nostalgia. Instead, he channeled his energy into catching up with the sharp-witted city kids who had a clear advantage in their studies. His father, known for his chaotic energy and unpredictable nature, had attended six different schools in Matsue, leaving behind a trail of stories that painted him as a free spirit. Takashi, however, was determined to carve out his own identity—not as the star athlete, but as the hardworking and earnest student, even if he wasn't the most graceful in the gym.

His country-bred strength didn't lend itself to the agility his classmates seemed to possess. In gym class, Takashi would charge at the vaulting horse with all his might, only to crash awkwardly into it. He would grasp the parallel bars, his face flushed with determination, only to struggle and fail time after time to pull himself up. Even on the baseball field, no position seemed to suit him. His classmates, amused by his clumsiness, affectionately gave him the nickname "Daikon"—like the large, bulky radish that grew in the fields of his childhood.

But despite these setbacks, Takashi's attention was drawn to the new currents of thought sweeping through the halls of Matsue High School. It was a time of intellectual upheaval, where Western ideas were beginning to take root in the heart of Japan. The air was charged with an energy he had never known, particularly when it came to science and philosophy. Darwin's theory of evolution, rapidly becoming the new gospel, offered a natural explanation for life that seemed to render the ancient stories of gods and spirits irrelevant.

Thinkers like Thomas Huxley, revered for his agnostic views, dismissed religion as outdated—a relic of the past, no longer necessary in the modern world.

At school, the teachers did not openly mock Shinto beliefs, but their subtle remarks often suggested that such spiritual tales were no longer useful. They would reference ancient legends, like that of a god slaying an eight-headed serpent, and imply that perhaps it was simply a poetic description of an ancient engineer's flood-control system. The message was clear: science, not mythology, was now the key to understanding the world.

By the time Takashi graduated, his beliefs had undergone a profound transformation. The gods and spirits that once seemed woven into the very fabric of Japanese life had faded into the background, distant and unnecessary. In their place, science—rigorous, clear, and unyielding—had become his guiding star. He envisioned returning to the countryside, joining his parents in their medical work, and transforming their practice into something modern and scientifically grounded.

Yet, Takashi's mind wasn't solely consumed by the cold precision of science. He found himself deeply moved by the power of music and literature, realms that opened his heart to emotions he hadn't known he could feel. The symphonies of Franz Schubert captivated him; the melodies, rich with sorrow and joy, seemed to speak to parts of him that words alone could not reach. At the same time, he discovered *Kokoro* (True Heart), a novel by Soseki Natsume, one of Japan's greatest literary figures. The story of a man caught between a rapidly changing world and his own inner turmoil resonated deeply with Takashi. The protagonist's struggle with isolation and despair, culminating in a tragic choice of suicide—a fate that Natsume himself would one day embrace—stirred an unsettling darkness in him. Though disturbed by the novel's bleakness, Takashi quickly pushed aside these troubling thoughts. He had a greater task at hand: preparing for Japan's grueling university entrance exams.

When the results arrived, Takashi was offered a place at some of the most prestigious universities in Tokyo and Kyoto. Yet, in an unexpected twist, he chose Nagasaki Medical College, a lesser-known institution. To many, it seemed like a curious decision—one that defied conventional wisdom. But for Takashi, it was never about prestige. It was about meaning, about pursuing something that resonated with his own values and vision. His choice raised eyebrows, but it felt right to him—authentic, true to the person he was becoming.

His parents, filled with pride and anticipation, sent him off with prayers at the family altar, their hopes for his success filling the room. They believed he was simply setting out to study medicine, not realizing the deeper currents of change that were about to sweep him away. What they didn't know was that Takashi's life was about to take unexpected turns. New paths would open before him, leading him far beyond the simple aspirations of medical school and into a future far more intricate and transformative than he—or anyone—could have imagined.

Chapter 3

At the Nagasaki Medical College

When Nagai first donned his student uniform—its dark fabric crisp and gleaming, the buttons polished to catch the light—he felt a profound mix of pride and seriousness. It wasn't just about appearance; the uniform carried weight. It symbolized something greater, a link between him and the European scholars Japan had long revered, especially those from Germany. During the Meiji era, as Japan eagerly embraced modernization, it looked to the West for guidance. Britain provided a model navy, while Germany offered a blueprint for education and medicine. The Prussian influence had taken deep root, and Japan, with its inherent values of order and discipline, found in Germany's structured methods and exacting logic a natural alignment with its own ideals.

For Nagai, this connection meant immersing himself in the dense German medical texts that would guide his education. He wasn't just learning medicine—he was absorbing a philosophy, one that championed precision, objectivity, and control. It was the science of healing, but seen through a Western lens, and Nagai was determined to master every facet of it.

The Nagasaki Medical College, modern and solid, stood at the foot of Mount Konpira, its green peak towering behind like a silent protector. The buildings, pale concrete against the lush natural backdrop, overlooked the calm expanse of Nagasaki Bay. Across the shimmering water, Mount Inasa rose with equal majesty, as if Konpira had a twin watching over the city. Yet, amidst this serene landscape, the massive

Urakami Cathedral loomed—its bell towers rang three times a day, their sound intruding upon the peaceful rhythm of the city with a foreign, almost discordant, call to prayer. To Nagai, raised in the logic-driven spirit of the new Japan, the cathedral felt out of place—an echo of an outdated worldview, spiritual noise in a time hungry for intellectual clarity.

What he couldn't yet comprehend was that the very structure he found so jarring would one day come to define a core part of his identity, shaping him in ways he couldn't yet foresee.

Behind the college campus stood the university hospital, a structure as stoic and purposeful as the education it supported—built of concrete and glass, a testament to the modern age. Nagai often found himself climbing to the third floor, where he would lean against the railing and gaze out over the rooftops of Matsuyama and Urakami below. The grey sea of tile roofs stretched before him, each one nearly identical, yet together they created a sense of visual harmony that soothed his restless mind. In those quiet moments, the city ceased to feel like a battleground of new ideas and clashing beliefs. Instead, it transformed into a still, tranquil painting—a peaceful world where time seemed to slow.

The academic year began in April, coinciding with the burst of color that swept through Nagasaki's streets as cherry blossoms and spring flowers awakened from their winter slumber. The air was warm and fragrant, heavy with the promise of new beginnings. It was in this vibrant season that Nagai would encounter one of the pivotal experiences of his early training. During an anatomy lecture, his professor unveiled a cadaver with the casual detachment of a man revealing an object of study. Without ceremony, he addressed the class: "Gentlemen, this is your subject. A body. A thing we can weigh, measure, dissect, and analyze. This—only this—is what a human is."

The words struck Nagai to his core. It wasn't that he rejected the spiritual; rather, he became convinced that science held the key to understanding everything of true value. To him, science was not cold or impersonal—it was a promise. A promise that humanity could leave behind the shadows of myth and superstition, that suffering could be understood and, perhaps, even conquered. Knowledge was the tool that could forge a better future. In Nagai's eyes, the world was on the cusp of progress, emerging from the darkened past, and he was determined to be one of those who carried the flame forward.

Yet, for all his dedication to microscopes and scalpels, Nagai was not merely a man of science. Deep within him, there was a soul that yearned for beauty, for music, for the written word. His days were consumed by the rigid demands of his clinical studies, but his nights were filled with the quiet escape of literature and music. The works of Franz Schubert resonated with him on a profound level—not because he could articulate the exact meaning of every note, but because the melodies stirred something deep inside, something he couldn't fully express. They felt like unanswered questions wrapped in sound, emotions too elusive for words.

When it came to literature, few works affected him as powerfully as the *Manyoshu*. This ancient collection of Japanese poetry, written more than a thousand years earlier, moved him not only for its lyrical beauty but for what it symbolized. It wasn't simply a book of poems; it was a reflection of Japanese identity itself. It gave voice to everyone—not just emperors and nobles, but also farmers, soldiers, mothers, and lovers. In the *Manyoshu*, every person's voice mattered. Every life was worthy of being heard.

To Nagai, the egalitarian beauty of the *Manyoshu* felt uniquely Japanese. Unlike the clinical, logical world of science, the *Manyoshu* held a truth that could never be dissected in a laboratory or measured by a microscope. In its verses, there was a depth that science could never reach—an emotional truth that resonated in ways logic never could. This contrast—between the precise, methodical nature of Western medicine and the emotional richness of Japanese poetry—became a quiet undercurrent in Nagai's life. He admired the analytical power of German medicine, but he also found himself clinging to the gentle humanity woven into Japan's oldest poems. It was this blend—one grounded in logic, the other in lyricism—that began to shape Nagai's worldview.

He was a young man with a scalpel in one hand and a poem in the other—constantly searching, questioning, dreaming of a future where both the body could be healed, and the heart understood.

What he didn't yet know was how deeply both would be tested.

As Nagai's medical studies deepened, something unexpected began to stir within him. Amidst textbooks and microscopes, he found himself turning more and more to the *Manyoshu*, not merely as a cultural relic, but as a quiet, enduring companion—almost sacred in its presence. The poems, ancient yet alive, hummed with the pulse of centuries. They shaped his thoughts like gentle rain shapes stone—slowly, persistently, but profoundly. They left their mark, not with force, but with a quiet, lingering beauty that seeped into his own writings like ink into fabric. The more he read, the more he saw himself reflected in those verses, and their emotional richness began to infuse his own work with a depth he hadn't expected.

For those unacquainted with Japanese poetry, it can be easy to miss just how much soul resides in so few lines. But in the *Manyoshu*, emotion isn't merely whispered—it's sung, sometimes with joy, but often with aching sorrow. Take, for example, a poem by Prince Ikusa, written during a lonely journey far from his wife. There are no grand displays of despair, no wailing in agony. Instead, he compares his heartache to a night bird crying alone, or a fire burning on a salt-stained shore—images so simple, yet so raw, they cut straight to the heart. It's the kind of longing that transcends culture, a universal ache that anyone, anywhere, can understand.

The *Manyoshu* is also brimming with devotion and resilience. One soldier writes with steadfast loyalty, expressing that it doesn't matter if he falls in the ocean or perishes in the mountains—as long as he dies in service to his emperor, he dies content. There is poetry not just in words, but in the fierce acceptance of duty. Nature, too, is a constant presence in these verses—clouds drifting like waves, the moon sailing through the stars like a silent ship. Love, in all its beauty and pain, finds its place: "I would face a double-edged sword and die without regret, if it be for you," writes one samurai, his devotion echoing through the centuries. And then, there's the playful humor: "The cruel girl walks by my gate, as if daring me to die of love!" It's the kind of teasing that transcends time, one we all recognize, even today.

Unlike Western poetry, Japanese verse doesn't rely on rhyme to create rhythm. Instead, it flows to the delicate count of syllables—structured, yet free. It thrives on suggestion and subtlety, leaving enough unsaid to invite the reader's heart to fill in the empty spaces. The famed American scholar Edwin Reischauer once marveled at this "excessively brief form," especially in the haiku. And no poet embodied it better than Matsuo Basho, whose seventeen syllables could capture entire landscapes and the complex emotions they stirred. One of his most iconic haiku paints a scene of profound stillness, broken only by the sound of cicadas so deafening, it seems to echo through stone itself. In these three lines, Basho doesn't just evoke sound—he evokes solitude, time, and memory, all at once.

By the spring of 1928, just as Nagai began his studies at Nagasaki Medical University, he found himself drawn into a poetry circle led by Professor Mokichi Saito—a celebrated poet who also happened to teach medicine. In Japan, poetry was not a pursuit reserved for the artistic elite; it was woven into the very fabric of daily life. Doctors, shopkeepers, and even tailors could be poets. It wasn't unusual—it was simply part of the culture. For Nagai, joining the group felt like a natural step, a way to merge his clinical precision with the emotional depth of poetic expression.

Yet, outside the academic world, Japan was faltering. The 1927 banking collapse had already shattered the economy, and by 1929, the global depression arrived with the force of a tidal wave. Factories slowed, exports dwindled, and hardship spread like a shadow across the country. High tariffs in the West smothered Japan's international trade, and the value of silk, the pride of rural production, plummeted. In small towns, families were struggling. At Nagai's own clinic, patients began bowing as they asked for more time to pay for their treatments. It tore at his heart. In response, Nagai took on extra shifts at a hospital far from home, trying desperately to make ends meet. Sleep and meals became luxuries, unpredictable and fleeting. The noble calling of medicine, once a symbol of hope and purpose, now pressed down heavily on his shoulders and those of his wife.

Despite the heavy burden of financial strain, Nagai's parents ensured their son never felt its weight. His allowance always arrived on time, accompanied by letters brimming with encouragement. "Focus on your studies," they urged, "and on your poems." And so, he did. Poetry became his quiet sanctuary, a retreat from the harshness of economic troubles. Through verse, he reconnected with something timeless, something steady. In the words of the ancients, he found not only solace but a growing pride in his Japanese heritage—not just in the blood that ran through his veins, but in the culture and spirit of his people.

This wasn't mere nostalgia—it was the forging of his identity. For Nagai, patriotism transcended the shallow gestures of flag-waving; it was about recognizing the beauty woven into the very soul of his country. One journey crystallized this feeling, turning it from an abstract thought into a living truth. He traveled to the historic port of Hakata, not for leisure, but to stand at the crossroads of history. It was here, in the 13th century, that Japanese warriors had confronted the full wrath of Kublai Khan's Mongol invasion.

The Mongol empire, forged by the relentless Genghis Khan, had swept through Asia and Eastern Europe, and Kublai, his grandson, expected Japan to fall just as easily. By 1264, he had established the Yuan Dynasty in China and by 1274, assembled a mighty fleet with ships from Korea, ready to cross the narrow sea and invade Hakata Bay. When Japan refused to submit to Kublai's demands, war was declared.

The Mongol forces landed, seizing nearby islands and pushing inland, but fate had other plans. A violent storm struck the bay, ravaging the Mongol fleet. With their forces crippled, Kublai's commanders withdrew, unwilling to gamble everything on a single, uncertain campaign. Yet, they had gained crucial knowledge of Japan's terrain and would return, better prepared.

Standing in the very place where these battles were fought, Nagai felt something stir deep within him. It was no longer a mere chapter in a history book—it was a living, breathing continuity. He could almost feel the warriors' footsteps beneath his own. The Japan of ancient poems, of samurai oaths and storm-battered battles, was not lost to time. It was alive—in the earth, in the collective memory, and now, within him.

After the Mongol invasion failed, Japan was thrust into a state of heightened alert. From the samurai leadership in Kamakura to the priests and monks in Kyoto, a profound spiritual mobilization spread across the nation. Shrines and temples became not only places of prayer but rallying points for the collective spirit of Japan. The message that reverberated was clear and unwavering: Japan was a sacred land, entrusted by the gods to its people, and its defense was not just a duty but an honor. Resisting the invaders was more than a military task—it was a divine act of devotion.

In anticipation of the Mongols' return, Japan's builders erected a towering ten-foot-high stone wall around Hakata Bay—a desperate yet determined attempt to prevent the enemy cavalry from landing and ravaging the countryside. And in June of 1281, they came.

The Mongol fleet, numbering over 150,000, was the most formidable naval invasion the world had ever seen. On June 23, the sky above Hakata darkened with the sight of black sails. But the Japanese did not wait in fear. Instead, they met the threat head-on, launching small, agile boats that darted towards the Mongol ships, striking swiftly and vanishing as quickly as they came. Outnumbered and outgunned, the Japanese were not outwilled.

The Mongols swiftly overran nearby islands, leaving death and destruction in their wake. Women were subjected to horrors that sought not only to conquer but to terrorize. They were bound by their wrists and left to hang from the prows of Mongol ships. The samurai, standing firm onshore, understood the unspoken truth: if the Mongols broke through, unimaginable horrors awaited their families.

Yet, despite the overwhelming odds, the samurai stood their ground. For nearly two months—from late June to mid-August—they fought relentlessly, using the stone wall as their fortress. The air was thick with the sounds of clashing steel and the cries of the wounded. The Mongols, with their superior tactics, advanced equipment, and overwhelming numbers, pressed on. The question was no longer if the Japanese would fall, but when.

Then, in an unexpected twist of fate, the heavens themselves intervened.

On the night of August 14, strange and ominous signs appeared in the sky—dark clouds, erratic winds, and an eerie stillness. By morning, the skies broke open, unleashing a furious storm. A monstrous typhoon swept across Hakata Bay. For two days, wind and waves tore through the Mongol fleet. Ships splintered like fragile twigs, masts snapped, and sailors screamed into the storm, only to be swallowed by the ocean. By August 17, the storm had passed, and the waters were calm once more. But the Mongols were gone.

What swords had failed to do, nature had accomplished. The Japanese called it kamikaze—the "divine wind." To them, it was not mere coincidence. It was proof that their land was sacred, that the gods themselves had intervened to protect it.

This story didn't just become a part of history—it became the heartbeat of Japanese identity. The belief that their homeland was watched over by divine powers filled the people with an unwavering sense of purpose and pride.

Years later, when Dr. Takashi Nagai walked along the remnants of that ancient stone wall during a visit to Hakata, the weight of history settled deeply in his bones. Despite being a man of science, trained in the rigorous world of empirical knowledge, something stirred within him—a reverence, a profound connection to the spirit of his nation.

One afternoon, Takashi walked into the tuberculosis ward, carrying a book he'd borrowed—a thick, heavy volume filled with grim statistics and even grimmer realities. Tuberculosis still cast a long shadow over Japan, and while many of his classmates avoided the subject, Takashi found himself drawn to it. To him, every book wasn't just information—it was a doorway to deeper understanding, a step closer to uncovering the truth. His friends often teased him for being a compulsive reader, but he didn't mind. Each page he turned was one more piece of the puzzle.

As he settled in for another long night of study, his routine was suddenly broken by the arrival of a telegram.

It was from his father. The message was brief—only two words: *Come home.* Two words, but they carried the weight of a storm.

His heart raced as he packed his belongings into a bag, instinctively tucking in a few trusted books. Perhaps he didn't need them, but he couldn't help it—it had become habit. As the train rumbled northward, the scenery outside blurred into insignificance, while his thoughts were sharply focused. His mind kept circling back to his mother. During the last holiday break, she had seemed strangely tired, her energy fading like a candle flickering toward its end. When he had asked if she was alright, she had laughed it off, teasing him for being too eager to find a patient to practice on. But beneath the laughter, Takashi had sensed something unspoken—something fragile, something slipping away.

When he finally stepped through the front door, his father's expression confirmed his worst fears. His mother had suffered a stroke. She was alive, yes—but barely. Lying on a futon, her body a still and silent shell, she could no longer speak. But her eyes—those eyes—held something fierce. As he knelt beside her, she looked at him as if trying to burn his face into her memory. No words passed between them. None were needed. In that single gaze, Takashi felt everything—love, pride, sadness, and a quiet goodbye.

And just like that, she was gone.

The silence that followed was unbearable. But the impact of that moment never truly left him. Years later, he would try to capture it in words:

"I rushed to her bedside. She was still breathing. She looked fixedly at me, and that's how the end came... Her eyes spoke to mine... saying: 'Your mother now takes leave in death, but her living spirit will be beside her little one, Takashi.'"

This was the moment that shook him to his core. A man who had once trusted only in things that could be measured, dissected, and proven—now found himself standing face-to-face with something he could neither explain nor deny. Her final gaze had shattered the walls of his material worldview. And in their place, something unnameable had taken root.

His teacher had praised Pascal's elegance, calling him the epitome of modern French prose. But for Nagai, what was truly captivating wasn't just Pascal's writing. It was the idea that Pascal wasn't merely a writer—he was a hybrid, a poet who dabbled in numbers, a scientist who sought to understand the soul. This duality intrigued Nagai. Yet, life moved on. School ended. New books arrived while old ones were pushed to the back of the shelf—both physically and mentally.

Years later, within the sterile, logic-driven halls of Nagasaki University's medical school, Pascal's name resurfaced—not in the pages of a philosophy textbook, but in a medical discussion. To Nagai's astonishment, Pascal had invented the syringe. The same man who wrote about fragile reeds and the vastness of the human soul had also created tools that pierced flesh. As he read further, Nagai learned that Pascal had been the mind behind the barometer, had debated the very foundations of geometry, and yet still found space in his life for mystical pursuits. It was a life lived at the crossroads of logic and longing, formulas and faith.

There was something in that contradiction that felt deeply familiar.

Restless and curious, Nagai sought out a copy of *Pensées*. At the time, he had no idea that this small collection of fragments would become far more than just an intriguing read. It would come to serve as a companion for his soul, a book whose words would echo back to him in the darkest, most uncertain moments of his life.

When the telegram arrived from his father—short, urgent, and foreboding—Nagai packed quickly. He grabbed a few clothes, stuffed a handful of books into his bag, and without giving it a second thought, slipped *Pensées* inside. It wasn't a deliberate decision. It just felt like something he needed to bring with him, like a compass that he didn't yet know how to use, but somehow felt better carrying.

After his mother's funeral, his grief was a heavy cloak, damp and suffocating, clinging to him like wet wool against skin. He didn't rush back to his studies. Instead, he chose the long way home—boarding a southbound steamer that hugged the coastline. The sea that day was restless, its gray skies pressing down, heavy with unspoken sorrow. As the boat sliced through the cold water, he stood alone on the deck, the wind tugging at his coat, the silence around him as thick and heavy as the air.

He pulled out Pascal's book and began to read—not to study, but to find something. Comfort, perhaps. Or understanding. Or simply a voice that didn't try to explain away the pain.

And within those pages, he found something that mirrored his own heart.

Reading Pascal in that moment wasn't about philosophy, French prose, or intellectual admiration. It was about feeling seen. Pascal, too, had wrestled with doubt, with suffering, with the paradox of trying to bridge the physical and the spiritual. He had sought to reason his way to God, only to find himself drawn instead by something deeper—intuition, yearning, mystery.

For Nagai, that boat ride wasn't merely a return to university. It was the quiet beginning of a transformation—one that wouldn't fully reveal itself for years, but which had already begun to reshape his thoughts, his feelings, and the way he would live. He was beginning to sense, faintly but unmistakably, that the real truth wasn't just to be found in lab measurements—but also in the silence between words, in the unspoken connection between a son and his dying mother, and in the thoughts of a long-dead philosopher who had also sought to make sense of life with both logic and heart.

And for the first time, he began to wonder if, perhaps—just perhaps—man truly is a thinking reed after all. Fragile, yes. But capable of thought. And through that thought, maybe even capable of something greater.

Chapter 4

Penses Impact

When Nagai first opened *Pensées*, he wasn't sure what he was expecting, but it certainly wasn't what he found. The book didn't follow the logical, structured format of the scientific texts he was accustomed to. There were no formulas, no clean laws to measure, no straightforward answers. Instead, it felt like stumbling into the private thoughts of a man wrestling with something deeper—a search for meaning, stripped of pretense. Pascal wasn't using a microscope to dissect the world; he was digging through the soil of the soul with his bare hands, trying to unearth something real and raw.

As Nagai turned the pages, confusion often replaced clarity. Words like grace, redemption, and original sin were foreign to him—floating in the text like distant stars in a foreign sky. The Bible references and philosophical allusions seemed almost out of reach, not just in a geographical sense, but spiritually too. He didn't have the cultural framework to fully understand them. And yet, oddly enough, it didn't matter. Every now and then, amid the unfamiliarity, a line would break through the haze and strike him with unexpected force. It wasn't as if Pascal was offering a clear answer; rather, he was pointing—gently but insistently—toward something deeper, something beyond what could be understood with just the eyes. It was a kind of truth that called for a different kind of seeing.

What truly startled Nagai wasn't just the content of Pascal's words, but the way he delivered them. At Nagasaki University, reason was revered, and logic ruled. Everything had to be measured, verified, dissected. But Pascal—this man of the West—seemed to mock the very thing Nagai had been taught to uphold. He warned against blind faith in reason, arguing that human logic was deeply flawed—susceptible to illusion, self-deception, and arrogance. Pascal used dreams as his metaphor: at night, we are deceived by the unreal and believe it to be real. But what if, he asked, our waking life was simply another kind of dream?

That thought hit Nagai like a stone skipping across the surface of a still pond, sending ripples of realization through him. He had heard a similar sentiment before, but not in the West—in the teachings of Eastern philosophy. Buddhist ideas of *maya*—the illusion of the world—described life as a fleeting dream, layered within another. In that moment, Nagai felt a bridge forming between Pascal's words and the teachings of the monks he had known in Kyoto, as if two worlds—so different yet so alike—were speaking the same quiet truth.

Pascal also warned of two dangerous traps that people often fall into when it comes to reason. One was the over-reliance on it, which led to cold skepticism and a sterile, disconnected life. The other was the complete rejection of reason, retreating into ignorance because it was easier. For Pascal, truth demanded something more—a delicate middle path, where the heart remains active and searching, unwilling to settle for the simplicity of easy answers. He called those who avoided this search deserters, not with anger, but with a deep, heavy disappointment. That word lingered in Nagai's mind. Was he truly searching for meaning, or had he, without realizing it, already given up?

Pascal believed that reason had its rightful place—useful for understanding the physical world, but entirely inadequate when it came to perceiving the things that mattered most. The higher truths, he argued, could not be grasped with logic or intellect; they had to be received, felt. He spoke of this understanding coming through "the eyes of the heart." Nagai paused as he read those words. In Buddhist iconography, the Buddha's forehead jewel is said to represent an inner eye—one that perceives the world not as it appears on the surface, but as it truly is. It was a striking parallel, a reminder that, across time and space, East and West seemed to be reaching for the same elusive mystery, albeit in different ways.

One line, in particular, clung to Nagai like mist to skin: *"The heart has reasons of which reason knows nothing."* It was beautiful, yes—but also deeply unsettling. It suggested that there were truths that could not be dissected, only felt. Felt deeply.

He set the book down for a moment, becoming aware of his own body again—the cries of seagulls, the rhythmic hum of the ship's engine, the ache in his stomach. Slowly, he pulled out his bento box and ate quietly, the warm rice grounding him in the present. Yet, despite the peace of the moment, his thoughts kept returning to Pascal. The book had shaken him, in a way he wasn't fully ready to understand. Was it the unfamiliarity of it all, or was it the fact that Pascal had asked him questions he had never dared to ask himself?

Nagai thought back to his childhood, to the first time he'd had a Western-style breakfast. His father had taken him on a trip, and there, on a shiny plate, was an unfamiliar meal. Knife and fork in hand, he had struggled with the new utensils, clumsy in his attempts. The food didn't taste wrong—it just didn't taste like home. Over time, though, he had grown to enjoy Western food. *Maybe Pensées* was like that, too. Maybe it required patience, time, and a willingness to adapt to something that didn't immediately feel familiar.

He closed his lunchbox and slowly walked along the deck. The ocean stretched out before him—an endless gray blur meeting the sky. His mind, however, kept circling back to one uncomfortable question: If reason couldn't lead you to God, and if faith required surrender, then how was one supposed to begin? Pascal had insisted that faith was a gift, something you had to pray for. But pray to whom, Nagai wondered, if you weren't even sure that anyone was listening?

It felt like a trap. To believe, you had to start by believing. Circular. Irrational. And yet, perhaps that was the point. Maybe it wasn't a riddle to be solved, but a door that had to be knocked on. Perhaps faith, as Pascal had said, wasn't an achievement at all, but rather a response—an answer to a quiet knocking, already echoing deep inside the soul.

Pascal had written that God gives just enough light for those who wish to see, and enough shadow to leave room for choice. Faith, then, wasn't a thunderbolt, but a whisper. A whisper that could only be heard by the heart, if the heart was still enough to listen.

Nagai leaned against the ship's railing, letting the wind sweep past his face. The horizon stretched endlessly before him, a vast, indifferent gray. It offered no answers—only silence. Yet, somewhere deep inside, a question began to form. Quiet at first, but growing in strength: *What if the whisper had already begun?*

Nagai often found himself haunted by memories of his mother. Since her passing, there was a lingering sense that she hadn't fully left him. It wasn't just grief—it was something far deeper, more unsettling. Was she still near in some way, or was this just his mind's desperate attempt to keep the emptiness at bay, weaving comforting illusions to protect him from the raw ache of loss?

One evening, unable to quiet the restless thoughts that gnawed at him, Nagai reached for *Pensées* once more. He had been drawn to Pascal's strange clarity before—the way Pascal captured the deep contradictions within the human soul: how we are both majestic and miserable, divine and fallen. He remembered a line that struck him: *"We are fallen kings, stripped of our crowns."* That thought stayed with him, lodged in his heart, reminding him of some hidden nobility within, some purpose, some thread of meaning behind the chaos of life.

But as much as he longed to embrace this vision, a quiet doubt clung to him like a shadow. He recalled a phrase he had once heard: *"A mouse cannot see the stars, and an earthworm cannot know flowers."* That was how he felt—trapped in a world too small to glimpse anything greater. He wanted to believe in Pascal's stars, in his invisible truths, but what if they were nothing more than bedtime stories? Beautiful, yes. Comforting, yes. But were they truly real?

Another memory crept into his thoughts—an old lecture hall, a stern professor quoting Marx: *"Religion is the opium of the people."* But the professor hadn't dismissed religion completely. Instead, he had added something that stuck with Nagai: *"Opium comes from a flower. It's beautiful. Many religions are beautiful too. But beauty can be dangerous when it seduces us into dreams. Don't wait for miracles. Don't count on lilies in the field. Face the world head-on. Truth lives in science, in the tangible, not in parables."*

At the time, the professor's certainty had impressed him. It was bold. It was unwavering. But now, years later, it felt too neat. Too clean. The world, as he was beginning to see it, wasn't so easily sorted into boxes. Truth wasn't always clear-cut.

He flipped through *Pensées* again, pausing on a section where Pascal spoke of Christianity. Pascal had written that Christ was both a refuge and a barrier—a shelter to some, but a scandal to others. Nagai thought of Japan's own history: how the shoguns had seen Christianity not as a faith, but as a threat. Tens of thousands had died for that belief in the

1600s, their loyalty to Christ branded as betrayal to the sacred essence of the Japanese nation. These martyrs troubled him. They were part of his country's history, yes, but they felt foreign to him. Alien. He didn't know whether to honor them or feel unsettled by their legacy.

Back in Nagasaki, Nagai buried himself in his studies. But no matter how many hours he spent with textbooks and microscopes, the ache didn't go away. His mother's death had left a hollow space inside him—quiet, unspoken, and impossible to fill. In Japanese culture, fathers were often seen as the family's pillar, the stern guide. But for Nagai, it was his mother's gentle strength that had left the deepest mark. Her warmth, her quiet kindness—those were the things that shaped him, even more than his father's strong hand.

He missed her in ways he couldn't explain. Not to talk about science or his studies—but to share the ache in his soul. To ask questions that had no answers. But she was gone. And that door was closed.

His classmates started to notice the change. The bright, curious young man who once championed science with boundless faith was now asking harder questions—uncomfortable ones. He had grown skeptical, not cynical, but searching. He wanted something more than clever theories.

One day in class, a professor confidently claimed that human consciousness was merely electrical currents running through nerves. Neat. Simple. Final. But Nagai raised his hand and asked—*Where's the proof? What does that really mean?* The professor's response was vague, built on assumptions and unproven ideas. It sounded a lot like other theories Nagai had read—ideas once declared as fact in one edition of a textbook, only to be quietly discarded in the next. Was science uncovering truth—or just rearranging its guesswork with more polish each time?

By his third year, Nagai was walking hospital corridors, observing patients at their most vulnerable. And something began to disturb him. Some doctors—brilliant, no doubt—seemed emotionally absent. They treated patients like broken machinery, puzzles to be solved. But suffering wasn't mechanical. It wasn't just something to be diagnosed and repaired. It was human. It was sacred. And their detachment, rather than healing, made the wounds deeper.

Still, he tried to live as any student would. He joined his friends for basketball games, climbed mountains on weekends, laughed over drinks. Outwardly, he looked the same. But inwardly, something was shifting. He felt a pull not toward theories, but toward older, quieter truths. He found solace in the poetry of Bashō, whose haiku spoke not of distant ideals but of beauty in the everyday—in a flower blooming beside a stone, in a bird's cry at dawn, in the steam rising from a teacup on a cold morning.

This new way of seeing the world didn't erase his questions—it deepened them. Why are we here? What does it mean to truly live?

Years later, Nagai would write of that time:

"For five years, a voice inside me never went silent. Day and night, it asked: 'What is the meaning of our lives?' I searched in books, in the lives of others. But the more I read, the more lost I became. Because meaning isn't something you can borrow—it must be found in your own life, through your own wounds, your own joys. My life is not anyone else's. And neither is yours."

That truth runs deeper than any lecture ever could. Too often, we try to answer life's hardest questions with borrowed words—quotes from wise men, passages from books. We think someone else's insight will crack the code. But Nagai understood something most of us learn only through pain: real meaning is personal. It doesn't come from outside. It grows inside us—from our struggles, our memories, our quiet moments alone.

Think of life as a piece of handmade lace. Not the machine-made kind, uniform and perfect. But the kind shaped by a single thread, moved patiently by hand. From a distance, it looks messy, tangled. But the one weaving it knows each twist, each loop. They all have their reason. That's how life works. It may look confusing to others, even to us sometimes. But there's a pattern, a purpose—waiting to be discovered. Not by anyone else. Just by us.

At the time, I didn't understand that. I thought the philosophers had the answers. I read them by the dozen, hoping for clarity. But the more I read, the more confused I became. So many of them wrote not to help, but to impress—offering complex ideas wrapped in elegant language, more like a performance than a path. I remember feeling more lost with each book I finished.

Many modern thinkers seemed to conclude the same thing: that life is an unsolvable riddle. A grand illusion. But over time, I began to see differently. Maybe life's deepest truths aren't meant to be wrapped in riddles. Maybe birth, life, and death are not abstract puzzles, but simple realities—direct, honest, and deeply human.

It was 1931, a few months after his mother had died, and Takashi was still studying at Nagasaki Medical University. Life at school felt calm. But far away, over a hundred miles northeast, his father was going through a different kind of storm—one that had nothing to do with the weather.

The wind blew hard from the north, cold and sharp, like it came straight from Siberia. Dr. Noboru Nagai walked slowly up the hill behind his house. Snow crunched under his boots, but he hardly noticed the cold. His mind was full of heavy thoughts—anger, hurt, and a deep sense of betrayal. When he reached the top of the hill, he stood in front of his wife Tsune's grave and closed his eyes in quiet prayer.

The night before, two men had arrived from Nagasaki. One was a professor from the medical university where Takashi studied. The other was a rich businessman from the Nagasaki Chamber of Commerce. The professor introduced the businessman as someone important and wealthy. Then came the surprising offer.

"Your son made quite an impression on my friend's daughter," the professor said. "He visited their villa at Mount Unzen, and the girl seems to like him. We think they would be a perfect match. If they marry, my friend is ready to send Takashi to Europe to study any medical field he wants. And to show his thanks, he'll give you a seaside villa in Nagasaki."

Takashi later shared what happened next:

"I got a telegram from my father. He told me to come home right away. I boarded the train, an eighteen-hour trip, feeling uneasy. When I got home, he was still seeing patients, and I had to wait. A nurse I didn't know brought me tea and sweets, bowing politely. I thanked her, but the house felt cold without my mother there."

When the patients finally left, Takashi's father came in. He opened his mouth a few times, trying to speak, but no words came. Then suddenly, his anger burst out.

"How could you sell yourself?" he asked, his voice shaking.

Takashi was shocked. "Father... I don't understand," he said.

"Don't act like you don't know!" his father snapped. "You really thought I'd agree to this? You think a man with honor sells his future for money?"

Takashi was confused. "Please, tell me what this is about."

"Tell you?" his father shouted. "I know you can choose who you marry. But to marry for money? To become a *yoshi*?"

In Japan, a *yoshi* is a man who marries into a family with no sons and takes their surname.

"What? Me—a *yoshi*?" Takashi asked, his voice shaking.

Like a man laying down his cards in a game, his father slapped two visiting cards on the table.

"These two came yesterday," he said. "They told me everything. Marry this rich girl, become a *yoshi*, and your life is set. You'll study in Europe, live in a villa, and I'll go fishing in Nagasaki. That's their plan!"

Suddenly, Takashi understood. He had gone to visit the professor's friend, not knowing it was a setup for a marriage meeting—a *miai*. He never realized it was meant to arrange a future for him.

His father looked him in the eye. "I told them, I may not have money, but I'll never sell my son for a villa by the sea."

Tears welled up in Takashi's eyes. Without thinking, he reached out and grabbed his father's hand—a hand that had healed many people, but never once taken a bribe. In that moment, nothing had to be said. Their bond grew stronger, not through arguments, but through the quiet strength of a simple handshake.

Chapter 5

The Suffering Christians

Back in Nagasaki for his third year of medical school, Takashi Nagai threw himself into preparing for the all-important final exams that awaited him at the end of his fourth year. These exams would determine his future as a doctor, so he pulled back from clubs and campus life, choosing instead to pour all his time and energy into studying. Yet, even as he buried himself in textbooks, deeper questions tugged at him—questions about the meaning of life, about God, and whether any of it really made sense.

As the spring semester of 1931 began, he decided to take a break—not from studying, but from the noise in his head. He packed a simple picnic lunch, slipped his weathered copy of *Pensées* into his bag, and set off alone into the hills. He was searching for clarity, or at least peace.

He found it—at least in setting—by a small, murmuring stream that flowed down from the mountains. There, with only birdsong and the breeze for company, he sat on a rock and opened Pascal's *Wager*. Like many of his fellow countrymen, Nagai admired French culture. He took pride in hearing the French speak highly of Japanese art and architecture. And as he read, he couldn't deny that Blaise Pascal wrote with striking insight and elegance. Still, there were moments that made him frown. Pascal's confidence in his Catholic faith sometimes rubbed him the wrong way. Could someone really believe so deeply, so boldly, in the face of all the violence and contradictions in religious history? The

Inquisition. The condemnation of Galileo. The brutal missions in South America. It all seemed too dark to ignore.

Then he reached the final line of *The Wager*, a line that stopped him cold:
"Only Christianity makes men both happy and lovable; the code of the gentleman does not allow you to be both happy and lovable."

That, he could not accept—not when he thought of his own parents. They were both kind and honorable. They loved deeply. They were good people. So how could Pascal dismiss their happiness and love as lesser or incomplete?

Still, something in the Frenchman's words wouldn't let him go. Not the logic, but the feeling. Pascal insisted that real certainty about God didn't come from reason alone, but from the heart. Faith, he said, was not something to be proven—it was something to be lived. And, in a quiet, almost pleading tone, Pascal invited the reader to begin—not by understanding everything, but simply by praying.

"If you feel even a flicker of what I say," Pascal seemed to whisper, "then start there. Pray. Attend Mass. Even if you don't yet believe."

As the sun warmed the spring valley and the air filled with the gentle song of the *uguisu*—the Japanese nightingale that Nagai had loved since childhood—he closed the book and finished his lunch. The stream sparkled under the clear sky, and the trees rustled with new life. It was all so beautiful, so harmonious, so alive. It couldn't possibly be an accident, he thought. Could it?

Maybe Pascal's idea of a Creator wasn't so far-fetched after all.

And then a new thought came, simple and sharp: **What if I tested it?**

He was, after all, a scientist. Why not try Pascal's advice—not as a believer, but as an experiment?

But asking a priest? That was too much. He wasn't ready for sermons or dogma or anyone trying to convert him on the spot. What he needed was a quiet, honest way to observe—to experience faith without pressure.

So, he came up with a plan. He would look for a Catholic family in Nagasaki, someone who might take him in as a boarder. That way, he could see faith lived out day by day. He could learn, ask questions when he felt ready, and quietly explore prayer on his own terms.

After a few quiet inquiries, he found just the place. The house was tucked away not far from the university, shaded by towering camphor laurels and ancient camellia trees—some so old they seemed to have watched over Nagasaki longer than the university itself. A simple gate bore the name: **Sadakichi Moriyama**.

Mr. Moriyama was a respected cattle dealer. He lived in the quiet home with his wife, while their daughter, Midori, worked as a schoolteacher and lived elsewhere. They seemed like an ordinary family—but their warmth, faith, and quiet strength would soon become one of the most defining parts of Nagai's journey.

But before their story could unfold, it was worth pausing. Because something had already begun to shift within Nagai. On that spring day by the stream, beneath the singing nightingale and the bright April sky, he had taken his first step—not toward a religion, but toward a deeper search for meaning, for truth, and perhaps, for God.

Among the many Jesuit missionaries who came to Japan, one name stands out for both his generosity and impact—Luis de Almeida. He wasn't your typical missionary. Before joining the Jesuits, Almeida had been a wealthy investor, deeply involved in the silk trade between Macao and Japan. But something shifted in him. Rather than continuing to chase profit, he chose to use his fortune to help those in need. He dedicated himself to the care of orphans and the sick, funding hospitals and orphanages out of his own pocket.

What made Almeida even more remarkable was his role in introducing surgery to Japan. At a time when Western medicine was virtually unknown there, his efforts opened the door to new possibilities in healthcare. While rumors swirled that the Jesuits were secretly building wealth through gold and silk deals, these tales were likely exaggerated. Still, such stories made their way into popular imagination—most famously in the novel *Shogun*, which painted the Jesuits as both spiritual emissaries and shrewd businessmen.

Then came 1579, a turning point in the Jesuit mission in Japan. That year, a new leader arrived: Alessandro Valignano. He was just 35, but already a man of great intellect and authority. Before joining the Jesuits, he had trained as a lawyer during the Renaissance—a time when reason and humanism were flourishing in Europe. Yet, it was his deep devotion to the Spiritual Exercises of St. Ignatius that set him apart. As novice master, he had mentored future legends like Matteo Ricci, who would later bring the Gospel to China.

Valignano's mission was massive: oversee all Jesuit activity in the East. But he approached this not with arrogance, but with humility and insight. He quickly understood something many others missed—that for Christianity to take root in Japan, it couldn't come as a foreign imposition. It had to be shared in a way that honored Japanese culture.

Looking back at the Jesuits' journey in Japan, what stands out is how much more they offered than just sermons. They built relationships through action—offering education, healthcare, and real compassion to those society often overlooked. Their mission became a bridge between worlds. And while not everyone trusted them—some viewed them with suspicion, as having hidden agendas—the impact they left behind is hard to ignore.

What's truly captivating is how the Jesuits navigated these cultural cross-currents. They weren't perfect, and their presence was sometimes controversial. But they tried, often sincerely, to meet people where they were. They learned the language. They respected local customs. They brought their faith not with force, but with a desire to understand.

Alessandro Valignano was especially ahead of his time in this. In an age when colonial powers often bulldozed over local traditions, Valignano took a different path. He believed the Christian message could—and should—be separated from European customs. It wasn't about making the Japanese Portuguese or Spanish. It was about making the Gospel meaningful in a Japanese context.

He told his fellow missionaries: don't just preach—listen. Don't just teach—learn. If you truly want people to hear Christ's message, speak in their language, walk in their world, and honor their values. Western knowledge—like astronomy or medicine—was worth sharing, but never as a way to claim superiority.

In the end, what the Jesuits did in Japan wasn't just a religious mission. It was a story of cultural respect, adaptation, and human connection. And through families like the Moriyamas, that legacy would take on a life of its own—quietly, but profoundly shaping the journey of faith for generations to come.

One of the most visionary aspects of Alessandro Valignano's work in Japan was his belief that Japanese Christians should be empowered to lead their own communities. He wasn't interested in building a European church in Japanese soil. He wanted something more meaningful—something rooted in respect. He challenged the common belief that European missionaries should hold all the authority. In his eyes, Jesuits were not to act as masters in Japan, but as students—humble learners in a culture rich with wisdom, history, and beauty.

To make that vision real, Valignano didn't just talk about respect—he showed it. He wrote a detailed manual on Japanese customs and etiquette, insisting that every Jesuit follow it. He even had traditional tea ceremony rooms built into Jesuit houses. At first glance, that may seem small. But it was a powerful gesture. It said, *"We are here not to change you, but to walk with you."* For Valignano, learning the customs wasn't enough. Honoring them was what mattered.

His dream was simple but bold: that Christianity could live alongside Japanese culture—not replace it, but grow within it. This idea, of integrating faith into native culture rather than forcing foreign identity, was radical for its time. But it struck a chord. Many Japanese thinkers and leaders, even in China, were drawn to it. It wasn't long before this respectful approach led to real conversions—among farmers, tradesmen, and even the elite samurai class.

One of the most remarkable converts was Ukon Takayama, a respected warlord, or *daimyo*, often called the "Japanese Thomas More." Takayama didn't just practice Christianity in private—he stood by it, boldly and publicly. When ordered to renounce his faith, he refused. As a result, he lost everything: his land, his title, and his home. In time, he was exiled. His loyalty to Christ came at a steep cost—just as it had for Thomas More in England.

But not everyone saw this growing faith as something to be admired.

As Christianity spread, especially among the samurai and commoners, fear began to take hold among Japan's rulers. At the top of that list was Hideyoshi—the most powerful warlord in the country. He had once welcomed the Jesuits, impressed by the Western knowledge they brought in fields like science, navigation, and medicine. But when he saw that the loyalty of Christian converts—especially samurai—was shifting from their feudal lords to Christ, whom they now called *Shukun* (Lord), he saw a threat.

The samurai code demanded total allegiance to one's *daimyo*. But Christianity taught that there was a higher loyalty, one that went beyond earthly rulers. For Hideyoshi, this was unacceptable.

So, in a shocking and brutal move, he acted.

In 1597, Hideyoshi ordered the arrest of twenty-six Christians in Kyoto. He had them marched through the bitter cold of winter, all the way to Nagasaki—a long, public journey designed to humiliate and terrify. When they finally arrived, he had them crucified. Not just killed—*crucified*. Publicly. Visibly. It was meant to send a message: *Defy the old order, and this is what will follow.*

But why Nagasaki?

Because by then, Nagasaki wasn't just another port—it had become the beating heart of Christianity in Japan. Founded as a small village, Nagasaki had grown rapidly since 1571 when it opened to European trade under the rule of Omura Sumitada—a Christian *daimyo* who believed deeply in the Jesuit mission. He used port fees to fund churches, schools, and even a seminary to train Japanese priests. The city had become a living example of what Christianity could look like when it took root in Japanese soil.

And that's exactly why Hideyoshi chose it as the stage for his warning.

The execution of the twenty-six was meant to crush the spirit of this growing community. But history shows us something else: it became a moment of profound faith and quiet resistance. These men and boys—some as young as twelve—died singing hymns, forgiving their executioners, and looking not to fear, but to their *Shukun*.

Their story, and the story of those who came before them, reminds us that faith doesn't exist in a vacuum. It grows in soil shaped by culture, by language, and by human hearts. And it survives—not through dominance, but through love, courage, and the unshakable conviction that some things are worth everything.

The execution of those twenty-six Christians wasn't just a single, tragic event—it was the spark that ignited a wave of brutal persecution across Japan. In the months and years that followed, the land that had once shown such promise for the Christian faith became a place of silence and shadows. The churches were closed, the priests hunted down, and the once-vibrant communities of believers were driven underground. What had begun as a bold vision—a dream of a Christian Japan that Valignano had poured his heart and soul into—was now fading, crushed beneath the heel of fear and power.

But even in that darkness, there is something that refuses to be forgotten.

Valignano's dream may not have survived the swords and decrees of the ruling warlords, but his vision still echoes through history. His idea—that faith must grow alongside culture, not against it—was far ahead of its time. It was more than strategy; it was a deep, human understanding that people need not lose their identity to find their soul. Though political forces tried to silence that dream, they couldn't erase the seeds he had planted. Today, his legacy still speaks to us: that faith, when lived with humility and respect, doesn't just survive hardship—it transforms it.

Among those who witnessed the unfolding tragedy were the Moriyama family—devout Christians living in Nagasaki. They were there when the twenty-six condemned men and boys arrived in the city, weary and barefoot from their long, freezing march. These weren't faceless victims; they were brothers, sons, priests, and friends. And yet, their captors planned to make them symbols of fear.

Hideyoshi, Japan's powerful ruler, had little personal belief in any religion. But he did believe in control. And he thought that public terror would be enough to break the will of Japan's Christians. So, he orchestrated not just an execution—but a spectacle. He wanted to send a message so loud, so horrifying, that no one would dare stand for this foreign faith again.

The people of Nagasaki were informed ahead of time. The date, the hour, the place—everything was made public. But instead of fear and silence, the streets filled with believers. Men, women, and children lined the roads—not to mock or turn away, but to whisper prayers, to call out blessings, to let the condemned know they were not alone. It was a quiet rebellion of love and courage in the face of cruelty.

The final walk led to Nishizaka Hill, not far from where the Nagasaki railway station stands today. There, stretched across the hill, was a row of crosses. They stood like grim monuments, carefully positioned to be visible from the harbor below. One by one, the twenty-six were tied to those crosses—held in place by iron bands and ropes of straw. And below each cross stood two samurai, their bamboo spears unsheathed, waiting in silence for the order to strike.

But the execution didn't begin right away. It was delayed on purpose—to stretch the fear, to twist the knife of dread, both for the prisoners and the hundreds watching from the hillside. The message was meant to be clear: this is what happens when you follow Christ.

But the message that truly echoed that day wasn't the one Hideyoshi intended.

From the crosses, songs of praise rose up into the cold air. Prayers were spoken. Forgiveness was offered to the very men who would soon end their lives. And among the crowd, tears flowed—but not just from sorrow. There was awe. There was defiance. There was faith.

What Hideyoshi tried to destroy became a testimony—etched not in stone, but in the hearts of those who witnessed it and in generations that followed. Christianity in Japan may have gone into hiding, but it never truly disappeared. It lived on—in whispers, in secret gatherings, in the quiet, unwavering hearts of people like the Moriyamas. And the crosses on Nishizaka Hill? They became more than instruments of death. They became symbols of a faith that refused to die.

In the heavy silence of that grim hillside, something unexpected happened.

One of the prisoners, his body already bound to the cross, raised his voice—not in a cry of fear, but in a song of praise. The words drifted across the stunned crowd: *"Praise the Lord, ye children of the Lord."* It was a psalm, sung with strength and peace. The thousands gathered fell into a hush. No one moved. They listened.

Then another voice joined in. One of the condemned began to chant the *Sanctus*, a sacred part of the Latin Mass sung by Christian communities all over Japan: *"Holy, holy, holy, Lord God of hosts..."* The chant echoed out over the bay, carried by the wind like a whisper from heaven.

And then came another voice—a Franciscan priest on a nearby cross. His words were simple, almost childlike: *"Jesus, Mary... Jesus, Mary..."* But they were enough. The crowd of nearly four thousand believers, overcome with emotion, picked up the litany and began to repeat it, their voices rising together until the whole hillside resounded with the names of Christ and His mother.

This wasn't fear. It wasn't surrender.

It was faith—alive, defiant, and unbroken.

Standing nearby, Hazaburo Terazawa, the official in charge of the execution, grew visibly uneasy. This was not what Hideyoshi had planned. The shogun had wanted a warning—a public shaming of Christians so fierce and final that it would crush all further resistance. But what Terazawa saw unfolding before him was the opposite: a display of unshakable devotion, a public act of worship in the face of death. The Christians were not humiliated. They were radiant. Fearless.

Then, one of the prisoners asked to speak.

It was Father Paul Miki—a thirty-three-year-old Jesuit priest, the son of a samurai general from Baron Takayama's household. He was respected across the land for his wisdom, his preaching, and his calm dignity. In that moment, he stood tall on the cross, his voice carrying clearly over the silent crowd.

"I am Japanese," he began, "and a brother of the Society of Jesus. I do not die as a criminal, but as someone who has taught the gospel of our Lord Jesus Christ."

There was no tremble in his voice. Only gratitude.

"I thank my God for this gift of death—for letting me lay down my life for Him. And to those who are watching," he said, turning his gaze over the sea of faces, "do you see fear in our eyes? You won't. Because we know where we're going. Heaven is real."

He didn't curse his killers. Instead, he offered them forgiveness. Even Hideyoshi. Especially Hideyoshi.

And with that, he began his farewell—not in protest or bitterness, but in prayer. He sang the words Christ himself had cried out from the cross: *"Lord, into Your hands I commend my spirit."*

At Terazawa's signal, the samurai stepped forward. Each one raised a long bamboo lance tipped with steel. Then, with a sharp cry, they thrust them upward into the ribs of the prisoners. One by one, the twenty-six were pierced.

For a brief moment, the hillside was silent.

Then the crowd exploded—not with chaos, but with grief, with fury, with something too raw for words. Cries of anguish rang out. Some wept. Others shouted. What was meant to be a lesson in fear had become a beacon of courage. What was designed to humiliate had instead glorified the Christian faith.

Terazawa turned and hurried away, his task complete—but shaken. He had witnessed something far greater than a simple execution.

In the days that followed, news of what had happened on Nishizaka Hill spread far and wide. And instead of stamping out Christianity, the execution did the opposite. The prestige of the faith rose. Many who had wavered now stood firm. Others, moved by what they had seen and heard, came quietly to ask for baptism.

The blood of the martyrs had not silenced the Church.

It had given it a voice.

Not long after the crucifixions, the ruler who had ordered them—Toyotomi Hideyoshi—died. With his death, Japan was thrown into a violent scramble for power. Feudal lords turned on one another in a ruthless bid for control. From this chaos rose Ieyasu Tokugawa, a cold and calculating leader who crushed his rivals and seized power. Unlike Hideyoshi, Tokugawa was not content with control—he demanded total submission.

And he saw Christianity as a threat.

To Tokugawa, the faith was more than a foreign religion. It was rebellion in disguise. He couldn't ignore the fact that even nobles like Baron Takayama had refused to abandon it. Even peasants had risked everything to cling to it. This was no passing belief—it was something deeper, something dangerous.

In 1614, once Tokugawa had fully secured his rule, he made his move. He strengthened the ban on Christianity. Priests and catechists were hunted like criminals. The government offered rewards—silver, land, or promotion—for anyone who betrayed them. But as more Christians chose death over denial, the shogun's cruelty escalated. Torture became policy.

And Nagasaki—once a vibrant hub of Christian life—turned into a city under siege.

Spies watched the streets. Soldiers patrolled the hills. Foreign priests who slipped into the country were quickly discovered—their strange accents and unfamiliar faces made them stand out. Those who were caught rarely lived long. The authorities interrogated them with unthinkable brutality.

Yet the faith refused to die.

Many Christians fled Nagasaki, scattering to offshore islands or remote places like Urakami—wild, forested regions far from the watchful eyes of the shogun. There, in the shadows, they quietly kept the light of their faith burning.

Among those who fled were the ancestors of a young boy named Sadakichi Moriyama.

They journeyed north from Nagasaki and found refuge in a rugged place where the Urakami River emptied into the bay. They took to fishing and farming. But their greatest work was in secret—they built an underground church. Not a structure of stone, but a community of souls bound together by purpose.

To survive without priests, they had to adapt. They assigned roles: one was the "water man," responsible for baptizing newborns. Another was the "calendar man," keeper of the sacred dates—Advent, Lent, Easter—so no holy season would be forgotten. And then there was the *chokata*, the spiritual leader. Always a man. Always chosen from the same family. The role passed from father to eldest son like a torch in the night.

Sadakichi's ancestors were the first to serve as chokata.

Generation after generation, they led their hidden flock—whispering prayers, preserving traditions, and risking everything to keep the faith alive. No churches. No sacraments. No foreign missionaries. Just courage, memory, and the quiet strength of belief passed from parent to child.

Two and a half centuries passed.

The Tokugawa shoguns ruled with an iron fist, never relaxing their hatred of Christianity. The system was ruthless. Surveillance was constant. Dissent was crushed. Still, the underground Christians endured.

In 1856, one of them—Kichizo Moriyama, the seventh chokata—was lured into a trap by the police. He was arrested, beaten, and tortured. They wanted him to confess, to betray his people, to deny Christ.

He refused.

And under that torture, he died. But he never broke.

His infant son survived. That child would one day grow into the man known as Sadakichi Moriyama.

The boy whose blood carried the legacy of centuries.

The boy born from silence, sacrifice, and a fire that could not be put out.

In 1858, Japan's long-held isolation shattered—not by choice, but by force. American warships, led by Commodore Perry, appeared on the horizon like steel dragons. Under threat of bombardment, the nation was forced to sign treaties it did not want. One of them, with the United States, opened ports like Yokohama and Nagasaki to foreign trade.

And with the merchants came missionaries.

European settlers began to build churches, their spires rising quietly among the tiled rooftops. But the shogunate was quick to respond. A strict decree was issued: these churches were for foreigners only. Japanese citizens were still forbidden from entering. Christianity, though present in plain sight, remained a forbidden faith—tucked away behind locked hearts and whispered prayers.

Still, hope had returned, however faint.

In February of 1864, Father Bernard Petitjean, a missionary from the Paris Foreign Mission Society, completed the construction of a small stone church in Oura, a southern district of Nagasaki. It stood beneath the now-famous Glover Mansion, a place immortalized years later in the opera *Madama Butterfly*. The new church was modest in size but sacred in purpose—a house of God rising not far from the sea.

What Father Petitjean didn't yet know was that just four miles away, hidden in the hills of Urakami, lived a silent community of Christians.

For centuries, they had kept their faith alive in secret. The memory of their last chokata, tortured and killed in 1856, was still fresh in their hearts. The scars of that grief made them wary. The sudden appearance of a Western priest felt like a dream—but could also be a trap.

They had been waiting for something like this.

Passed down through generations was a prophecy of sorts—three signs by which the faithful would recognize the true Church when it returned to Japan. The first: the priest would be celibate. The second: there would be a statue of the Virgin Mary. And the third: the Church would obey the Pope in Rome.

Without all three, they would remain hidden.

Then, on a quiet market day, a few believers from Urakami made a bold decision. They ventured closer to the foreigner's church. The streets buzzed with trade and conversation, but their eyes were fixed only on one thing.

One of them, heart pounding, slipped through the open doors of the Oura church.

Inside, silence. Stone walls. Wooden pews. And at the front—there she was. A statue of the Blessed Virgin Mary, holding the Christ child gently in her arms. Just as their ancestors had described her.

They asked around about the foreign priest. Was it true he lived alone? Was he unmarried?

The answer came quickly—yes. The tall Frenchman in black robes kept no wife, no family. He lived simply, serving only the Church.

A third sign remained. And outside the church, nailed beside the entrance, was a harsh warning from the government: **Japanese are forbidden to enter. Severe punishment awaits those who disobey.**

The sign confirmed it all.

Only a faith under the Pope—one that still stood in defiance of earthly powers—would provoke such a warning.

Everything their ancestors had taught was true.

The Church had returned.

The young boy who had inherited the title of *chokata*—leader of the hidden Christians—was still too small to speak or decide. The responsibility fell to the elders, but they remained locked in quiet debate. Was this new foreign church truly of the same faith they had preserved in secret for generations? Or was it a trap?

Their wives, however, had grown weary of hesitation. They had seen enough. The signs were clear. The time for hiding was over.

So, on a gray morning thick with low clouds, they took action.

It was March 17, 1865.

Gathering quietly at the shore, several women from Urakami climbed into fishing boats. The wind was cold, the bay still. They sailed three miles down the eastern edge of Nagasaki Bay, dressed as ordinary fisherfolk heading to the city for food and goods. No one would suspect anything.

They landed just past Dejima and began their silent journey up the hill. The city stirred around them—vendors, porters, and guards—but they walked with heads low and hearts pounding. When they reached the stone steps of the church and saw no sign of government officials, they climbed quickly and slipped inside.

Inside the dim sanctuary, Father Bernard Petitjean sat alone, reciting his breviary. His voice barely moved the air.

He had come to Japan with dreams in his heart. As a seminarian in Paris, he had been inspired by the stories of Japanese martyrs—Baron Ukon Takayama, Lady Tama Hosokawa, and countless ordinary men and women who had chosen death rather than deny Christ. He had imagined meeting their descendants. But since his arrival, Japan had greeted him with suspicion and silence.

His church was finished. But it felt empty. No converts. No seekers. Only stone walls and silence.

Until now.

He looked up, startled. A group of women in weather-worn clothes had entered the church. They moved quietly across the tatami mats, their faces marked by years of caution and hidden faith. One of them stepped forward. Her name was Yuri, meaning "lily."

She looked into his eyes.

"Where is the statue of Holy Mary?"

Father Petitjean froze. His heart caught in his chest. Could it be? Was this happening?

Before he could respond, another woman stepped forward. Her name was Teru—meaning "luster"—and her voice carried both gentleness and urgency.

"Our hearts and yours are the same," she said.

Then again, she asked, louder this time: "Where is the statue of Santa Maria?"

He could barely find his voice. But he nodded and whispered, "Ah, yes... yes. Please. Come with me."

He led them quietly across the church to a side altar along the eastern wall. And there she stood—*Santa Maria*, the Virgin Mary, holding the Child Jesus in her arms.

Teru gasped. Her hands trembled. Her voice broke through the silence, full of awe, full of tears.

"It's her! It's her!"

She pointed to the statue with reverence, as if greeting a long-lost friend.

"Yes... it is her," she said again. "She holds the Child Jesus in her arms."

The weight of centuries seemed to fall away in that moment.

They had found the Church.

And Father Petitjean, standing beside them, realized what had just happened. Though the language had shifted, though years of isolation had changed their words, their hearts had remained faithful. Their courage, their memory, and their love had kept the faith alive in silence.

Across time, across pain, they were one.

It didn't take long for Father Petitjean to learn where the Hidden Christians of Urakami gathered. It wasn't in a grand hall or a quiet chapel. It was a cattle shed—a plain, muddy shelter at the edge of the Moriyama fields. That humble building, which smelled of straw and livestock, had become their sacred ground.

He wasted no time. Quietly, he sent messages to key members of the secret community—the calendar man who tracked holy days in secret, the water man who passed coded messages, and the elders who had guarded the faith through silence and danger. Their reply came with a warning: discovery meant death or exile. The authorities would show no mercy.

But Father Petitjean would not be stopped.

He disguised himself as a farmer. Then, after sunset, he made his way through the shadows to the shed. Inside, hidden by darkness and the scent of hay, he stood on dry straw to cover the muck and celebrated Mass. The Holy Eucharist had returned to Urakami, not in grandeur, but in secrecy—in simplicity.

And that meant everything.

The Japanese Christians, deeply aware of symbolism, were moved to tears. To them, this was not just a secret Mass—it was a mirror of Bethlehem. Like the Holy Family once turned away and forced to find shelter in a stable, they too had clung to faith in the cold corners of a rejecting world. For generations, during Advent, they had told their children the story and even laid extra hay in their own sheds on Christmas Day. The story had stayed alive in whispers, in gestures, in hope.

But shadows don't last forever. Eventually, light exposes all things.

Rumors reached the authorities in Nagasaki: there was a French priest among the Hidden Christians.

The timing could not have been worse. The Tokugawa shogunate, now crumbling after centuries of rule, was desperate to preserve its grip on power. Rebels were rising to restore the Emperor and rid Japan of foreign influence. In a panic, the shogunate ordered the local officials: crush Christianity once and for all.

And so, in the early hours of July 15, 1867—at exactly 3 a.m.—soldiers marched through sheets of rain, their lanterns flickering like ghostly eyes in the dark. One by one, they arrested the Christian leaders. Sixty-eight were taken that night.

Then came more.

Soon, every known Christian in Urakami—3,414 souls, from newborns to the elderly—was seized and scattered across the country. The goal was clear: destroy the community. Break their unity. Shatter their spirit. And if they refused to abandon their faith, they would be tortured.

Some were. Some died. Others were forced to watch loved ones suffer. The camps were brutal. The conditions inhuman.

Less than a year later, the Tokugawa regime collapsed. Emperor Meiji rose to power, promising to modernize Japan. But freedom did not follow for the Christians.

The new government, eager to present a united Japan to the Western powers, saw Christianity as dangerous. They needed loyalty to the Emperor. Shinto, not Christ, was to be the soul of the nation. The Hidden Christians, though now out in the open, were seen as traitors—hearts loyal to a foreign faith.

And the persecution continued.

In the camps, many died. Starved, beaten, or simply broken by years of cruelty. But news of their suffering began to leak out. Foreigners in Nagasaki raised their voices. The Western press caught wind. Soon, diplomats from France and beyond demanded answers.

Finally, in 1872—five years after their arrest—the Urakami Christians were allowed to return.

But what they came back to was devastation.

Six hundred sixty-four of them had died in the camps. The rest came home sick, worn, and heartbroken. Their homes were gone. Their land was wild with weeds. Their boats, tools, and every belonging had been stolen or destroyed.

They stood at the edge of the paddies, staring at the broken land they had once tended with pride. And they wept.

The soil was the same, but the life was gone.

Yet even in their sorrow, one thing remained untouched.

Their faith.

Chapter 6

The Bells of Nagasaki in Urakami

When the French priests arrived in Urakami, they brought not just hope, but change—deep, irreversible change. The old ways, the quiet but strong leadership of the Hidden Christian community, began to fade. Men like the *head man*, the *water man*, and the *calendar man*—figures who had kept the faith alive through whispers, signs, and hidden rituals—slowly vanished from the heart of village life. Their roles, once vital, were now replaced by new customs, new people, and unfamiliar traditions.

The last of those sacred leaders passed away in 1856. His death didn't just mark the end of a life; it marked the end of an era.

His son, shaped by suffering and silence, had grown up in exile during the brutal years of persecution—a time they called *Babylon*. After years away, he returned to Urakami when the exiled Christians were finally allowed to come home. With quiet strength, he worked hard to rebuild what had been taken. He restored the family's cattle business, married, and slowly carved out a new life in a changed world.

By 1907, his eldest son, Sadakichi, was ready for his own journey. He set off for Ukujima, a remote, wind-swept island about 200 miles west of Nagasaki. Though part of the Goto Islands, Ukujima stood apart. It was known for its harsh isolation—and its tragic past. Long ago, during the dark days of the Tokugawa persecutions, Christian families had fled to its shores, hoping to find safety. But wounds lingered. Fear remained. The locals, though descended from people of faith, still viewed Christianity with suspicion. They had learned to survive by staying silent. Outsiders, especially Christians, were seen as dangerous.

Into this tightly guarded world came Sadakichi—and it didn't take long for his life to take an unexpected turn.

He fell in love.

Her name was Tsumo Akagi, a strong-willed island girl with wind-burned cheeks and black hair like polished stone. But their love sparked more than whispers. Tsumo's father, a traditional farmer deeply rooted in local customs, was outraged. He wanted nothing to do with a Christian from Nagasaki. To him, Sadakichi represented everything risky, everything foreign. When the arguments at home became unbearable, Tsumo ran away—boarding a cattle boat to Nagasaki in search of freedom.

Her father chased after her, furious and heartbroken. But Tsumo wasn't ready to be dragged back into the life she had fled. She escaped again. Finally, exhausted and defeated, her father disowned her.

Heartbroken but not alone, Tsumo returned to Nagasaki. Only one person opened the door to her—Sadakichi.

But even in Nagasaki, peace was hard to find. Sadakichi's family didn't welcome her. His mother, especially, was bitterly against their relationship. Tsumo, in their eyes, was a *mishinja*—an unbeliever, a woman without faith. Worse still, the women of Urakami mocked her. They whispered behind her back, called her *"the Crow,"* laughing at her deep black hair and her sun-darkened skin—the marks of a life spent under the harsh winds and salt air of Ukujima.

But love, real love, holds firm.

Despite the pressure from all sides—family, neighbors, traditions—they married. In 1908, their daughter was born. They named her **Midori**, a name that spoke of life and new beginnings.

Their love story was far from perfect. It was complicated, tangled in culture, faith, and loss. But it was real. And it endured.

In a time when it was easier to give in, Sadakichi and Tsumo chose each other.

And that choice—quiet, bold, and full of grace—became its own kind of legacy.

Time passed, as it always does. And when Sadakichi's father passed away, he left behind more than just the family cattle business—he left a home built on courage, sacrifice, and quiet faith. The old house, tucked away in a corner of Urakami, had once been a lifeline for Hidden Christians. But now, in the modern world, its walls stood silent, its sacred past slowly fading from memory.

By late 1931, a young medical student named **Takashi Nagai** stood in front of that very house. He knew nothing of the stories it held. For him, it was just a place he hoped to rent—modest, well-kept, and close enough to the university.

He had no idea that within those walls, generations had whispered forbidden prayers in the dark. That mothers had baptized their babies in secret. That elders had kept the flame of faith alive when discovery meant torture or death.

To him, it was just a house.

Nagai adjusted his uniform—its brass buttons gleaming in the afternoon sun—and knocked gently on the wooden door. "*O jama itashimasu,*" he called politely. *Excuse me for disturbing you. Is anyone home?*

Moments later, the door creaked open, and a woman appeared—her once jet-black hair now streaked with soft gray. It was **Tsumo**, older now, but still carrying the quiet strength of her younger days. Her sharp eyes softened when she saw the well-mannered student before her, standing with his back straight and shoes polished.

He introduced himself with a warm smile, explaining that he was looking for a place to stay while studying medicine nearby. Tsumo listened patiently, then nodded and said gently, "I'll have to speak with my husband first. He's out in the shed with the cows."

She knew well that such decisions weren't made lightly.

Later, when she passed along the request, **Sadakichi** barely looked up from his work. "We don't usually take in boarders," he said, matter-of-factly. That was the end of the conversation—or so it seemed.

But two days later, Nagai returned, this time bowing even lower, his smile a little brighter, and his voice more hopeful. Something in his quiet determination touched Tsumo. He didn't seem like someone looking for convenience—he seemed like someone looking for a place to belong.

She brought the matter up again.

This time, Sadakichi paused. Just the Sunday before, the priest had preached about welcoming the stranger—about how we never know when we might be entertaining someone sent by God.

"Maybe the Lord did send him," Sadakichi murmured thoughtfully. "What do you think, Tsumo?"

Tsumo gave a small nod, her heart already leaning toward kindness. "Let's take him in," she said.

And so, with a grateful heart and a bag of books in hand, Takashi Nagai moved into the upstairs room. As he unpacked, he hummed an old folk song from Kyushu, unaware of the sacred echoes that still lingered in the beams above his head—the prayers, the tears, the hope of those who had lived and worshipped in secret before him.

For now, all he felt was a quiet peace—a sense that, somehow, he was right where he was meant to be.

Living with the Moriyamas became more than just a stop on Takashi Nagai's journey—it became a turning point in his life. Years later, he would write about this season in his books, recalling how those days quietly reshaped his heart and mind.

Each morning, just before sunrise, the soft chime of cathedral bells would drift through the old wooden house. At exactly 5:30 a.m., the bells rang out, waking Nagai gently from his sleep. He soon fell into the rhythm of the Moriyama home—early prayers whispered in the local singsong dialect of Nagasaki, daily routines steeped in peace and purpose. At noon, the bells rang again. Then once more at 6 p.m.—calling everyone to pause and recite the Angelus. It was a sacred rhythm, like the heartbeat of Urakami itself.

Sometimes, Nagai joined the family for meals. Around the table, Sadakichi would speak passionately about Christianity, especially after a little warm sake. At times, his intensity overwhelmed the young medical student. But even then, Nagai couldn't help but admire it—the fire in Sadakichi's words, the love for a faith that had endured so much. Still,

Nagai wasn't ready to dive in completely. He preferred to take slow, quiet steps, discovering Christianity on his own terms.

One day, three months into his stay, Nagai sat in a lecture hall when the topic of the "Nagasaki martyrs" came up. The professor brushed them off as little more than fanatics. It was a common enough opinion, and Nagai didn't feel surprised. But that word—*fanatics*—didn't sit right with him anymore.

He thought of the Moriyamas. Their kindness. Their unwavering faith. Their Sunday rest, where even laborers paused to be with their families—a practice unheard of in most of Japan at the time. It struck him: Urakami was quietly ahead of its time.

He remembered the kindergarten near the cathedral, run by Catholic sisters for over sixty years—one of Japan's very first. There was also the orphanage, the schools, and the devoted priests and nuns who ran them. Their care and educational standards rivaled the best the government could offer. It reminded him of something older, something deep in Japan's roots—like the Buddhist monks who had once shaped the nation's spirit through their temples, their teachings, and their art.

Nagai felt a deep respect for the Christian presence in Urakami. But he also carried a quiet concern.

He had read about Europe's history—the Crusades, the Inquisition, the persecution of thinkers like Galileo, and even the church's role in justifying slavery and colonization. These darker chapters lingered in his mind. Could any religion, no matter how pure its beginnings, turn dangerous when given too much power?

Maybe the professor was right, he thought. Perhaps even the most beautiful faith could carry the seeds of something harmful, if left unchecked. It was a troubling thought—and one that Nagai couldn't easily shake.

Then, one afternoon, Nagai heard a curious rumor.

The bell ringer at the cathedral, an old man with a rasp in his breath and a kind smile, was said to possess a hidden collection of Christian relics—objects that had survived centuries of persecution. Intrigued, Nagai paid him a visit.

The bell ringer led him to a quiet, dim room. Inside, time seemed to stand still. Crosses, old rosaries, and faded paintings filled the space. But what stopped Nagai in his tracks was a small, haunting image—**Maria Kannon**.

She was a blend of two worlds: the Virgin Mary, mother of Christ, and Kannon, the Buddhist goddess of mercy. Soft, compassionate eyes. A gentle face. Somewhere in the design, almost hidden, was a tiny cross.

Centuries ago, when Christianity was outlawed, the faithful had adapted. They disguised Mary as Kannon, crafting ceramic images that passed as Buddhist art to avoid suspicion. To outsiders, it was just another household statue. But to those who believed—it was their hope, their prayer, their secret act of defiance.

As Nagai gazed at the image, he felt a quiet awe. There, in that dim room, he saw the resilience of a people who had risked everything to keep their faith alive. He saw creativity born out of danger. Courage hidden in plain sight.

And for the first time, perhaps, Nagai began to understand that faith wasn't just about belief—it was about love strong enough to survive in silence, in symbols, in secret.

Nagai's interest grew even more when the bell ringer, noticing his curiosity, offered to show him around the cathedral. It was a massive building, stretching 230 feet long—the biggest cathedral in the entire Far East. It could hold thousands of people. The old man spoke with quiet pride as he shared the story of the cathedral's past—a story filled with struggle and strong faith.

He remembered his own childhood in 1872. That was the year his family returned to Urakami after being forced to live in internment camps for many years because of their faith. Life was tough when they came back. Most of their tools had been stolen, so they had to use broken pieces of pottery and tiles just to dig the ground and plant crops.

Their dream was to build a house on a hill that looked over Urakami. But the land they wanted had once belonged to a government official who had arrested and imprisoned their religious leaders. Still, they didn't give up. After years of hard work, they saved enough money to buy the land. They tore down the old building and built a small wooden church in its place.

By 1895, with the help of a dedicated priest—who didn't even have any training in architecture—the community started building a larger stone and brick cathedral. Every family helped. They carried stones from across the river, cut wood from the mountains, and even the women and children made thousands of red bricks by hand. Skilled workers carved statues and decorations from solid granite.

Building the cathedral wasn't easy. Money and materials were always running out. Sometimes work had to stop completely until they could gather more supplies. But even with all these difficulties, the cathedral slowly began to rise. Finally, after twenty-two years, in 1917, it was finished. By then, Japan's economy was improving, and the country was supporting the

Allies in World War I—though they hadn't suffered much compared to others.

As the church bells rang at 6 p.m. for the Angelus prayer to Mary, Nagai saw something that moved him deeply. Workers in the fields stopped what they were doing. Their hands were rough and worn from hard labor, but they knelt down quietly, joining their hands in prayer. Even a young girl in the distance stopped moving, standing still as the sound of the bells filled the air.

In that peaceful moment, Nagai's thoughts drifted. The scene reminded him of a painting by Millet, one of his favorite artists—paintings that showed farmers praying in the fields, filled with calm and quiet faith. The people of Urakami, like the figures in Millet's art, seemed to have a deep and certain belief in something greater than themselves. Nagai, a student filled with questions and doubts, felt the difference. He admired their faith, but also felt sad, realizing he didn't share the same certainty.

Suddenly, a loud sound broke his thoughts—a young cow was mooing loudly. It had arrived from the Goto Islands the night before and had been restless ever since. The animal had caused a scene trying to run away and had been tied up in a stall. Its cries had echoed all night, and even now, it was still uneasy.

Nagai looked at the cow and felt an unexpected connection. In a way, he was like that animal—restless, searching, and unsure where he truly belonged. Both of them were longing for something just out of reach, trying to find a place to call home—but not quite sure where that was.

With a deep sigh, Nagai sat back down at his desk and opened a medical textbook. He was getting ready for his lectures. The book was written in German, full of facts and clear explanations. Its exactness and order gave him a strange kind of comfort. This was the world he knew well—the world of science and logic, where things followed rules and made sense.

But even as he focused on his studies, something inside him felt unsettled. There was a quiet uneasiness in his heart. He couldn't explain it, but he felt that something important was missing—something deep and meaningful. He just didn't know what it was.

Chapter 7

Beyond this peaceful scene

In the early days of 1932, Nagasaki came alive with the hope and joy of a new year. The scent of *omochi*—soft, sticky rice cakes offered in celebration—filled the air. The streets shimmered with color as families traded their everyday clothes for bright, elegant kimonos. Laughter echoed through alleyways as children, dressed in brilliant reds and blues, darted about playing *battledore*, their parents watching with soft smiles and full hearts. It was a rare pause—a moment of pure, unburdened happiness. For a little while, the troubles of the outside world felt far away.

But just beyond the hills and coastlines, storm clouds were forming.

Far off in Manchuria, tensions were rising fast. What once felt like distant news slowly grew into something too big to ignore. China was growing angry with Japan's increasing presence in the region. In protest, Chinese citizens began boycotting Japanese goods—hurting businesses back home, especially in cities like Nagasaki, where the economy was already under pressure. Western countries added to the strain with their own trade barriers. And then, in late January, Japan's Kwantung Army attacked Shanghai. The battle that followed was long, bitter, and unresolved—ending only weeks later with a fragile peace treaty. The ink had barely dried before it became clear: this was only the beginning.

Back in Nagasaki, however, life went on. The streets still felt safe, the cherry trees still waited for spring—and for Nagai, the war seemed like another world. His eyes were fixed on something much closer: the national medical exams. These weren't just ordinary tests—they were the final hurdle after nearly two decades of hard work. In Japan, schooling began at six and stretched endlessly through rigorous years of education. Now, at twenty-four, Nagai stood at the edge of it all.

From January to March, the festive spirit faded into silence among the students. No more firecrackers or New Year sweets—only long days and sleepless nights of study. Internal medicine, surgery, ENT, ophthalmology, gynecology, dermatology, urology, psychiatry, pediatrics—nine intense subjects that would be tested first on paper, and then in front of professors with real patients. There was no room for error.

But as he always had, Nagai rose to the challenge. He passed each exam with distinction and earned the university medal—one of the highest honors a student could receive. When the university asked him to deliver the graduation speech, it was a proud moment not just for him, but for everyone who had watched his journey from the sidelines.

Full of excitement, he wrote to his father. He hoped to return home and work at his side, to finally give back to the man who had sacrificed so much. But the reply he received was gentle, firm, and full of wisdom.

"Your mother worked so hard to help you become a doctor," his father wrote. "Now you've been given a place at the university. I am proud of you—but you must stay and continue your work there."

The words stung, but they also stirred something deep in Nagai. For a while, he let go of the heavy thoughts that had been weighing him down—the questions of purpose, of faith, of what kind of man he was becoming. He focused instead on his speech, on the message he wanted to share with his classmates.

He knew this moment mattered. He wanted to speak not just with knowledge, but with vision—with a heart full of both respect for Japan's traditions and urgency for its future. Japan was still struggling with diseases like tuberculosis, still far behind the West in many areas of medicine. His speech would not just be a farewell—it would be a call to action. A plea to his fellow doctors to dream bigger, reach higher, and bring healing not just to bodies, but to a nation searching for its place in a changing world.

Sitting alone at his desk, Nagai dipped his brush into black Chinese ink. As the scent of the ink rose faintly in the air, he felt a quiet connection to generations past—those whose thoughts had been shaped by centuries of poetry, wisdom, and tradition. In this space, surrounded by silence and simplicity, he could finally breathe. Here, his words weren't confined to clinical charts or the rigid grammar of German medical texts. Instead, he wrote in the elegant language of his ancestors, a language that carried emotion, spirit, and soul.

As he scribbled down the first lines of his graduation speech, something stirred deep within him. For all the precision and power of science, something was missing—something he couldn't diagnose or dissect. The heart of a nation, the spirit of its people, and the soul of its culture—these mattered just as much as scalpels and stethoscopes. Medicine could heal bodies, but what about the things science couldn't touch?

And so, with quiet determination, he began to write. Not just as a doctor-in-training, but as a son of Japan—rooted in its traditions, and hopeful for its future.

But life, unpredictable as always, had other plans.

The graduation celebrations had been long awaited. After months of intense study and sleepless nights, the students deserved a night of release. They chose Tsutenkaku—a famous Chinese restaurant in Nagasaki that lived up to its nickname, "the heavenly palace." That evening, the air buzzed with laughter, music, and the clinking of glasses.

Geishas welcomed them—graceful and distant at first, their painted faces unreadable. But as the night wore on, the mood shifted. The women began to laugh, sing, and dance, pulling the students into a whirlwind of joy and abandon. Sake flowed like water. Chinese spirits warmed their bellies. Even European wines found their way to the table.

Nagai, ever the quiet scholar, surprised everyone. He drank confidently, keeping pace with the liveliest of them. A geisha from Sasebo, bold and charming, gravitated toward him, clearly intrigued. When she teased him about his drinking stamina, he just smiled and poured another. For the first time in months—maybe years—he felt completely free.

And then, it happened.

With a grin and a drunken bow, he stood to perform his signature party trick: the "Dance of the Mudfish Catcher." Everyone roared with laughter. The hours slipped by unnoticed, the city outside fading into a blur. By the time Tsutenkaku closed, the students spilled out into the streets like children set free, singing and cheering under the quiet stars of a Nagasaki night.

But for Nagai, something began to unravel.

The streets tilted. The sky seemed too wide. His steps grew heavy and uncertain, and he found himself wandering without purpose. Was he walking home? Was he even still himself?

The familiar city around him suddenly felt distant, almost unreal—like a dream he couldn't quite wake from.

He made it to the tram stop, only to realize the last tram had already left. Still grinning, still lost in his tipsy bravado, he flagged down a taxi. But when it came time to pay, he reached into empty pockets. No matter. He was about to graduate. He had earned a university medal. And the girl from Sasebo had looked at him like he was someone important. Life felt like a celebration with no end in sight.

Rain began to fall—a light, cold drizzle that soaked his clothes and sobered his mood. He crept quietly into the Moriyama household, careful not to wake the cows or the family. Slipping into his room, he collapsed onto his futon, mumbling with a drunken smile, "Mudfish all... let's lie at the bottom of the lake for a while." Then silence.

Morning arrived like a hammer.

A sharp light pierced the window, and his head throbbed with each heartbeat. Everything hurt. He barely responded when someone called him for breakfast. Instead, he groaned and pulled the blanket over his face. He thought it was just a hangover.

But something was wrong.

Terribly wrong.

When he finally managed to sit up, the world around him had gone eerily quiet. The usual sounds—the rustling, the voices, the distant streetcars—were gone. He blinked. He turned his head. Nothing.

He couldn't hear.

Panic gripped him.

He stumbled his way to the hospital, each step heavier than the last. His friend, the matron, saw him arrive—pale, sweating, and confused—and rushed him to a bed. A doctor was summoned. The diagnosis came fast: severe inflammation in the middle ear, possibly meningitis.

The matron's face was grave as she delivered the news. "It's serious," she said. "If it spreads… it could take your life."

He was moved to a private room immediately, and a top ear specialist was called. As the hospital buzzed around him, Nagai lay in bed—half-deaf, disoriented, and unsure of what would come next. The boy who had written so passionately about Japan's future just days before now faced a future he couldn't even hear.

When the professor entered the room, Nagai immediately knew who he was. This was the same man who had once tried to arrange a marriage between him and the daughter of a wealthy man. But now, lying in bed with a high fever, Nagai didn't think about how strange that was. He was too weak, too tired to care. The professor performed a spinal tap and looked at the results. He let out a long, low whistle—he couldn't believe what he saw.

Nagai, once the top student, full of health and energy, was now seriously ill. His condition was dangerous. If something wasn't done soon, he might die. There was only one option—a risky surgery. It might save his life, but it could also damage his brain. Just days ago, his future had looked so bright. Now, everything seemed uncertain and fragile.

The surgery helped to stabilize him, but he wasn't safe yet. For days afterward, Nagai drifted in and out of sleep, sometimes unaware of where he was. He hovered between life and death.

In Japan, when someone is very sick in the hospital, a close female relative usually stays with them. This helper is called a **tsukisoi**. She comforts the patient, helps with small things, and keeps them company through the night. Since Nagai had no family in Nagasaki, the Moriyama family found someone else to help. She was an older woman from Urakami—a peasant with a kind heart and a strong body, like the women in Millet's paintings. Though she didn't know Nagai personally, she stayed by his side and prayed for him, softly saying the Rosary in her gentle Nagasaki accent. Her voice calmed his mind, and even in his weakness, he felt safe near her.

Little by little, Nagai began to recover. The fever left, and his thoughts became clearer. But something had changed. He couldn't hear from his right ear anymore. The illness had damaged it permanently.

The graduation ceremony happened without him. Another student gave the speech he had spent so much time writing. For the first time in his life, Nagai felt completely empty—his body was weak, his mind exhausted, and his heart heavy.

During his slow recovery, Nagai found peace in old Japanese books. One that stood out was **"The Ten Foot Square Hut"** by Kamono Chohei. He had always liked it, but now, its words meant much more to him. The book began with the line:
"Ceaselessly the river flows… The eddying foam gathers and then is gone, never staying for a moment. Even so is man and his habitat."
He finally understood what the writer meant. Life keeps moving like a river, and nothing—no achievement or happy

moment—can stop it. Everything passes, whether we want it to or not.

When spring came, the cherry blossoms were in full bloom. Their beauty was stunning—light pink, soft, and pure. People gathered to admire them, to enjoy their brief season. But their time was short. A few days later, the petals fell to the ground and were crushed under people's feet. Their beauty faded, forgotten by many in the rush of daily life.

In the same way, Nagai's graduation speech had been forgotten. The words he had written with so much hope and pride had been lost in time. No one remembered. He had dreamed that his speech would be a proud moment. Now it felt like it didn't matter. His stomach turned—was it life's cruelty that made him sick, or was it the painful truth that his pride had been misplaced? The question stayed with him.

Even though the operation saved his life, Nagai's body was still weak. He moved between sleep and waking, often unsure if he would survive. The tsukisoi, the old woman from Urakami, continued to care for him. In Japan, this role is more than just helping—it's about giving emotional support, too. The tsukisoi does small things with great kindness: she fixes the blanket, gives water, and gently massages sore muscles. She stays close, quietly giving the patient strength and comfort.

Though she didn't know Nagai, this woman felt sorry for him. She saw a young man who was sick and suffering, and she stayed, praying the Rosary in her soft voice. Her words were full of faith and peace. Nagai, half-awake, listened to her voice and found calm in the prayers. Even as he struggled between life and death, those simple prayers gave him comfort.

As time passed, Nagai began to get better, though the illness had taken its toll. His right ear would never hear again—a lasting mark from the disease. The ceremony had taken place without him. Another student had stood at the podium and read his speech. A deep sadness settled in Nagai's heart. His energy, his ambition, all seemed to be gone. His once strong body felt weak and worn out, and he carried the scars of what he had been through.

In the quiet that followed his illness, Nagai turned to the comfort of the old classics. Japanese literature, with its gentle focus on the shortness of life and the quiet passing of time, had always touched something deep in him. Now, it spoke even louder. One piece in particular, *The Ten Foot Square Hut* by Chohei Kamono, written back in 1212, echoed through his thoughts. The words he had once read for their beauty now struck him like a truth too clear to ignore:

"Ceaselessly the river flows… The eddying foam gathers and then is gone, never staying for a moment. Even so is man and his habitat."

Back then, he had admired the lines for their poetry. Now, they cut deeper. The river kept flowing, always forward. The foam—bright, swirling, alive—vanished in seconds. Just like people. They appeared, lived their short lives, then disappeared without leaving much behind. Even blossoms on the trees, so lovely in spring, fell quietly to the ground and were soon forgotten.

And what about him? Nagai, who had once dreamed so boldly, who had aimed so high? He now saw that the life he had worked so hard to build—the top grades, the big plans, the speech he never gave—had slipped through his fingers like running water. All of it, gone. And what remained?

A strange silence. A deep ache. But also, maybe, a small window of clarity. In a world where nothing stays forever, perhaps the only thing that truly matters is how we live in the time we're given.

Chapter 8

X=ray Technology Obsession.

In the spring of 1932, Professor Itsuma Suetsugu sat alone at his desk in a quiet corner of Nagasaki Medical University. The room was dim, the air heavy, and the feeling in his chest even heavier. What had once been a heart full of hope now carried the quiet ache of disappointment.

Just a year before, he had walked into the university with big dreams and a clear vision. He wanted to bring Japan to the forefront of modern medicine by building a top-notch radiology department. It was a bold idea—radiology was still new, even in Europe—but Suetsugu believed in its potential. He believed it could save lives, change lives. He had studied in Germany, at Saint George's Hospital in Hamburg, one of the best in the field. He had learned the science, absorbed the knowledge, pushed through the language barrier with textbooks and research papers written in German. And yet, back home, none of it seemed to matter.

What hit him hardest wasn't the struggle to master the science—it was the people. Behind the polite greetings and formal speeches, he could feel it: the quiet pushback, the closed doors. His colleagues, many of them older, set in their ways, looked at him not with admiration, but with suspicion. To them, radiology wasn't a leap forward—it was a threat. A cold machine that might replace the warmth of their stethoscopes and decades of experience. Change, no matter how promising, often feels like betrayal to those comfortable in the old ways.

Suetsugu had not expected the silence in the hallways, the sidelong glances, the way conversations stopped when he entered the room. He had thought they would welcome progress, that they would see the same future he did. Instead, he found himself alone, carrying a dream that suddenly felt much heavier than before.

The university's treatment of Suetsugu's efforts had quickly become more disappointing than he could have ever imagined. A year ago, after returning from Germany full of enthusiasm, he had been promised full support for his new department. Instead, he found himself in a shabby, barely furnished corner of the medical school. There were no resources, not even the most basic amenities. His request for a simple sign marking his department as "Radiology" was flatly denied by the University Council. It was as if his work didn't matter—not to the administration, not to his colleagues, and not to the students.

The students, caught up in their own academic pressures, barely spared a thought for the importance of radiology. Their minds were consumed with exams, their futures hanging by a thread, and Suetsugu's lessons were little more than a footnote in their studies. When radiology was barely included in their exams, it felt like the final straw for his already fragile spirit. In frustration, Suetsugu graded their assignments harshly—many failed, including one student, Nagai.

By late spring, Nagai's health had improved significantly, though he remained in the hospital. One afternoon, a messenger from the university arrived with urgent news. The visitor, understanding Nagai's hearing loss, sat beside him and relayed the university's decision. Because Nagai had lost hearing in his right ear, he was no longer fit for stethoscope duties, a crucial part of a doctor's work. But there was an alternative: they offered him a position as an assistant to Dr. Suetsugu in the fledgling radiology department.

Suetsugu's relentless complaints about the neglect of his field had finally forced the university's hand. His harsh grading had done what words alone couldn't. Nagai was shocked by the offer, but the reality was clear: turn it down, and his future at the university would be uncertain. Despite his reservations about Suetsugu's eccentricities, Nagai reluctantly accepted.

Weeks later, Nagai sat in the small, cluttered office beside Suetsugu, who was explaining his vision. "X-ray technology is the future of medicine," Suetsugu said with quiet but unwavering passion. "Japan is nearly forty years behind Europe in this field. We can't keep pretending we're ahead. We must face it head-on." His voice grew serious, and he locked eyes with Nagai. "But we're not there yet. We can't control the rays fully. There are risks."

Suetsugu slid a photograph across the desk—a portrait of Dr. Holzknecht, a radiology pioneer in Vienna who had mentored him. "This man gave everything to this field," Suetsugu said, his voice lowering. "He lost one finger to radiation. Then another. Eventually, they amputated his arm. These," he pointed to the worn notes next to the photo, "are his instructions on how we can protect ourselves from radiation. This is the price of progress."

Nagai skimmed the dense German notes, struggling to make sense of the technical language. Suetsugu noticed and gave him a rueful smile. "It's hard to read, I know," he said gently. "After the amputation, Dr. Holzknecht had to write with his left hand. I've seen a memorial in Hamburg University—a stone tablet with the names of over a hundred people who died from radiation exposure. Doctors, technicians, even a nun-scientist. All martyrs, giving their lives so we could move forward." His voice grew even more somber. "These are the people who will lead us to the next step in medical technology."

Suetsugu paused, his gaze sharp. "And yet, there are no names from Japan on that memorial. That's our duty, Nagai-kun. We must step into this field, no matter the risks. We have to make sure every major hospital in Japan has safe, effective X-ray machines."

His voice softened, a rare moment of camaraderie. "It won't be easy. We'll have to fight for every inch." He leaned forward, speaking with urgency. "Have you heard of Pierre and Marie Curie? They were so poor that Marie had to take a teaching job just to survive. The world's foremost female scientist, forced to teach high school students basic math. Can you imagine?"

He paused again, his expression changing to one of quiet determination. "I'm not offering you fame, Nagai-kun. I can't promise you recognition. All I can offer is hard work and complete disregard from the world around us. You'll be pushing this forward alone. And yes, there's a real risk to your health." He smiled faintly, his eyes lighting up. "But you'll be a pioneer. You'll be part of something that could change the world."

Suetsugu leaned back, his tone shifting to something almost playful. "We're on the cusp of discoveries that will last forever, Nagai. Politics? That's fleeting. It's built on lies and things that fade. But truth endures. Look at history. The Mongol Empire—Genghis Khan built a vast empire, but it's gone now. No land. No lasting legacy. Just this." He recited a haiku, his voice rich with reverence.

"Natsu kusa ya tsuwamono domo no yume no ato!" The words from Basho's poem painted an image of a battlefield once filled with ambition and pride, now overtaken by the quiet growth of summer grass. Nature's slow reclaiming, an enduring reminder of how fleeting human efforts can be.

As Nagai pondered the weight of the haiku's meaning, the professor's words began to settle in. He realized that his place in this journey was far more than just a job. It was a step into history, into something that could last.

Fully immersed in his new role, Nagai stood beside Suetsugu as their first patient arrived—a young woman with striking, wavy hair, an uncommon sight in Nagasaki. As Suetsugu explained the procedure to him in German, they watched as the barium fluid traced its path through her body, revealing the cause of her discomfort: intestinal worms. Nagai couldn't help but wonder about her life. What would her suitor think if he knew this intimate detail about her health? Would it change the way he saw her?

The next patient was a teacher, gravely ill with tuberculosis. He begged for a clean bill of health—a desperate plea to keep his job and provide for his family. In the midst of Japan's economic depression, losing one's livelihood was more than just a blow; it was a catastrophe. The weight of the world seemed to hang on a single diagnosis.

And in that moment, as Nagai stood there with Suetsugu, he realized that their work—this nascent radiology department—wasn't just about science. It was about life, about hope, about the human struggle to survive and thrive, even in the face of overwhelming odds.

Over lunch, the conversation turned to finances. Suetsugu leaned in, his voice lively as he discussed their struggles. "In America," he said, "both the government and corporations fund scientific research. Here, we're still fighting just to be noticed. Each x-ray costs seven yen—that's about four days' wages for you, Nagai-kun. We need funding to make this more affordable."

His voice grew more passionate as he spoke about the future. "Do you know what American scientists are working on? Atomic research. It's the next big thing in our field, and the potential is huge. Ernest Lawrence at the University of California built a machine called a cyclotron. It's massive, four times the size of all our buildings put together." Suetsugu's excitement was clear, and Nagai began to feel the spark of interest. He would soon become deeply captivated by atomic science, radiation, and the endless possibilities of atomic energy.

By mid-December 1932, the cold had set in, and the hospital was poorly heated. Yet Nagai found himself staying late, absorbed in his radiology research. He couldn't quite reconcile his new passion with his earlier indifference toward the field. But tonight was different. Instead of his usual late hours in the lab, he left early to join the Moriyamas for Christmas Eve dinner. Though Christmas wasn't widely celebrated in Japan, Nagai accepted the invitation out of respect for his hosts. It was his first time celebrating, but he was eager to experience it.

The Moriyamas' home was traditional, with a low dining table placed just above the tatami mats. Everyone sat in the formal seiza position—legs folded beneath them, backs straight, feet flat on the floor. Moriyama, the father, invited them to relax. "Dozo, O raku ni, please sit comfortably," he said, and the men shifted, crossing their legs in front of them, while the women stayed in the rigid seiza posture.

Midori, the Moriyamas' daughter, was home for winter break. Her name, meaning "verdant," reflected her youth and vitality. Nagai couldn't help but notice her thick, shiny black hair, a feature passed down from her mother, Tsumo. Known as "the Crow" for her dark hair, Tsumo came from a long line of farmers and fishermen from Ukujima, a heritage that had shaped Midori's beauty. Her darker complexion spoke of the hard lives her ancestors had led.

Midori didn't say much that evening, but her grace was undeniable. Nagai remembered the photos Tsumo had once shown him—pictures of Midori excelling in sports and volleyball. That athleticism still showed in her movements, as though her past achievements were quietly woven into her present grace.

Moriyama, a little tipsy from sake, shared stories of his Christian ancestors who had endured persecution. "Every Christmas Eve," he said, "we gather in a cow shed, which we call the natara." The natara was a secret meeting place for Japan's Hidden Christians, with a special vocabulary created by Japanese Catholics, a mixture of Latin, Portuguese, and Japanese. This secret language couldn't be found in any dictionary, a testament to the strength of their faith.

Moriyama's voice grew more animated as he spoke of their traditions. Before midnight mass, the natara would be cleaned, food prepared, and a charcoal stove set to heat water. They had to be careful, as police often patrolled the area. Lookouts would warn the group of any raids. If the authorities arrived, the Christians would quickly turn the gathering into a Buddhist memorial to avoid detection.

The most moving part of the evening, Moriyama explained, was when the elders retold the nativity story. They spoke of Mary and Joseph, rejected from every door, until they found shelter in a humble barn. This retelling wasn't just tradition; it was a living connection to the past, reminding them of the resilience of faith, especially in times of hardship.

Moriyama sighed, looking at Nagai. "We face our own challenges with the police these days, but compared to our ancestors, we have it easy. At least tonight, we can celebrate Mass openly at the cathedral." With a hopeful look, he leaned in and asked, "Sensei, why don't you join us for midnight Mass tonight?" Since the Sunday Nagai had asked to stay with them, Moriyama had been praying for his conversion. He had even encouraged his family to pray for Nagai, believing that perhaps his presence among them was no accident.

Midori glanced at Nagai, seemingly holding her breath, waiting for his response. Nagai had never considered Christianity before, but the warmth and sincerity of the Moriyamas touched him. A thought from Blaise Pascal drifted into his mind: "Kneel down and go to Mass." To his surprise, he found himself answering, "Yes, I'd like to go with you tonight."

The cathedral was alive with energy despite the relentless snowstorm outside. Nearly five thousand people had gathered, their figures blending into a sea of bundled coats and bright kimonos, creating a striking contrast against the dim, flickering candlelight. Farmers, laborers, and their families had dressed in their finest, each adding a splash of color to the otherwise somber scene. Nagai stood among them, overwhelmed by the sheer power of the collective voice as they sang in unison. But it wasn't the sound alone that held his attention—it was the deep silence that followed each song, a silence that seemed to pulse with a life of its own. In that quiet, Nagai felt something—a living presence, something beyond the walls of the Urakami Cathedral. He later described it as a moment of sudden realization, a feeling he couldn't quite place but that stayed with him long after the Mass had ended.

For Nagai, the idea of emptiness wasn't new. As someone steeped in Buddhist thought, he had long pondered the concept of *Mu*, a character symbolizing nothingness, often interpreted as the absence of anything tangible. The very nature of existence, in this view, is rooted in *Mu*—a reminder that everything we are, from our bodies to our very thoughts, is borrowed from the world around us. Nagai often thought about how his life, from his accent to his mannerisms, was shaped by the people who had come before him, and even more so by the things others had given him. In the quiet of the cathedral, surrounded by the hum of collective worship, he found himself musing on the Buddhist belief that even our bodies are not truly ours. The navel, positioned perfectly for us to see every day while we bathe, was the body's subtle reminder that our very existence is a gift—received without merit, unearned.

But there was another form of *Mu*, one that seemed to transcend the physical and venture into a spiritual realm beyond understanding. Nagai's mind drifted to the writings of Blaise Pascal, who had written about the "Absolute, Infinite God," a being beyond human comprehension. Pascal's thoughts echoed in Nagai's mind: our senses and reason are limited, and no matter how hard we try, the true nature of existence remains elusive. And yet, Pascal had suggested that while our reason might never fully grasp the truth, our hearts could still experience it. Nagai couldn't help but feel a certain tension. Could this rejection of reason, this embrace of the ineffable, lead to the same blind fanaticism that had caused so much harm throughout history? Or was there something more to this elusive truth that reason alone could never uncover?

The priest's voice pierced through Nagai's contemplations, calling the congregation to attention. As the words flowed, Nagai felt himself shaken—almost as though he'd been struck by a Zen master's bamboo staff. The priest spoke of the humility of the Holy Family, of the power in their acceptance of suffering. Nagai's own selfishness, his materialistic tendencies, and his assumptions about life seemed to dissolve in that moment. The priest's words hit home in a way that resonated deeper than any academic or intellectual insight ever had. The humility of Christ's family was a mirror to his own self-centered view of the world, and the realization was jarring.

As the Mass drew to its conclusion, the congregation stood and began to sing the *Credo* in Latin. The music, devoid of the polished complexity of famous composers, felt raw—alive with the voices of the people, rising as a collective force. Nagai couldn't shake the unsettling feeling that gripped him. Was it a natural reaction to what felt like "fanaticism," a fervor that seemed foreign and almost disorienting? Or was it something deeper—something about the raw, unwavering faith of these simple people who, with their modest devotion, could stand with certainty, while he, a man of reason, found himself adrift?

As the singing faded, the smell of incense filled the air, drifting lazily across the flickering candles, bringing with it a nostalgic feeling of tenderness. The fragrance reminded him of *haru-gasumi*, the mist that clings to the mountains of Japan in spring, gentle and soft, a fleeting reminder of nature's quiet beauty. The chime of bells broke the silence, and the congregation knelt in unison. Nagai's gaze moved across the room, and the tiny candle flames seemed to pull him into a distant memory—one from a university vacation when he and a few friends hiked through the mountains. That night, as they sat around the fire, Nagai would often look up at the stars, feeling as though the constellations were playing a silent symphony, a music only his heart could hear. Those stars, like the candles before him now, whispered of something beyond—a presence, a mystery that words could not touch.

The Mass was over, but Takashi Nagai's mind wouldn't settle. Back at the Moriyama home, wrapped snugly in a thick quilt, his body begged for rest, but sleep kept its distance. Though he had been awake nearly a full day, his thoughts were anything but tired. His mind buzzed like the skies during Nagasaki's kite festival in April, with ideas zipping and colliding like paper dragons in a windstorm—each tugging for attention, none giving way.

He had just emerged from a Mass that felt more like a haunting medieval mystery play than a conventional religious service—overwhelming, beautiful, and profound. The emotional currents it stirred within him collided violently with his rational mind, trained in the scientific method. He admired the unwavering devotion of the five thousand souls present—mostly simple workers—who moved effortlessly from profound silence to soul-stirring hymns, like the tide flowing in rhythm with the moon. Yet, another part of him, the clinical, skeptical thinker, kept its distance, wary of what it saw as the subtle manipulation of emotions disguised under the veil of piety. History had shown him the dangers of unchecked belief: the Crusades, militant Buddhist sects, the fanaticism that had seized parts of the Islamic world. He had learned to be cautious when religion promised answers that were too simple or demanded obedience too absolute.

And yet, the memory of the Presence that had settled over him during the Mass refused to leave. It was not a sensation he could dismiss or explain away, though his professors might have reduced it to terms like autosuggestion or mass hysteria. But Nagai was not the first thinker to wrestle with this tension. His thoughts drifted to Blaise Pascal—a mathematician, a believer, a realist. Pascal had warned against blind emotionalism but still clung to the notion of a loving God. If Pascal, with his logical brilliance, could hold both belief and doubt in delicate balance, perhaps there was room for such a contradiction in Nagai too.

An odd image crossed his mind—Pascal, not in 17th-century France, but in Urakami, wandering through the streets as though he belonged there. Nagai frowned, both amused and perplexed. No, that was absurd. Pascal belonged in Europe, perhaps near the towering Saint George's Cathedral in Hamburg. Before he could unravel the strange mental mix-up, exhaustion finally overtook him, and his relentless thoughts gave way to sleep.

By the following evening, after a grueling day in the radiology department, Nagai was too drained to analyze his thoughts further. He collapsed onto his futon, barely managing to undress. But just as the house quieted down, a new storm began to stir.

Midori, lying downstairs, awoke in agony, sharp pains twisting in her stomach. Her mother, instantly alert, guessed the cause: intestinal worms. It wasn't an unusual affliction in 1930s Japan, where hygiene was often inadequate. Few homes had modern plumbing, and the practice of fertilizing crops with human waste—carried in sloshing "honey buckets"—was common. The pungent smell often preceded its sight. Vegetables grown this way carried hidden dangers—worms that burrowed into the body, wreaking havoc from within.

Without hesitation, Midori's mother administered medicine. But this time, it offered no relief. The pain intensified, and Midori began to cry out, her face twisted in agony, pale as winter's frost.

Outside, snow fell thick and relentless. Getting a doctor at this hour seemed impossible, but her father, Sadakichi, didn't hesitate. He climbed the stairs and knocked gently on Takashi's door, bowing deeply in apology even as he explained the emergency. Within moments, Takashi was by Midori's side. A single glance was all he needed—he recognized the signs of acute appendicitis. Time was now their enemy.

He stood to leave, but paused. In the corner of the room, Sadakichi had lit a candle beneath a statue of the Virgin Mary, whispering, "It's all part of God's plan. Who knows what blessing might come from this?" The words struck Takashi—not so much for what they said, but for the calm conviction that radiated from Sadakichi.

"We need to get her to the hospital—now," Takashi said, his voice urgent. He braved the storm and made his way to the local school, where he knew an old night watchman might still be awake. The man answered the door and allowed him to use the phone. Takashi quickly dialed the hospital, his voice sharp with anxiety. "This is an emergency. Get me to the ER now!"

A colleague confirmed they were preparing for surgery. Relieved, Takashi hurried back to the Moriyama home, where Midori lay shivering beneath layers of blankets, her face contorted in pain. Calling a cab in this weather was futile. Time was slipping away.

Takashi turned to Sadakichi. "O-to-san," he said, the respectful title for "father." "If you lead with the lantern, I'll carry Midori."

Midori hesitated. The idea of being carried through the snow by a man—especially an unmarried one—was unthinkable in ordinary times. But these were not ordinary times. With no one in sight and the storm cloaking them, she nodded weakly.

Takashi gently lifted her onto his back. She was lighter than he had imagined. As they stepped into the night, Sadakichi's lantern bobbed ahead, casting warm patches of light across the snow-covered ground. The world seemed muted under the heavy blanket of white, their muffled footsteps the only sound.

Suddenly, a dog burst from a side street, barking furiously. The three of them froze. Takashi shouted, startling the animal, which quickly retreated. For a brief moment, the silence returned—broken only by Midori's labored breathing against his neck. With renewed determination, Takashi resumed his pace.

They reached the hospital, its windows glowing softly against the storm, steam rising from a nearby vent like curling smoke signals. "They're ready," Takashi thought. "We made it."

Seven minutes after she was wheeled in, the surgery was complete. The appendix had been on the verge of rupturing, a near disaster narrowly avoided. A nurse handed the specimen—preserved in a bottle of formaldehyde—to a stunned Sadakichi, who could only stare at it, as if the life-saving moment had yet to sink in.

Not long after, Tsumo arrived, her arms wrapped around a bundle: bedding, toiletries, and a furoshiki—an all-purpose cloth. She handed it to Takashi with a graceful bow. "A gift for the doctor," she said softly, her gratitude in her eyes more than her words.

Takashi took the bundle, but it was the surgeon who untied it first. Inside, nestled carefully, were wine, ham, and sausages. The surgeon raised an eyebrow, intrigued by the unusual offering. With a flourish, he poured two glasses of wine and handed one to Takashi.

"To your sweetheart's quick recovery," he said, a mischievous grin tugging at his lips.

Takashi flushed deeply. "She's not my sweetheart," he replied quickly, his voice betraying a flicker of awkwardness.

The surgeon chuckled. "Come on. You carried her through a snowstorm like she was made of glass. That kind of care isn't just duty—it's something more. You should be proud of that."

Takashi didn't argue. He just raised his glass, the weight of the surgeon's words settling heavily in his chest. His mind wandered back to the night's events, to the strange intertwining of life and love, of faith and sacrifice. It was as though the chaos of the crisis had revealed something deeper—belief, purpose, and connection—tangled together like the kites that flew in the skies of April. They twisted, collided, and, perhaps, just perhaps, lifted us a little higher than before.

Chapter 9

Please come back. I will be praying for you

It was January 1933 when the postcard arrived. Thin, impersonal, and cold—its blunt message struck like a quiet blade to the gut. No warmth, no ceremony—just a stark command: report for duty with the Eleventh Hiroshima Regiment. For Dr. Takashi Nagai, nestled in the calm, predictable rhythms of his research in Nagasaki, it felt like a thunderclap on a clear day, shattering the fragile peace he had cultivated for himself.

Japan's generals had once painted the Manchurian campaign as a swift, easy victory. But as the months dragged on, that illusion unraveled. Resistance from the Chinese forces was stronger than anyone had expected, and the news that trickled back to Nagasaki grew darker each day—names of the fallen, numbers that seemed to stretch into infinity, stories that unsettled even the most loyal hearts.

For Nagai, who had spent the last few months immersed in his research, chasing the elusive answers of science with quiet hope, the abrupt shift felt like stepping off a well-trodden path into a dense, impenetrable fog where nothing could be seen or trusted. His microscope, once his only focus, now seemed distant and insignificant. The world of sterile labs and rabbits had given way to one of violence and uncertainty. The summons yanked him from his orderly life. The experiment he had left unfinished now felt like a metaphor—his whole life, perhaps, was hanging on a cliff, a sentence left incomplete, lost to a war that he never asked for.

His last night in Nagasaki should have been a celebration—a farewell, maybe even a distraction from the looming storm. His old basketball teammates from medical school gathered in a small tavern, trying to laugh away the tension, their glasses raised, voices growing louder as the night wore on. But all of it fell apart when the tavern owner's daughter approached him to refill his sake. As she did, she suddenly broke down, sobbing openly, her grief raw and unrestrained.

Her tears weren't quiet or polite—they poured from her like a relentless rainstorm. She had seen this scene too many times: young men leaving with uniforms and smiles, only to return as nothing more than names on a wooden tablet. Her sorrow seeped into the room, turning the air colder, and the laughter from before became an awkward echo.

Nagai slipped out quietly, his footsteps crunching softly in the snow as he walked the streets of Nagasaki, blanketed now in a thick silence. The familiar sights felt different—empty, almost as though the world was holding its breath. He passed the same path he had walked just weeks before, when he had carried Midori in his arms, her fragile body pressed against his chest. Her breath had whispered against his skin. The memory of her lingered—warm and bittersweet. Was she just a friend? A life he had saved? Or something more? His heart, restless and unsure, didn't care for labels. It only ached.

Back at the Moriyama home, everything felt strangely final. It was as though the very air was heavy with goodbyes. Takashi climbed the stairs to his room, thinking perhaps he should pour himself a drink and let the night slip quietly away. But before he could, the soft sound of footsteps echoed down the hall, and a voice—gentle and familiar—whispered, "Gomen kudasai."

It was Midori. She stood in the corridor, dressed formally, her figure a stark contrast to the delicate vulnerability she usually showed. She was seated in the seiza position, her hair spilling forward like a veil.

"I came to say goodbye," she said softly, her voice laced with the weight of something unspoken. "And to thank you again... for saving my life."

Nagai lowered himself across from her, at a loss for words. She extended a thick wool sweater toward him—one she had knitted during her recovery. It was a parting gift, warm and sturdy, meant to fight off the bitter cold of the Manchurian winter. But there was more to it than just practicality. It carried her hopes, her prayers that he would return—that he wouldn't become just another name on a memorial.

For a moment, Midori seemed almost unreal to him—like a delicate piece of spring about to be swallowed whole by winter's harsh embrace. Without thinking, driven by something deeper than logic, he reached for her hands. They were warm but trembling, the pulse of life running strong beneath her skin. And then, almost instinctively, he kissed her—softly, deeply, as if he were trying to answer a question he hadn't known he was asking.

When he pulled away, his heart raced. He searched her face, hoping for some clue, some answer. But all he saw was the glimmer of unshed tears, pooling in her eyes.

She bowed her head, her voice barely above a whisper: "Please come back. I'll be praying for you every day."

And just like that, she was gone—slipping away down the stairs, the soft rustle of her kimono the only sound left in the room.

Nagai stayed there, alone, as the silence stretched between them. The kiss still hung in the air, fragile as a secret. Guilt washed over him—had he crossed a line? What if she had wanted something different? What if he had jeopardized everything—the trust she had placed in him, the respect of the Moriyamas—for a fleeting moment of longing? He didn't know. War, after all, had a way of making every choice feel both necessary and reckless at the same time.

Chapter 10

The Summon

Not long after his quiet visit to the brothel, Dr. Takashi Nagai was summoned to the commandant's office. He expected routine paperwork or perhaps a new assignment. Instead, a junior officer waved him in with a look that was equal parts curiosity and suspicion.

"Who is this Midori?" the officer asked, tapping a small file on the desk. "And what exactly is your relationship with her?"

Nagai straightened instinctively, caught off guard. "She's just… someone I know, sir. Nothing serious."

"Just someone?" the officer said, raising an eyebrow. He smirked slightly, clearly seeing through the formality. Nagai felt the heat rise to his face. The officer reached under the desk and pulled out a pair of gloves and a small, worn book.

"You can keep the gloves," he said, almost teasing. "But this—" he held up the Catholic Catechism, "—this stays with us. Special Affairs wants to take a look. If there's anything questionable in here, we'll be having another chat."

Nagai took the gloves gently. They carried a soft scent—faint and familiar, like a trace of the night they'd last been together. It wasn't perfume exactly, but something warmer, quieter. A fragrance that wrapped around his memory and pulled him somewhere far away. It's strange, how memory works—how a single smell can break open a part of you you thought was buried.

Three days passed. Nagai returned, tense and bracing for reprimand. Instead, the same officer handed the book back, a little shrug in his voice.

"Special Affairs says it's just complicated Christian nonsense," he said. "But if you've got time for fairy tales, make sure you've already memorized your Soldier's Manual."

But it didn't feel like nonsense.

The Catechism wasn't loud. It didn't try to convert him with thunder or guilt. It simply asked—quiet questions, like someone speaking gently across a dark room: Why are we here? Why is there suffering? What happens after death?

Before drifting into agnosticism, Nagai had searched for answers in Japan's spiritual history. He had studied the lives of Kobo Daishi and Dogen—men who had left everything behind in search of something eternal. He admired their discipline, their simplicity, their courage to seek beyond borders. But still, something was missing. A single question haunted him through it all: What is truth, and how do we recognize it when it finally stands in front of us?

Then, one night, he reached the Ten Commandments in that little book.

And something broke.

Not from fear. But from recognition.

"I felt like a man covered in filth," he would later write. "If there was a God, and if there was a devil, then I had been marching under the devil's banner my whole life—pride, greed, lust, anger. These weren't abstract ideas. These were me."

On the last day of his leave, Takashi Nagai drank like a man trying to silence something screaming inside him. Six bottles of sake, loud laughter, friendly backslaps—all of it a mask. A performance. Behind his eyes, though, was something else entirely. The kind of emptiness that laughter couldn't touch.

Later that night, slouched in a corner of Nagasaki's glowing nightlife, he watched the world spin in meaningless circles. Neon lights. Passing faces. Nothing that felt real. *What's the point?* he asked himself. In a few months, he could be dead—in some cold trench in Manchuria, or from an infection in the field hospital, or maybe worse: alive but hollow. Existing, not living.

And yet, through the noise in his mind, one quiet thread refused to snap.

Midori.

A woman of few words but deep faith. She had told him she would pray for him every day. And even though he wasn't sure he believed in anything, her promise had stayed with him. There's something powerful about someone praying for you when you don't even believe in prayer. A promise like that—maybe it *is* a kind of prayer, after all.

Two years later, his diary picks up again—but now it's written from the edge of hell.

Manchuria.

The "glorious victory" the brass had promised was now a slow-motion collapse. A mess of mud, fire, and human wreckage. Nagai wasn't holding a rifle, but his weapon was no less brutal—a scalpel. He was saving lives, sure. But he was also cutting away parts of people. And sometimes, what he cut away stayed with him longer than any scream.

The hospital was more a butcher's shop than a place of healing. Blood everywhere. The stench of rot. So many amputations. Young men with no legs. Teenagers with half their faces missing. And every time he had to tell a soldier that a limb had to go, it felt like he was sawing away a piece of his own heart.

But one case haunted him beyond all the others.

A young soldier—blinded, deafened by an explosion—woke up thrashing, terrified. He couldn't hear, couldn't see, had no idea where he was. He thought he'd been captured by the enemy. He screamed until his voice broke. And then he began to beg. Over and over again, he begged Nagai to kill him. Just end it. Please.

Nagai would never forget that voice. Or the way the boy's hands shook.

As his unit pushed deeper into enemy territory, they passed the wreckage of towns and villages. The snow didn't hide the dead. Bodies—soldiers, civilians, children—lay frozen in grotesque stillness. In one village, he saw children clinging to the lifeless forms of their parents. Their eyes were wide and dry—too shocked to cry, too broken to understand.

Whatever noble reason had brought him there—defending Japan, resisting communism, protecting the homeland—crumbled in his hands like ash.

Science. Reason. Logic. These were the things he had trusted once. But now? They felt empty. *What's the point of progress,* he thought, *if it can't stop men from tearing each other apart?*

And still, through all the horror, something inside him held on. Barely.

He wanted to believe that all this pain meant something. That the lives lost weren't just statistics. That the guilt clawing at his chest could be transformed into something other than despair. But faith? That scared him too.

What if belief is just another drug? he wondered. *Like morphine for the soul?*

He'd seen another doctor lean on morphine just to get through the day. Was religion any different? Just another way to numb the unbearable?

And yet, he kept thinking about men like Blaise Pascal. Dogen. Kobo Daishi. He didn't admire them because they had everything figured out. He admired them because they *asked*. They stayed with the questions. They didn't escape the tension—they lived inside it.

Nagai wasn't ready to believe. Not yet. But something had changed.

The questions no longer felt meaningless.

And somewhere far from the battlefield, in a quiet home in Nagasaki, a woman still prayed for him. Every day. Without fail. Without knowing whether her prayers were heard.

And somehow, just that—just *her*—was enough to keep him going.

Chapter 11

Father... I don't even know why I came.

When Richard Wagner wrote *Tannhäuser*, he wasn't just composing music. He was peeling back the layers of something ancient and raw—a war every human heart eventually faces.

In the opera, Tannhäuser is a knight—not just battle-worn on the outside, but bruised deep within. Tired of the weight of the world, he runs toward Venus, the goddess of sensual pleasure. For a time, her embrace feels like relief. Her world offers escape. No guilt, no questions—just the rush of feeling. But it doesn't last.

What first felt like freedom turns into a golden cage.

Tannhäuser starts to feel it in his chest—the hunger for something real, something lasting. Not just pleasure, but peace. Not just touch, but truth. His soul begins to ache. He wants to leave—not just Venus, but everything she stands for. All the noise. All the false promises.

And in the end, it's not a sword or a sermon that saves him. It's the prayers of Elizabeth—the woman who loves him not with desire, but with devotion. A love that doesn't burn out, but holds on. Through her sacrifice, Tannhäuser finds hope again. A way back.

Years later, and on the other side of the world, a man named Takashi Nagai stepped off a ship in Nagasaki.

He wasn't returning whole. The war had taken things from him—things that didn't bleed but still hurt. Part of the pain was out there in the world. But most of it? It lived inside him now.

As he stood on the dock, the sea air wrapped around him like an old memory. But Nagai knew something else, too. He was at a crossroads—not just of roads, but of the soul.

There were two Nagasakis waiting for him.

One was loud and easy to find. The Nagasaki of distraction. Maruyama's red lanterns. The buzzing nightlife of Hama no Machi. Warm sake. Smiles from strangers whose names you'd never remember. This city pulled him close and whispered in his ear: *Forget. Laugh. Drink. You've earned it. Just live for now.*

But beside it—quieter, steadier—stood another Nagasaki.

A city woven with prayer. Patience. Suffering that had bloomed into something sacred. The Urakami Cathedral rose like a promise, its bells echoing not entertainment but endurance. The Hill of the Twenty-Six Martyrs stood in solemn silence, reminding all who passed of those who had once bled for something they couldn't see but still believed in. At Oura Church, pilgrims bent low in reverence. Not out of fear—but out of love.

And there, hidden in plain sight, were the Franciscan monks—men who had followed Maximilian Kolbe into a life of silence, service, and simplicity. In their hands, faith wasn't a sermon. It was bread, shared with the poor. It was wounds tended to quietly. It was mercy, not myth.

This wasn't the realm of Venus.

This was the city of Mary.

She didn't promise pleasure. She offered peace.

And Takashi Nagai stood between them.

One city told him to numb the pain.

The other told him to carry it—and find meaning in the weight.

Here's a more emotionally resonant, deeply human version of your passage—still faithful to the original but drawing out the inner tension, the quiet heartbreak, and the sacred turning point:.

It felt like standing at the mouth of a river that had split in two. One stream shimmered with ease—familiar comforts, the quiet pull of old habits, the kind that dull pain without healing it. The other was harder to look at. A steep climb. Worn stone steps. The path of repentance.

Tannhäuser had Elizabeth—the woman who loved him when he didn't deserve it, whose prayers pulled him back from the edge. For Nagai, it wasn't a saint or a sermon calling him back. It was a memory.

Midori.

He had left her when he went to war. Not just physically—he had walked out on her love, her faith, her quiet devotion. She had offered him something steady. Something sacred. But at the time, he had been too restless to recognize it. He treated her heart like it was just another moment to enjoy and forget. A soft place to land, nothing more.

Now he was back, not whole but hollow. War had broken something in him. And he wasn't hoping for romance or comfort. He just wanted to say *sorry*. She deserved that much.

Maybe after seeing her, he'd walk to the cathedral. Maybe he'd finally start to figure out who he was now—and who he might still become.

When she opened the door, it wasn't joy that crossed her face.

It was silence.

For a long moment, neither moved. Neither breathed. Nagai, who had once stood tall in lecture halls, who had spoken with clarity about medicine and life and death, now stood wordless.

So instead, he removed his coat. Slowly. Carefully. Then, with both hands, he laid the wool sweater she had knitted for him—years ago, before the war—gently on the tatami mat.

That sweater had clung to him through Manchuria's biting winters, soaked in sweat, in blood, in memory.

Midori didn't rise. She sat perfectly still. Straight-backed. Her hands resting quietly in her lap.

Nagai remained standing, awkward, unsure, like a boy waiting for judgment.

Finally, he bowed and muttered, "Thanks to you, I didn't catch the flu. So... thanks."

No answer.

Then, slowly, she leaned forward. Picked up the sweater. Pressed it to her chest.

The room was cold, but the silence was colder.

He waited.

Still, she said nothing.

Then, with the calm of someone who had already let go, she stood up.

"Where are you going?" he asked, voice small.

She paused. Her voice was gentle, but it carried weight. "I don't suppose it's of much use to you now."

And with that, she walked away. Into the back of the house. Barefoot. Silent. Like a ghost fading into the walls.

That's when he knew.

Midori hadn't waited for his love. She had waited only for his soul. She had prayed. She had hoped. But she had also prepared herself for this moment—the return of a man she once loved, now barely recognizable. A man she no longer needed. A man she had already released.

Her chapter in his story was over.

He stepped outside, heart raw, shame clinging to him like the winter air. Pulled his coat around him. And began the walk toward the cathedral.

The stone stairs felt steep. Every step a confession. Every breath a kind of penance.

When he reached the rectory, he stood at the door for a long time before finding the strength to speak.

"Gomen kudasai," he called out, voice trembling. "May I come in?"

The door creaked open.

There stood Father Moriyama. Older now. Slower, maybe. But his eyes still held that same quiet warmth. He had been the one who led the Christmas Eve Mass years ago—before war, before ruin.

He looked at Nagai. Really looked. And smiled.

Not with pity.

With recognition.

Not as if seeing a fallen man, but a brother finally coming home.

He reached out, took Nagai's hand, and led him inside. The room was lined with books. The light was soft. The air felt safe.

And for the first time in years, Nagai felt like he could speak the truth.

And be heard.

They sat quietly, the weight of the silence not uncomfortable, just heavy—like a blanket soaked in rain.

Nagai shifted slightly, unsure of what to do with his hands. His eyes drifted to a calligraphy scroll on the wall bearing the kanji for "Moriyama." He hesitated, then asked, "Excuse me… are you related to a man named Jinzaburo Moriyama?"

Father Moriyama chuckled softly, a sound like wind stirring dry leaves. "Jinzaburo? That was my father. Let me guess—he caught you in one of his endless stories?"

A smile flickered across Nagai's lips, small and tired. "Maybe once or twice."

They laughed, though Nagai's laughter was brittle—thinned by exhaustion, bruised by everything he had seen and done. The war had taken more than his strength. It had scraped his soul raw.

Now he sat here, stripped of all the masks he once wore. No more doctor, no more soldier, no more man of ambition. Just a man trying to remember how to be human.

The words came slowly.

"Father… I don't even know why I came. I shouldn't be here. I shouldn't waste your time."

His voice was quiet. Almost apologetic.

"I've lost the peace in my heart. Maybe I've lost the right to it."

He looked down, ashamed.

"I've committed nearly every sin in your catechism. Maybe even the one they say can't be forgiven."

There was no performance in his voice. No drama. Just truth.

Plain. Worn.

He had gone looking for meaning in pleasure and come back empty. He had chased after freedom only to find himself enslaved by his own desires. Now, all he wanted was for someone to hear him. Not fix him. Not preach. Just hear.

And maybe that's how redemption begins—not with fireworks or choirs, but with one broken person daring to speak their pain out loud.

Father Moriyama didn't rush to respond. He didn't flinch. He didn't reach for holy water or hurried reassurances. Instead, he simply watched Nagai, his eyes full of quiet understanding.

Without a word, he rose and walked to the stove, lifting the kettle with practiced hands. The room filled with the soft sound of boiling water and the calming scent of green tea.

He poured two cups.

O-cha—the old comfort of a weary land.

Nagai took his with both hands, fingers trembling. The warmth soaked through his palms and up into his chest, grounding him.

The priest's silence wasn't passive. It was invitation. It said: *You're safe here. Speak when you're ready.*

And slowly, Nagai began.

He told the story of his atheism—how sure he had once been that there was no God. He spoke of his mother's death and how it had cracked something open in him. He shared his struggle with Pascal's wager, the tug-of-war between reason and hope.

He admitted how he had tried to drown the ache: in alcohol, in fleeting lovers, in nights that blurred together until he forgot who he was trying to forget.

"Sometimes I wonder if there's a God," he said quietly. "If there's something after all this. But it never lasts. The certainty never stays."

Then, looking up, voice soft as a breath, he asked, "Shinpu-sama… what made *you* so sure? Why did you become a priest?"

Father Moriyama didn't answer right away. He didn't give him doctrine. He didn't quote scripture.

Instead, he told a story.

A family story.

A story that carried weight like stone and wind and tears.

He spoke of the year 1864, when Christianity had again been outlawed. His grandparents—faithful believers—were arrested, stripped of their rights, and dragged away in chains. His grandmother had died behind bars in Sakura Machi Prison. His grandfather not long after, in Tsuwano.

Their son, Jinzaburo—only twenty-two, unmarried, grief-shaken—had stepped into their place. Not out of glory. But out of love. Out of conviction.

That legacy—the bloodline of quiet martyrs and steadfast hearts—had shaped him. Carried him. Called him.

Father Moriyama told the story not to impress, but to show Nagai something deeper:

Faith doesn't always begin with answers.

Sometimes, it begins with loss.

With silence.

With a cup of tea and the courage to speak broken truths aloud.

In Tsuwano, a town where Shinto was strongly followed, the government was determined to make the Christians return to their old faith. When words didn't work, they used torture. Jinzaburo and other Christians were forced into a frozen pond in the middle of winter. They were held under the ice until they almost drowned, then pulled out and put near a fire to warm up—only to be thrown back into the freezing water again. Many could not bear the pain and gave up their faith for food and warmth. But Jinzaburo stayed strong. He spoke clearly and bravely, and he refused to give in. The authorities focused on him. They needed to break him.

The head officer, Morioka, a former samurai, became angry with Jinzaburo's strength. So, he came up with a cruel plan. He decided to hurt Jinzaburo's younger brother, Yujiro, who was just fourteen and deeply loved by his older brother. They dragged Yujiro away, stripped him, and beat him. They tied him to a cross, poked him with sharp bamboo sticks, and mocked his Christian faith. For two weeks, they poured cold water on him and gave him no food. His body couldn't take it anymore. Though Morioka only meant to scare him, the boy was dying. The officer, seeing what he had done, asked himself, "Am I still a man, a samurai, if I torture a child to death?"

They brought Yujiro to his sister, Matsu, who was in the women's prison. She held him in her arms, trying to warm him up. When Yujiro opened his eyes, he saw her tears and whispered, "Please forgive me for crying out like a coward."

Before he passed away that day, Yujiro told Matsu things that would stay in the family's heart forever. People didn't think he was just saying things from pain. They believed his words came from God—like the special wisdom that God sometimes gives to children. He told his sister she would return to Urakami and that she must take care of the children left without parents. Matsu did just that. She became one of the first Catholic nuns in modern Japan and gave her life to caring for orphans.

Yujiro also said that Jinzaburo would live and have a son who would become a priest. And he was right. Jinzaburo survived, returned to Urakami, got married, and when his first son was born, he rushed to the French priest's house holding the baby. "Shinpu-sama," he said, "a boy. Please pray that he becomes a priest." The red, crying baby was blessed that day—and he grew up to be Father Moriyama.

Father Moriyama looked at Nagai and said, "My faith was handed down to me by my family. But I've also met many people who were once atheists and later found God. You admire Pascal, and I agree—his thoughts about prayer are very meaningful. You also spoke of Dogen, the Zen monk. Many scholars from Kyoto visited his mountain monastery, hoping for deep conversations. But he would simply tell them, 'Tada suware. Just sit and meditate.'

"There was a French priest who helped me when I was studying to be a priest. He often quoted Origen, an early Christian thinker who said the Gospel of John is the heart of the Bible—and that we can only understand it if we rest on Jesus' chest, like John did. He meant that prayer is the way to know God. Christianity isn't about knowing everything like in science. It's about meeting the mystery of God through prayer. I'll show you how to begin that kind of prayer later."

Then he added gently, "You said you fear you've sinned against the Holy Spirit. But you haven't. That sin means completely rejecting God forever—and it's very rare. The God we believe in, the one my French teacher called the 'good God,' is the Father who runs to welcome the lost son. Jesus came to save sinners—not to push them away."

Midori was always strong and calm, both in class and in life. But Nagai's sudden return shook her deeply. When he showed up at her doorstep, she was overwhelmed. Later, alone in her room, she placed his cardigan at the foot of the family crucifix—a cross that had been passed down through seven generations of faithful Christians. She cried and prayed: "Jesus, here is his cardigan. I asked you to bring him back, and you did. Thank you. I know I love him, Lord. But someone wiser than me should be his wife. Maybe you're smiling at me now for even dreaming of marriage with him. Now that he's safe, I'll meet the men my parents and the matchmaker suggest. I offer this pain as a prayer—that he finds faith."

She felt completely drained. To clear her mind, she left the house and walked to the nearby cathedral. Outside, there was a stone statue of the crucifixion. As she passed, she looked up at the sorrowful image of Mary, Jesus' mother, and whispered in her heart, "You always said yes to God. Help me say yes too. But why is life so painful? I feel lost. Please show me the way."

Inside the church, she knelt and took out her Rosary. It was Friday, the day to pray the sorrowful mysteries—prayers that matched the sadness in her heart. After about twenty minutes, she lifted her head—and saw someone familiar. It was Nagai, kneeling at the front, deep in prayer. At that moment, it felt as though Christ whispered to her, "Midori, your task is complete. He is with me now. You must let go."

That day, her genuflection felt heavier than ever. Letting go of Nagai was one of the hardest things she had ever done. Every Sunday, when she saw him at Mass, her heart would ache with a feeling she couldn't quite explain. At twenty-five, an age when most Japanese women were already married, she had said no to many suitors. But she never told her worried parents the real reason—that she couldn't even think of marrying while Nagai was still at war in Manchuria.

Still, she agreed to step away from her full-time teaching job. She moved back home and started taking a few classes at Junshin, a local Catholic school for girls. The name meant "pure heart."

Spring came again. The sweet songs of the uguisu, the little bush warbler, filled the air, and cherry blossoms colored the town. But none of it moved Midori. Her heart was somewhere else.

Nagai had returned to his old job in the hospital's x-ray department. But all his free time was spent reading the Bible, studying the catechism, and talking to Father Moriyama. He was learning everything he could about the Catholic faith—its prayers, its teachings, and its way of life.

Helping him through this journey was a humble man from Urakami. He wasn't a scholar. He knew little about philosophy, but his heart was full of kindness and quiet wisdom. At the hospital, he worked as a janitor. But to Nagai, he was a teacher, a true *sensei*.

Chapter 12

I've argued with my father. He's sure I'm lost.

By the summer of 1934, Japan's countryside was bursting with life. The fields were deep green, the skies painted with swallows that swooped and soared like brushstrokes on a living canvas. On the surface, everything looked calm and beautiful. But underneath, a quiet storm was growing in the hearts of many Japanese people.

Writers, teachers, and deep thinkers felt something shift. The hope they once had in Western ideals—especially the bright promises of things like Roosevelt's New Deal—was beginning to fade. That dream, borrowed from America, now felt like a lie. And the sense of betrayal hung in the air like summer heat.

The Great Depression had already brought deep pain. Japan's economy was still bleeding. Then the West made things worse, slamming their doors shut with high tariffs. Trade dried up. Factories slowed down. Families struggled to survive. But worse than the money troubles was something deeper and harder to name—a growing realization that the West didn't see Japan as an equal. To them, Japan was always the outsider. Always "other."

That wound had been there for years. After World War I, Japan had stood beside the Allies, had fought and bled as part of the winning side. At the Versailles Peace Conference, they believed it was their moment to be seen, heard, and treated fairly. They proposed something simple and powerful: a racial equality clause. Just a basic statement that all people, no matter their race, deserved equal respect.

But the answer was a loud and painful "no." The biggest pushback came from Australia's Billy Hughes, who feared it would challenge his country's white-only immigration policies. The message was clear: equality was for white nations only. Japan, no matter its strength or sacrifice, wasn't welcome in that club.

Even though the war had ended, the old racist fears hadn't. Germany's "Yellow Peril" posters may have been taken down, but the same ideas had just put on suits and sat behind closed doors in quiet meetings. The rejection wasn't just political—it was personal. And for many in Japan, it marked the beginning of a new and bitter resolve.

After being humiliated on the world stage and shut out of the global economy, Japan turned inward. The glow of liberal democracy faded into something cold and distant. In towns and cities across the country, people began to turn their backs on the Western model they had once admired. The dream no longer fit. Divorce rates climbed. Crime grew bolder. People blamed jazz, Western movies, and scandalous headlines for unraveling the values they had once held sacred.

To the growing conservative voice in Japan, this wasn't freedom—it was moral decay. It was everything they feared the West would bring: chaos, corruption, and a loss of soul.

Among Japan's thinkers, the shift was unmistakable. Where they had once lifted glasses to democracy and openness, they now spoke in new tones—of strength, purity, and national honor. Nationalism and militarism were no longer whispered in dark corners; they had become proud and public dreams. Japan, they said, must rise. No longer would it beg for respect from Western powers who grouped it with the colonized and looked down on it. If the West wouldn't see Japan as a partner, it would learn to fear it instead.

As this new wave of pride swept through the nation, it carried with it a renewed devotion to Shintoism—the old heartbeat of Japan. In quiet places like Urakami, where a small Catholic church stood quietly beneath the hills, this shift cast long shadows. Christianity, with its foreign roots and its teachings of peace and humility, started to look suspicious. To many in power, it seemed un-Japanese. Almost like a quiet rebellion.

And right in the middle of this storm stood Dr. Takashi Nagai.

He was a man of medicine and science, trained in the newest techniques. But more and more, he found his heart pulled toward the message of Christ. It wasn't loud or dramatic—it was quiet, slow, deep. A still, small voice that kept asking him questions he couldn't ignore. But as his faith grew, so did the risks.

His work at the state-run university hospital began to feel fragile. There were whispers behind his back. Sideways glances in staff meetings. And then the message came from home: his father was calling.

In Japanese culture, when the patriarch summons you, it's not a request—it's a command. As the eldest son, Nagai carried the family's past and future. He was expected to honor the ancestors, tend their graves, carry their names forward. So when he told his father he had become a Christian, it wasn't just a disagreement. It was betrayal.

"You shame our blood," his father said sharply. "How can the ancestors rest, when their heir walks away from the old gods?"

Nagai didn't raise his voice. He didn't argue. He just spoke quietly, gently. He tried to explain that even the ancestors had once searched for truth. That the gods of old weren't always there—they had been discovered, one step at a time, just as he was now discovering something new. Something true.

But his father's heart didn't move. For him, Shinto wasn't just religion—it was Japan itself. It was sacred, ancient, immovable. And so, with that wall between them still standing, Nagai left. He didn't win the argument. He wasn't even sure he'd made the right choice. All he knew was that something inside him was changing.

In his confusion, he turned to an unlikely teacher—a janitor at the hospital. The man kept a rosary in his pocket and memories of persecution in his eyes. He didn't offer comfort. He offered something harder: Scripture.

"If anyone comes to me and does not hate his father and mother... he cannot be my disciple."

The words hit like a stone. Not because they were cruel, but because they were clear. Faith, he realized, wasn't meant to be safe. It wasn't about feeling good. It was about choosing—really choosing—what you believe is worth everything.

Looking back on this moment in Nagai's life, I can't help but think that faith doesn't always bloom in peace. Sometimes it takes root in the middle of conflict—between love and duty, family and conviction. Nagai's story is about more than religion. It's about identity. It's about the silent battle between who we are and who we are called to be. And that struggle—quiet, painful, beautiful—is one many of us face in our own way.

The next morning, Takashi Nagai walked with purpose yet hesitation. His steps led him to the quiet home of Jinzaburo

Moriyama—a man weathered by years, refined by suffering, and known for a wisdom others pursued like a rare spring in a dry land.

Nagai spoke. Words poured out of him like rain breaking after drought. Doubts. Questions. Inner storms he could no longer quiet. Moriyama listened without interruption. He didn't rush to respond. Instead, he offered a story—one he had carried in his heart through many winters.

It went back to the dark days after Tsuwano—the prison, the interrogations, the quiet martyrs. Years later, a letter had arrived. Unexpected. Unsettling. It was from a man named Brother Morioka. He had something to confess.

His father, the letter said, had been the official who led the Christian persecutions at Tsuwano. The same official under whom thirty-six believers had perished—including Moriyama's younger brother, Yujiro.

But this wasn't just a confession—it was an appeal. Morioka, now a Christian himself, wanted to meet. To seek reconciliation. He enclosed money for the journey. Moriyama didn't hesitate.

They met and walked together to the old prison grounds. The buildings had vanished, but not the weight. The past still breathed there. The pond remained. So did the low stone wall where Yasutaro, a friend and fellow believer, had died in a wooden box during a brutal winter—twenty days of exposure, silence, and slow agony.

For Moriyama, it wasn't just memory. It was presence. That place still pulsed with pain. As they stood together, the past pressed against them, cold and relentless.

Without a word, Moriyama dropped to his knees. The weight was too much. Beside him, Morioka fell too—head bowed to the earth, bearing grief not even his own. A sorrow passed down like a family name.

And still, Moriyama did not turn him away. He opened his arms and held the son of the man who had helped kill his brother.

"Your father thought he was protecting Japan," Moriyama said softly. "To him, our faith was a threat. But in the end, he understood the cost. He carried Yujiro's body to my sister with his own hands. I've prayed for him every day since. I believe Yujiro has too—from heaven. Your faith tells me his death wasn't in vain. God was there. Even then. Even there. Suffering doesn't get the final word—not when we trust Him."

They sat in silence. Tea arrived. The conversation turned. But the weight of that moment stayed with Nagai like a stone in the chest.

As he walked home along the quiet edges of Mount Konpira, he felt the battle inside him rage again. Baptism wasn't just a ritual. It was a break—a severing from the deep roots of his upbringing. To accept Christ felt like betrayal. Not of ideas, but of family. Of his father. Of the ancestors whose names were still honored with incense and prayer.

There were doubts of the mind as well. He had read the Germans—Nietzsche, Feuerbach, even some of the liberal theologians. What if they were right? What if belief was just projection?

And then, there was his future. Radiology was a young science. He stood at the edge of something important. If he waited—just a little—perhaps he could serve the Church more powerfully later. Maybe this wasn't the time. Maybe delay wasn't cowardice, but wisdom.

But then again—maybe not.

That night, Takashi Nagai sat cross-legged on the tatami mat, the quiet of his home pressing in around him. He opened Pascal's *Pensées*, letting the stillness fill him. But he barely had time to turn a page before one line shot out at him—bright and sharp, like a flare cutting through the darkness: "There is enough light for those who desire only to see, and enough darkness for those of a contrary disposition."

It wasn't just words. It was a revelation. A quiet, piercing truth that unraveled him. He realized that the waiting he had cloaked in the guise of wisdom was, in fact, fear—raw, gripping fear. And fear, he knew, was no light at all.

With his chest tightening, he rose. The familiar weight of it settled over him—like the heaviness before a battle fought in distant lands, in Manchuria. He didn't pause. Without hesitation, he turned toward Father Moriyama's house, his resolve steadying with each step.

"I don't know if I'm worthy," he said, his voice faltering but resolute, "but I want baptism, Shinpu-sama."

Father Moriyama studied him with a calm that seemed to hold back centuries of wisdom. Baptism, he knew, was sacred. It couldn't be rushed. But there, in Nagai's eyes, was sincerity that could not be ignored.

"I've argued with my father," Nagai continued. "He's sure I'm lost. And the longer I delay, the more we both suffer. Please, examine me. Decide if I'm ready."

Father Moriyama listened. Thoughtful questions, quiet pauses. And then, at last—a gentle consent. Baptism would come in the weeks ahead, before the first rays of morning light reached the cathedral.

June arrived in a soft veil of rain. The seasonal storms had come, and Japan's skies were thick with water. Water dripped from eaves and leaves as Nagai made his way through the puddled streets, his steps reverberating in the stillness. The cathedral stood ahead, an imposing silhouette against the overcast sky—Western, foreign, strange.

His father's voice echoed in his ears: *"You're abandoning who you are."*

Inside, three figures waited: Father Moriyama, a quiet janitor-catechist, and a broad-faced farmer in worn robes—Midori's cousin, chosen as godfather. Together, they entered the baptistery, where the font awaited—an ancient stone basin that held both promise and danger.

Nagai hesitated. Could he truly renounce everything? His past, his heritage, the familiarity of the world he had known? Was he choosing to become a stranger in his own land?

The salt touched his tongue—sharp, unsettling—a reminder of purification, of dying to the old self. And then the Latin words—the same language that once felt cold, foreign, and distant—now carried the weight of something beautiful. Like music. A thread connecting him to a family that stretched across oceans and centuries. These were the sounds of Bach and Beethoven. Of saints long gone and martyrs who had given all. He wasn't losing himself. He was finally becoming who he was always meant to be.

He took the name Paul Miki, honoring the Japanese Jesuit martyr who had given his life on a cross in Nagasaki. Miki had embodied everything Nagai aspired to—faithful to Christ, loyal to Japan, courageous to the very end.

Midori? Her prayers had never wavered. Father Moriyama had known of her quiet love and had hinted to her cousin, the farmer-matchmaker, that something was blooming between them. When both admitted their feelings, the cousin had arranged the introductions—the traditional way.

But Nagai had his own confession. "My work in x-ray diagnosis carries risks," he said, his voice steady. "It's still a young science. Many radiologists have died of cancer. She must know that before she agrees to walk beside me."

Midori's response was simple, unwavering. She clung to the words of Ruth:
"Where you go, I will go… your people shall be my people, and your God, my God."

To her, the risk was nothing compared to the life they could share together.

"I will walk with him," she told the cousin. "Wherever the road leads."

Nagai knew the path would break his father's heart. But he still went to two of his father's closest friends—Dr. and Mrs. Furuse—and told them everything. He had become a Christian. He wanted to marry Midori. Would they speak to his father?

They agreed. And when they met Midori, her calm presence, her unwavering gentleness, won them over. They traveled north to Mitoya, and somehow—whether by providence or the passing of time—his father gave his reluctant blessing.

But the wedding felt like something foreign to the elder Nagai. Latin chants, unfamiliar robes, the ceremony held before the sun had even risen. It was nothing like what he had imagined for his son.

Yet Midori brought with her something powerful: *wa*. That deep, uniquely Japanese sense of harmony. Peace—not just as the absence of conflict, but as the presence of balance and goodwill. She quietly built relationships, visited the family home, honored traditions without ever compromising her faith.

By the time their first child was placed in his grandfather's arms, something had shifted. The past hadn't been erased, but the wounds had begun to heal.

Wa had returned.

Chapter 13

The Graceful wife

In the uncertain years of the mid-1930s, Takashi found himself struggling in a world that seemed to be falling apart around him. Working as a junior staff member in a radiology unit, he earned only forty yen a month—a sum that barely covered his own bare necessities, let alone the needs of a family. Midori's father had passed away, and with him, the family's main source of income—raising cattle—had slowly crumbled. To make matters worse, Japan's economy was spiraling. Exports were plummeting, imports surged by nearly a third, and the yen lost half its value in just six years. It felt like trying to fill a leaking bucket—no matter how hard they worked, the money just never stretched far enough.

But Midori wasn't one to sit idly by and wallow in despair. Instead of focusing on what had been lost, she turned her attention to the earth beneath her feet. With unwavering determination, she reclaimed their barren pastureland and transformed it into a thriving vegetable garden. Her name, "Midori," meaning "green," seemed like a gift from the universe. It fit her perfectly. Her hands worked magic in the soil, coaxing life from the ground when the world outside seemed drained of hope. While the country trembled under the weight of economic despair, Midori's garden became a sanctuary—a tiny oasis of life and order. She grew potatoes, onions, radishes, sweet potatoes, barley, and two kinds of cabbage. Their meals came from her bountiful rows of leafy greens, and any extra harvest she gave away without a second thought. Generosity flowed from her as naturally as the plants she nurtured.

Yet, as much as she loved the earth, Midori's heart beat with even greater passion for sewing. It was there that her creativity truly blossomed. After marrying Takashi, she became his personal tailor, replacing his once-ordinary wardrobe of rayon shirts and factory-made socks with hand-sewn garments made from cotton, wool, and silk. She even crafted his gloves and underwear with such care. One of her creations—a beautifully designed tweed coat—caught the attention of a local dressmaker, who displayed it as a showpiece in her shop. Takashi, ever the thoughtful observer, couldn't help but see his wife as the "capable woman" described in Proverbs 31—industrious, talented, and filled with a quiet strength that seemed to make everything she touched bloom.

Midori's elegance wasn't something she learned from fashion magazines or movies. It was ingrained in her, woven into the very fabric of her culture. For centuries, Japanese women had been admired by foreigners for their quiet refinement, shaping the artistic soul of the country. While many women in Europe were still denied an education in the Middle Ages, Japanese women were already writing poetry of remarkable depth and beauty. Some of the greatest early works of Japanese literature, like *The Tale of Genji* by Murasaki Shikibu, were penned by women. From this rich literary tradition arose a cultural ideal: the woman as gentle, graceful, and strong—like bamboo that bends in the wind but never breaks.

This ideal wasn't confined to noble courts; it seeped into every corner of Japanese life. Tea ceremonies, flower arranging, and embroidery weren't just hobbies—they were rites of passage, teachings every girl learned as naturally as walking or speaking. Midori herself held diplomas in both ikebana and sewing, and she had a deep appreciation for the subtle beauty of the tea ceremony. After her marriage, she transformed their home into a small school, where, by night, students came to learn the arts of flower arranging and needlework.

Takashi would often watch her work in the garden, dressed in her monpe pants—loose, durable trousers that had become the uniform for working women during the war years. To Midori, appearance didn't matter. She didn't care about looking polished or refined, even when former students from the elegant Junshin school passed by in their kimonos. They would bow respectfully and call out, "Good afternoon, Sensei." Midori, with the dirt still on her hands and sweat on her brow, would return the bow with a humble smile before returning to her work. Her grace wasn't in her clothes or her shoes, but in how she carried herself—her dignity was a part of her, as natural and unshakable as the earth beneath her feet.

As time went on, Takashi's career flourished. He helped establish Radiology as a full-fledged department, earning recognition for his research on kidney stones, even publishing in a medical journal. But with success came a price. Takashi became more withdrawn, often losing himself in his work. Days would go by in silence, his clothes would pile up, and his desk would be buried under papers. Then, in a flash of realization, he would call out, "Midori, can you help me find that report from Kyoto University?" She would always respond with patience, understanding that his absent-mindedness was a mark of his dedication. To her, his work wasn't just a job—it was a mission, a calling, a duty.

At home, Midori held everything together. She managed the budget, did the shopping, handled the banking, oversaw her night school, and tended the garden. She was the quiet force that made their lives run smoothly. On Sundays and holy days, the Nagais would listen to Father Moriyama preach about the humble life of the Holy Family in Nazareth. His words struck a deep chord in them. He said that holiness didn't come from grand, dramatic acts—it bloomed from the small, repeated actions of love: cooking a meal, folding a shirt, planting a seed.

These homilies took Takashi back to his own childhood. He remembered how his mother used to say, "When you look at a bowl of rice, see the entire universe in it." She taught him to see not just the rice, but the farmers who grew it, the craftsmen who shaped the bowl, the parents who made sacrifices to bring it to the table. To her, every meal was sacred. And she would end the lesson by folding her hands in prayer and murmuring, "Namu Amida Butsu"—a reminder that we depend on more than ourselves.

And when I think of their lives, it feels almost revolutionary. In an era marked by war, inflation, and uncertainty, Takashi and Midori built a life grounded in simplicity, duty, and love. No flashy gestures. No perfect Instagram moments. Just real, honest effort—and a deep, unwavering respect for each other's role. Their story isn't just a glimpse into pre-war Japan. It's a timeless reminder that grace often hides in the simplest of places: a hand-sewn sock, a freshly tilled row of radishes, a quiet prayer whispered over a bowl of rice.

There's something deeply moving in the groundedness of their lives. It celebrates the unsung beauty of a life well-lived.

Nagai didn't grow up confined to a single spiritual path. While his roots were in Shinto, faith in Japan often flows like a river with many streams. His household held space for both the rituals of Shinto and the quiet wisdom of Buddhism. His mother, a woman descended from samurai, was especially influenced by Zen. She didn't just know about Zen—she lived it. From the monks at the nearby temple, she absorbed lessons she passed on to her son, not through lectures, but in quiet conversations over tea or shared moments at home.

One of those early teachings was about a word everyone says without thinking—"arigato"—thank you. But to her, it wasn't just a word of politeness. She explained the deeper meaning of the kanji—*difficult to exist*. A monk at their temple had once shared that meaning with her. What we receive, he said, doesn't come easily. Whether it's a loaf of bread, a simple kindness, or love itself—someone, somewhere, gave something up so that we could have it. This version of gratitude carried weight. It wasn't just manners—it was an awareness of sacrifice, of the invisible hands that make our lives possible.

Another important word in Nagai's childhood was *shigoto*—work. His mother didn't just define it; she explained its meaning deeply. The parts of the word—"shi" and "goto"—suggested that true work isn't just about labor, but about service. She helped him understand that tasks like cleaning a floor, treating a patient, or fixing a neighbor's fence weren't about showing off. They were about contributing something useful to the world. Nagai quietly absorbed this lesson, carrying it with him throughout his life, especially when he became a doctor.

In the years that followed, Nagai's talent in radiology became more and more noticeable. Under Professor Suetsugu, the new head of the department, Nagai began to stand out. As doctors became more interested in X-rays, Nagai's ability to explain them clearly made him in high demand. His lectures were practical but insightful, and soon he was speaking to full rooms of doctors eager to learn. His hard work didn't go unnoticed, and he was soon asked to help write a new textbook. Before long, he was promoted to chief of medical staff at the university hospital. The role brought him recognition, but it also added more responsibility.

Despite his busy professional life, Nagai's heart was drawn in another direction. One day, a man named Tagawa, a Christian from Urakami, invited him to learn about the Society of Saint Vincent de Paul. Nagai wasn't quick to join; he wanted to understand the group's origins first. He learned that the group was founded by Frédéric Ozanam, a 19th-century French intellectual who, like Nagai, had struggled with doubt before fully embracing faith. That resonated deeply with Nagai. Ozanam wasn't some untouched saint—he was a real person who had wrestled with questions, and that made his compassion feel genuine.

One story about Ozanam stayed with Nagai. It was about a moment when Ozanam walked into a shabby church in Paris and saw the famous physicist André Ampère—a man who had spent his life studying the laws of nature—praying. That moment struck Nagai. If someone like Ampère could have faith, then maybe science and religion weren't enemies. Perhaps they were just different ways to understand the same mystery.

With this conviction growing, Nagai joined the Society. His first mission took him to Kaminoshima, a small island village. What he found there wasn't romantic—it was difficult. Almost everyone had trachoma, an eye disease that leads to blindness. Nagai didn't just feel sorry for them; he got to work. He organized regular trips to provide care and even brought colleagues along when he could convince them. This wasn't charity for show—it was real, hard work mixed with compassion.

One visit left a lasting impact on Nagai. A woman and her son were hiding in the mountains, shunned by society because she had gonorrhea. She was almost blind, living in a run-down shack with only a few chickens. When Nagai first arrived, she rejected him. But he didn't give up. He returned the following week, not as a doctor with a diagnosis, but as someone offering food, clothes, and kindness. Slowly, she started to open up.

As Nagai was leaving, the woman said something surprising: she could smell plum blossoms. It was a small thing, almost nothing, but Nagai knew it meant something. Despite her suffering and isolation, she could still feel beauty. Nagai climbed the mountain, found a plum blossom, and brought it to her—not to fix her, but to remind her that she still had the right to appreciate the beauty around her.

Later, Nagai wrote in his journal about that moment. He realized that to truly help someone, you needed more than medicine. You needed to see their humanity, to restore their dignity. True compassion wasn't just about treating wounds—it was about reminding people they still mattered.

In February 1935, Nagai was working late in a freezing lab. There was no heat, but he kept going, driven by his sense of duty. By morning, he had a sore throat and a fever. His wife, Midori, urged him to rest, but Nagai had promised to help with a surgery and refused to back out.

He arrived at the hospital shivering and dizzy. Before going into the operating room, he stopped for an injection from a specialist. But as he entered surgery, something felt wrong. His vision blurred, nausea hit him, and his heart pounded. He tried to focus, but the room spun.

Apologizing, he staggered out. Outside, he collapsed, vomiting dark blood. Struggling to breathe, he realized his body had reached its limit. This wasn't just exhaustion—it was a warning. A turning point.

Sometimes, life humbles us quietly—through wisdom, the scent of a flower, or the teachings of a parent. But sometimes, it humbles us through collapse, when our bodies remind us we're not invincible. For Nagai, that night was a wake-up call. It would make him rethink his health, his life, and his way of serving others.

Professor Suetsugu immediately rushed to help. He laid Nagai down and gave him another injection, but things didn't improve. Nagai slipped into unconsciousness, his face swelling, blood pooling beneath his skin. The professor realized Nagai was suffering from anaphylactic shock—a severe allergic reaction. His face was so distorted it was almost unrecognizable. His breathing was shallow, barely there.

A priest from the cathedral soon arrived. He leaned close, speaking softly, but with conviction. Though Nagai could barely open his eyes or speak, the priest's words reached his heart.

"Child of God," the priest said gently, "turn back to the One who gave you life. Offer this suffering to Christ, who took our pain upon Himself. Let us pray—not just for healing, but for peace, for the grace to accept whatever comes."

In the haze between life and death, Nagai found enough strength to whisper his sins. The priest listened, then offered absolution and anointed him with oil. The warm, earthy scent of the oil felt sacred, almost otherworldly, reminding Nagai of incense rising in a church or the scent of old wood in a quiet temple. Instead of fear, he felt a calm, a sense that even if this was the end, he wasn't alone.

Midori's small, trembling hand took his. Her tears soaked his skin. In that moment, full of weakness and love, something inside him stirred: the desire to live. A voice nearby called out, "Pulse 130, breathing 36." Another injection. Maybe it would work. Maybe not. But Nagai felt ready.

"If I die," he thought, "this isn't such a bad place to go. Surrounded by those who care. Surrounded by love."

A memory from Confucius came to him: "If you understand the Way by morning, you can face death peacefully by evening." Now, he understood.

Against all odds, Nagai survived. But the experience changed how he saw life. Before, death had seemed far away, something that happened to others. But now, it felt close. Personal. Real. That single moment, caused by a tiny injection, had shown him just how fragile life is.

He remembered the old metaphors from Japanese poetry—life like a dewdrop on grass, or like smoke rising over the cremation grounds. Beautiful. Temporary. Vanishing before you can hold it.

From that day, he changed. He found himself drawn more to the Bible, spending quiet time in the cathedral, not out of fear, but out of a new appreciation for the peace that faith brings. Something deeper had taken root in him.

But his asthma didn't go away. It stayed, a constant reminder, lurking in the background. A gust of wind, the smell of animals, even laughter or rich food could trigger an attack. Every day felt like walking a tightrope.

One snowy evening, his chest tight, Midori urged him to stay in bed. But just then, a knock came at the door—a messenger had news of a farmer in Ippongi, struggling to breathe from his own asthma attack.

Midori begged him not to go, but Nagai was already determined. She helped him dress warmly: thick socks, a padded kimono, gloves, a cotton mask, and his Wellington boots. He grabbed his doctor's bag and walking stick, joking that he looked like a traveler from Siberia. Then, he stepped out into the cold.

The path was steep and slippery, but Nagai climbed slowly, controlling his breath. When he reached the farmer, the man was hunched over, gasping for air, his eyes full of desperation. He couldn't speak, but his eyes said it all. Nagai knelt beside him, gently holding his arm, and whispered, "You're going to be all right." A quick injection of adrenaline and camphor worked wonders. The man's color returned, and his breathing steadied. Nagai left him with some medicine and a simple farewell: "O genki de—get well."

But the snow was falling harder now. As Nagai turned to head home, he thought it would be easy—downhill, after all. He picked up his pace. That was a mistake.

Halfway home, his chest tightened. His lungs screamed for air. He stumbled, barely able to see, and fell into a pit dug into the hillside—a potato storehouse. The snow covered him like a cold, suffocating blanket. He tried to reach for the syringe in his bag, but his hands were shaking too much. Darkness surrounded him. Seven hours until morning. No one would be out in this storm.

He was no longer the doctor. Now, he was the patient—alone, helpless, scared.

Then, a flicker of light appeared. A lantern. A figure in the storm.

A voice called through the wind, "Is that you? It's you, isn't it?" Midori.

"Yes," he whispered, barely able to speak.

She found his bag, filled the syringe, and gave him the injection. The effect was immediate. It felt like someone had lifted a heavy weight off his chest.

He collapsed into her, his head resting on her body, thinking, So this is what it feels like when a soul is pulled from purgatory into light.

Midori didn't hesitate. She was ready to carry him home. Though she called him Shujin—"Lord"—out of tradition, everyone knew she was the one who quietly ran their household. She managed the finances, handed him his allowance, and organized their life with a gentle but firm hand.

Now, she took charge again.

She knelt down, wrapped in her thick monpe pants, and told him to lean on her back. With one strong push, she stood, balancing him and the lantern. The snow swirled around them, but she kept moving forward, her steps steady. The soft glow of the lantern lit the snow like a quiet hymn.

As he swayed on her back, Nagai remembered another time, another crisis, when she had carried him. She was never large or strong in the way people expect, but like bamboo in a storm, she bent without breaking. Always steady. Always holding him up.

Chapter 14

But what peace? What justice

In the early years of his marriage, Dr. Nagai was consumed by his work. As Japan's political climate grew increasingly tense, he remained largely unaffected, buried in the demands of teaching, publishing scientific papers, and advancing his research in X-ray technology. There was little room in his life for the chaos unfolding around him. It was during this time, on April 4, 1935, that his world shifted in the most personal way. His son, Makoto, was born. The name "Makoto" means "truth" or "honesty," and it was a name chosen with deep care, symbolizing the parents' fervent hope that their son would grow to embody integrity, even in the face of an uncertain future.

But outside their quiet home, Japan was anything but peaceful. The nation was divided, its leadership fragmented among three powerful forces. Emperor Hirohito, once expected to follow the firm rule of his grandfather, Emperor Meiji, was now relegated to a more symbolic role. His father, Emperor Taisho, had been seen as weak, and Hirohito was groomed more as a figurehead than an active ruler. Meanwhile, influential politicians, bankers, and industrial magnates were gaining some ground in Japan's democracy, but their influence was limited—less than half the population had the right to vote. The third and most powerful force, however, was the military. Driven by a sense of divine mission, the military leaders were determined to push Japan toward global supremacy, with both their arms and their economy.

Those who dared to speak against the military's aggressive expansion—especially their controversial invasion of Manchuria and growing military budget—did so at great risk. Seven outspoken critics were murdered, their deaths a chilling message to anyone who might dare oppose the military's ambitions. When Hirohito protested these killings, his mentor, Prince Saionji, reminded him that the emperor was not meant to interfere in government matters. Reluctantly, Hirohito complied. With the threat of violence quieting dissent, the military's grip on the nation tightened. The press was heavily censored, and law enforcement became an arm of the military's agenda. The kenpeitai, the secret police, began to monitor and control civilian life, crushing any resistance. Even Father Moriyama, a devoted Christian, found himself blacklisted, his faith seen as a dangerous foreign influence, and his name smeared with accusations of espionage.

In the midst of this turbulence, Dr. Nagai and his family lived, quietly, with their hopes for a future built on truth and integrity, unaware of how swiftly their world would change.

In the summer of 1937, as the Nagai family celebrated the arrival of their baby girl, Ikuko, the world around them was already changing. That very night—July 7—Dr. Takashi Nagai hurried through the streets of Nagasaki, eager to meet his daughter for the first time. The city buzzed with the festivities of Tanabata, the Festival of Stars. Paper lanterns cast a soft glow along the roads, while bamboo poles swayed in the breeze, heavy with colored streamers and small slips of paper bearing handwritten dreams and wishes.

As Nagai made his way home, the atmosphere pulled him in. The air was filled with the joyful sound of children singing in their bright kimonos, their voices carrying the story of a princess in the heavens and her forbidden love for a humble herdsman. According to the legend, once a year, the stars would align, and the two lovers would meet again—a tale of longing, of love separated by distance, a heart aching for something just out of reach.

To Nagai, that story felt like more than a simple romance—it spoke to something deeper. It stirred a yearning he felt in his own soul, a longing for something spiritual that he believed was slowly being forgotten by his country. While the people of Japan poured their hearts into fleeting wishes tied to bamboo branches, Nagai couldn't help but feel they were chasing after shadows, distracted by temporary beauty. In his heart, he wished they could see beyond it—to the eternal light he believed had once shone over Bethlehem. But instead, it seemed that the country was turning its gaze to another star—the red one, the planet that symbolized war and conquest.

The very next day, Nagai's sense of unease deepened. A harsh news bulletin crackled over the radio: Japanese forces had exchanged gunfire with Chinese troops near the Marco Polo Bridge in Beijing. War had begun. And in a cruel twist of fate, it seemed that the spark for this conflict had been lit on the very day of Tanabata—a festival Japan had borrowed from China, the very nation it was now at war with.

As the military leaders embraced the war with swelling pride and bold predictions, Nagai felt only dread. Not long after, a postcard arrived for his wife, Midori, bearing life-altering news—Nagai had been promoted to first lieutenant and assigned as chief medical officer for the Fifth Division. Orders had come: he was to deploy to China immediately.

Within weeks, he was gone.

For the next two and a half years, Nagai worked tirelessly on the front lines, documenting his experiences in letters and journals. These writings would later become a vivid record of the brutal realities of wartime life. When his unit first arrived in China in August 1937, they found themselves in hostile terrain, not far from the Great Wall. The narrow valley they entered was met with sudden, violent resistance. Gunfire rang out from the surrounding hills, and in mere moments, four hundred men were either dead or badly wounded. Their radio, weapons, food, and medical supplies were all destroyed. Cut off from any support, they were alone.

With casualties mounting and no help in sight, Nagai worked quickly to set up an emergency field hospital inside a damaged tent. When he informed his commanding officer of their dire situation, the reply was grim: unless someone could break through enemy lines and reach headquarters that night, they would not survive another two days.

Without hesitation, Nagai volunteered for the task.

Under the cover of night, he slipped into the wilderness, fully aware of the danger he faced. The twelve-mile journey to the nearest base was treacherous, the first stretch especially so, with Chinese troops patrolling the area. Crawling over jagged rocks, sliding through dense underbrush, and even allowing the river to carry him for stretches, he pressed on, each step a reminder that one wrong move could be his last. By the time he reached headquarters, soaked and exhausted, his only thought was to get help. Reinforcements would be sent immediately. But when he was ordered to accompany them back, he declined. His duty was to the wounded still waiting for him.

On his way back, something shifted within him. Perhaps buoyed by his earlier success, he noticed the landscape more keenly. The Great Wall curved along the horizon, shrouded in morning fog, while golden fields stretched endlessly before him. Passing an apple tree, hunger pushed him to shake the branches, letting a few ripe fruits fall. But just as he bent to pick them up, a bullet whizzed past his ear—a warning shot from a hidden rifle. Heart pounding, he left the apples behind and dashed for cover.

By the time he returned to camp, reinforcements had arrived, and the Chinese forces had pulled back. The wounded were evacuated, but Nagai couldn't shake what he had seen. In the faces of the Chinese villagers, he saw his own family—children who resembled Ikuko, women who reminded him of Midori, and old men who looked like his father. The lines between "enemy" and "neighbor" blurred, and for the first time, he questioned everything.

In his journal, he wrote:

"They say this is a just war—that killing the enemy is not murder. That it is done for peace and righteousness. But what peace? What justice?"

His inner turmoil deepened. One day, he witnessed a fellow surgeon telling a wounded soldier that his arm would need to be amputated. The man burst into tears. "That arm is my life," he said, "I play the violin." Another time, Nagai treated a young soldier who had been shot through both cheeks. Unable to speak, the boy looked at him with pleading eyes. Nagai turned to a corpsman. "Find something soft for him to eat," he said. Hours later, the boy returned with honey—but his face and hands were covered in bee stings. He had fought off a hive to bring back something sweet for the wounded.

These moments, these glimpses of human resilience and tenderness amid the brutality of war, left an indelible mark on Nagai. The war, he realized, was not just a clash of nations—it was a clash of human nature, revealing its darkest cruelty and its quietest, most profound bravery. And through it all, something deep inside him was changing.

He reflected on how different he felt compared to his earlier years, during the conflict in Manchuria. Back then, he had been torn apart inside. But now, in the heart of an even bloodier campaign, he had found something strange and unexpected: peace. Not the kind promised by political leaders, but a quiet certainty deep within.

One evening, he prepared to operate on a Chinese prisoner whose foot had become blackened with infection. As he cleaned the wound, something stirred inside him. There was no anger, no disgust—only care. He looked at the man and felt no distinction between them. In his journal, he wrote:

"I did not come to China to win battles or defeat enemies. I came to treat the wounded—Japanese or Chinese, soldier or civilian. All are worthy of compassion."

As the conflict raged on in China, civilians were caught helplessly in the tide of war. Many were left wounded or maimed as battles swept through their towns and villages. Children lost limbs, parents were torn from their families, and entire communities were left in ruins. Witnessing this suffering up close, Dr. Takashi Nagai felt compelled to organize a group of volunteers to provide basic medical care to the injured and displaced. He documented their work through photographs, sending them back to his hometown of Nagasaki. The images stirred hearts, especially among the faithful at Urakami Cathedral, where the local Saint Vincent de Paul society quickly mobilized. Donations began to pour in—boxes of food, warm clothes, and small toys meant to offer a flicker of joy to children who had already seen far too much.

To Nagai's surprise, several branches of the Vincentian society were already active within China. These local groups became crucial partners, helping him distribute the donated goods more effectively. But despite these efforts, trust was in short supply. When Nagai first began assisting Chinese civilians, he encountered deep suspicion. The Chinese had every reason to be wary—many feared the Japanese military, and some even eyed Nagai with anxiety, imagining that he might be hiding a grenade in his sleeves. The tension cut both ways, as the Japanese doctors also sensed an unspoken hostility from the locals. Still, as the days passed and his presence remained steady, fear began to give way to fragile trust. Slowly, people started coming to him for help, and the invisible wall between them began to crack.

The war dragged on, and the Japanese army found itself increasingly stretched thin. Rather than face the better-equipped Japanese forces head-on, Chinese commanders adopted guerrilla tactics—quick, unpredictable strikes followed by retreats into the countryside. Meanwhile, winter bore down hard. The cold became a silent killer, felling soldiers whose spirits had already been battered by endless marching and constant danger. Alcohol became the only escape for many, a way to dull the ache of the freezing nights and relentless fighting. But Nagai had left such habits behind after marrying Midori. Instead, he turned inward, finding comfort in his writing.

Poetry had once come naturally to him, but in the rawness of war, his verses changed. The elegance of traditional Japanese poems gave way to blunt and honest imagery. "Good poetry," he once mused, "doesn't tell you everything. It should leave you with silence between the lines." Still, the lines he wrote were vivid and immediate. One poem captured a haunting moment: "Young Communist soldiers, lifeless on the hillside, as bellflowers bloom around them." The contrast between death and nature's quiet persistence struck him deeply.

His journals from that time oscillate between rage and sorrow. After tending to the body of a fallen soldier he had come to respect, Nagai poured out his grief—not just for the man, but for a system that had sacrificed so many promising lives to blind nationalism and empty slogans. Yet more often than not, he chose to write about the quiet dignity he saw in ordinary soldiers—those far removed from the decisions of high-ranking officers. He also took note of the beauty around him, from sweeping mountains to the vibrant traditions of local villages, finding in the Chinese landscape a hidden grace.

His spiritual life, too, was evolving. Raised in the traditions of Shintoism, with its quiet reverence and simple rites, Nagai had also been shaped by Buddhist practices, especially the rhythmic chanting at funerals: "Namu Amida Butsu"—a prayer of surrender and dependence. As he grew in his Christian faith, Nagai didn't discard these earlier influences. Instead, he reshaped them into what he called a "Christian Nenbutsu." He would quietly repeat verses from the Psalms or lines from the New Testament—short, powerful phrases that became anchors for his soul.

Many nights, while working in makeshift operating tents, he found himself surrounded by the wounded. Fatigue pressed on him from every side. In those moments, he turned to Scripture. "The Lord graciously restores the dead to life" became a phrase he clung to. Another came from Isaiah: "For your sake we are killed all day long… regarded as sheep for the slaughter." These words didn't just comfort him—they steadied him, helping him focus amid the chaos and noise of war.

The Japanese word "Nenbutsu" carries with it the sense of being fully present—"heart" and "now" woven together. For Nagai, practicing this form of prayer meant resting in God's immediate presence, the one who once spoke to Moses: "I Am Who I Am." He came to see this prayer practice not as a retreat from suffering, but as a path through it. It gave him a stillness that no battlefield could shake. He often recalled Pascal's reminder: "Don't just read Scripture—pray it."

In time, Nagai realized something profound: the violence around him was loud, but the quiet words of Christ were louder in his heart. He remembered the teachings of Jesus—not in grand theological terms, but in the simplicity of everyday examples. "Look at the birds... and the lilies," Jesus had said. Those lines stayed with him. In those small moments of silent prayer, Nagai found peace. It wasn't the peace of resolution or escape—it was the kind that lets you keep going, even when the world seems to be falling apart.

Much like Buddhist monks use prayer beads for the Nenbutsu, Nagai carried his Rosary with him everywhere. To him, it wasn't just a string of beads; it was like a pocket-sized chapel. During long marches or rare moments of calm, he would hold the beads and pray. When words failed or his mind was too scattered, the rhythm of the Rosary brought him back to center.

One memory from that time never left him. It was Christmas Eve, 1939. The Chinese army had launched a surprise attack, wounding hundreds of Japanese troops and surrounding the rest. The situation was desperate. The officer in charge, weary and drawn from hunger, pulled Nagai aside. "If they strike tonight," he said grimly, "we're finished." Then he gave a grim order: "Place the wounded around the flag. Soak their blankets in gasoline. If capture becomes certain, set it all ablaze. We cannot allow the enemy to take them or our flag." The man's voice broke—this was not a command he wanted to give, but he saw no alternative.

Nagai said nothing. He turned to his assistant and quietly instructed, "Start preparing the wounded to move. But leave me alone unless something urgent happens. I need to pray." He walked a short distance away, knelt on the frozen ground, and began to pray the Rosary. Bead by bead, he let go of the weight of that night—the unbearable decision, the fear of death, thoughts of Midori and their children. Each prayer became an offering, a surrender to a will greater than his own. He lost all sense of time.

Hours later, a young soldier approached, bowing deeply. "Sir," he said gently, "a message from command. A relief force has arrived. We're saved."

Relief came, but not without cost. Not long after, a letter reached him from Midori. Her words were always a balm, but this one cut deep. Their daughter Ikuko had died. So had Nagai's father. The war that had kept him away now exacted a more personal price. Grief swept over him like a flood. The weariness he had carried for years—through jungles and snow-covered hills—finally broke through. He longed not for sleep, but for escape, for silence, for some corner of the world where the pain might finally stop.

It was a spiritual reckoning. Not a crisis of faith, but a plunge into its deepest, most painful depths—the kind of darkness where even prayer feels hollow. Yet, even there, in that deep well of sorrow, Nagai did not let go. He prayed, not to escape the pain, but to carry it with grace. And that grace, however faint, helped him rise once more to care for others—both Japanese and Chinese—with the hands of a man who had seen too much, yet still chose to heal.

Chapter 15

One day, this place might not exist

When Nagai first set foot in China, he was struck by how much the local artwork reminded him of home. The scrolls, the pottery, the brushstrokes in the paintings—so many of the designs felt familiar. Bamboo and pine, for example, were motifs he knew well, symbols of strength and resilience, enduring through the harshest winters and scalding summers. But it wasn't the bamboo or the pine that lingered most in his thoughts. It was the plum blossom—small, delicate, and seeming almost out of place against the biting cold. Yet there it was, blooming boldly in the last days of winter, as if to say, "Spring will return." To Nagai, it wasn't just a flower; it was a quiet promise.

During January 1940, with spirits low among the troops, the plum blossoms dotted the landscape like whispers of hope pushing through the despair. Their silent resilience reached beyond just the Chinese and Japanese soldiers—it touched everyone who laid eyes on them. And then, one morning, Nagai received unexpected orders: a postcard directing him to report for immediate repatriation in Canton. The news stirred something deep within him—an inner thawing of emotions long buried, feelings that had been locked away beneath the weight of war.

A week later, as he stood alone on the deck of the ship carrying him back to Japan, the coastline came into view. He recognized the shape of Dannoura, the site of the 1185 battle between the Genji and Heike clans. The legendary clash had always fascinated him—not for its strategy or its outcome, but for what it represented: the downfall of arrogance. The Genji's victory had given birth to a saying still whispered in Japan: "The proud Heike fall."

As the ship sailed on, Nagai couldn't help but draw a comparison between the ancient Heike and the modern military leaders of Japan. He had seen the toll the war had taken—how the army was stretched thin, battered, and broken. Yet when he arrived, a commanding officer quickly reminded them, "Do not speak of the war's true state. We must preserve morale." The words stung. It felt like a denial of reality, a refusal to face the truth. But Nagai kept quiet, his heart heavy with disillusionment, as the ship neared the docks at Shimonoseki.

On shore, a crowd had gathered. Through the sea of faces, Nagai spotted her—Midori. She stood motionless, her expression weary, her eyes heavy with sorrow. No words were needed for him to understand the pain she had borne in his absence—the loss of his father and, most painfully, their young daughter, Ikuko. Japan's home front had been ravaged. Food was scarce. Fuel nearly gone. Medicine in short supply. Children were dying—not from bombs, but from hunger and neglect. Little Ikuko had been one of them. Midori had believed she had failed as a mother, as a wife. The guilt had consumed her, and it was clear in the way she stood before him, looking lost and hollow.

As Nagai descended the gangplank, all he wanted was to pull her close, to hold her, and to run away together—to escape the war, to return to the quiet life they had known in Nagasaki. But the army didn't wait. Their reunion was brief, and the words they exchanged were few. He was immediately sent to Hiroshima. There, at the barracks, another officer's lecture awaited him, reminding the men not to speak the truth about the war's devastation. As the officer spoke,

Nagai's mind drifted back to the faces he couldn't forget: his assistant Kawahara, the blind Chinese girl he had helped, the terrified mothers screaming for their children, the young boys dragged into battle. The upper ranks—well-fed, comfortable—reminded him again of the Heike: secure in their positions while the ordinary people, those at the bottom, paid the price.

Sometime later, Nagai was awarded the Order of the Rising Sun. But before he reported for his next duty, he took a brief trip to Mitoya to visit his parents' graves. Standing there by the earth that covered them, he remembered the quiet life they had led—full of kindness, humility, and service to others. A line from the Gospel echoed in his heart: *"Those who show love to the least of these will inherit the kingdom."* It brought him comfort. Their humble home, once a refuge for struggling farmers, still stood nearby, a symbol of their compassion. He bowed before their graves, thanking them for the strength they had given him, and asked for their prayers as he moved on to a new chapter in Nagasaki.

On the train bound for Nagasaki, Nagai tried to distract himself, but his thoughts refused to quiet. He couldn't shake the faces of those he had met in China—the wounded, the forgotten, the innocent. Each one haunted him, each one a reminder of the cost of war. In his pocket, his Rosary lay, and slowly, almost instinctively, his fingers wrapped around the beads. With each bead he touched, he whispered a prayer for those whose lives he had encountered, those whose suffering had etched itself into his soul.

As the train neared the lush green slopes of Mount Unzen, a deep stirring began to rise in his chest. He was almost home. His heart raced as Isahaya station came into view. There, waiting for him, was his son, Makoto. The boy rushed toward him, but when Nagai reached down to lift him, Makoto stiffened, pulling back, not responding to his father's embrace. The small, subtle gesture cut him deeper than any words could. It was a painful reminder that the war had changed them all, perhaps forever.

That night, lost in a quiet storm of joy and sorrow, Nagai opened his worn copy of Pascal. The French philosopher had written of humanity's tragic greatness and smallness, and how only Christ could reconcile them. The words resonated deeply within him. He took up his writing brush, his hand steady despite the weight of the moment, and on a blank page, he wrote: *"The Son has returned me safely to Nagasaki—to serve the Father's glory."*

Back at the university, Nagai dove back into teaching radiology. His energy quickly returned. He was soon promoted to professor, and his lectures—while challenging—drew crowds of eager students. But beneath the surface, a quiet dread gnawed at him. Japan was on the brink of disaster. There weren't enough doctors, and disease—especially tuberculosis—was spreading like wildfire. In response, Nagai launched a citywide X-ray campaign to catch the disease early. The results exceeded expectations, offering a rare glimmer of hope.

But even as he worked tirelessly on public health initiatives, Nagai couldn't escape the pull of his other passion: radiation research. Together with a small group of fellow scientists, he explored the hidden world of atoms. It wasn't just scientific curiosity—it was reverence. "A microscope once revealed to us a world hidden from the eye," he wrote in his notes. "But the atom is a thousand times smaller. Compared to it, Earth is as massive as an apple compared to a grain of dust." In these quiet moments of discovery, Nagai felt an intimate connection to God. His laboratory, once a place of sterile experiments, had transformed into a sanctuary of sorts.

Once, while studying kidney crystals under the microscope, an overwhelming urge to kneel overtook him. In that still, sterile room, he felt the presence of holiness—no less real than in any chapel. His time away from science had only deepened his thirst for truth. The lies of war, the brutality, had made honesty feel sacred. Slowly, his writings began to find their way into print once more.

Midori, as always, read every article. Nagai found it touching—and even a little amusing—that she pored over his dense, technical reports with the same focus as if they were love letters. She would sit on the tatami mat, her posture straight, brows furrowed, eyes serious, her rough hands stained from working the garden. To him, she had never looked more beautiful. He often watched her in silence, pretending to read, feeling an overwhelming pride as she struggled to understand his complex work—and sometimes, when she finally grasped it, she wept.

Midori wasn't just his wife—she was a force of nature in her own right. When the government mandated the creation of a Women's Neighborhood Association, Midori was not only elected leader of their block but also became the head of all eighteen branches in their district. Nagai admired her strength, her resilience, even as his thoughts grew darker.

The war had taken a darker turn. Nagai had begun to take notes on the rise of fascism. The alliance between Japan and Hitler's Germany unsettled him, but it was the appointment of General Tojo—nicknamed "the Razor"—as prime minister in October 1941 that truly chilled him. Something about Tojo unsettled him. It felt as though Japan was following the same path the Heike had once walked—proud, blind to its own impending fall. Like the Heike, Nagai feared that Japan would soon pay the price for its arrogance.

On the morning of December 8, 1941, Nagai and Midori made their way up the slope toward the cathedral, the air cold and still with the weight of winter. The feast of the Immaculate Conception imbued the morning with a quiet, sacred gravity. As they walked, Nagai confided in Midori. His heart was heavy with unease, and he spoke in a low voice about the deteriorating negotiations between Japan and the United States. There was an urgency in him, a sense of dread he couldn't shake—a feeling that mirrored the crushing weight he had once carried in China when he had been forced to commit unspeakable acts on the battlefield.

Inside the church, incense swirled in the soft glow of candlelight, and the Latin prayers echoed, carrying a peace that felt too far from the turmoil in his heart. As the prayers rose, Nagai whispered his own desperate plea—that somehow, the war with America might still be averted. He understood the pressures Japan faced—the oil embargo that had driven the country to a corner—but still, he hoped. Like Admiral Yamamoto, he saw the embargo not as justification for war, but as a dangerous spark that could ignite a fire they might never be able to extinguish. He feared, deep in his bones, that if Japan chose war, it would be a road to ruin.

After Mass, Nagai walked home through the narrow streets. Factory workers were already heading to their shifts at Mitsubishi. He watched their tired faces and slow steps. A heavy thought filled his mind—if war really started, Nagasaki wouldn't be safe. The city was too full of factories, too important. It would surely be a target.

Midori had breakfast ready when he arrived. It was a special meal for the feast day: miso soup with sweet bean paste, warm rice with strips of seaweed, and a rare treat—grilled sea bream. Nagai ate quickly, trying to push away the uneasiness in his chest. A few minutes later, he left for the university.

He hadn't gone far when a loudspeaker crackled nearby. A voice shouted out big news—Japan had attacked the United States and Britain. A man walking by raised his fist and cheered, "Banzai! It's finally begun!"

But Nagai didn't move. He stood frozen. The words didn't bring him pride or joy. Instead, a cold feeling spread through his body. Something deep inside told him the world had just changed—and not for the better. His hands began to tremble, not from the cold morning air, but from a deep fear. He felt, without a doubt, that what had started that day would lead to something terrible.

He looked around at the street, the houses, the people walking by—and a dark thought came to him: *One day, this place might not exist anymore.*

He couldn't know then how true that thought would become. Just a few years later, the very road he was standing on would be near the center of a disaster the world would call *ground zero*.

Chapter 16

No need for that, Nagai-kun. You've carried more than anyone could ask

That same morning, Dr. Nagai stood in front of his third-year students, ready to give a lecture on x-ray diagnostics. But as he looked across the room, something in his heart held him back. His face stayed calm, but there was a heaviness in his voice that made the students sit a little straighter. This wasn't going to be just another medical class.

He didn't start with formulas or machines. Instead, he spoke from a deeper place.

"The future is no longer far away," he said softly. "War isn't a maybe anymore. It's already begun. Some of you will be sent to the battlefield. Others will stay behind, working in hospitals and aid stations that may one day be bombed. No one—none of us—will be untouched by what's coming."

The classroom went still.

"This isn't the kind of war we can keep outside our homes or our work. It's not just soldiers fighting soldiers. We are now facing two of the world's greatest powers—America and Britain. Many of you will lose people you love. And until you've seen war with your own eyes, you can't understand what it takes from a person. What we saw in China… that was only the beginning. What's coming will be much worse."

His voice wavered, not with fear, but with memory.

"We'll be cut off from the world. No international help. We'll have to invent, adapt, survive with whatever we have. Our work as doctors won't stop—but it will become more painful, more lonely, and harder than anything you've known."

As he spoke, his mind wandered to a small hospital in China near the Yellow River. He remembered the children's ward. It used to be full of laughter and games. He had brought sweets and toys—gifts sent from the Vincentians in Nagasaki. But the children were quiet. Some had lost arms. Others had burns and deep scars. Their eyes no longer lit up when he handed them candy. They only stared, silent. Something inside them had been taken—something no medicine could bring back.

He blinked, returning to the classroom. His students were still watching him—eyes wide, unsure whether to speak or stay silent.

Wanting to ease the tension, he offered a line that had given him strength through the years. "Confucius once said, 'If you find the way of truth in the morning, you can face death with peace by evening.'" His face softened. A quiet smile followed. Then, he gently shifted back to his notes.

"Now," he said, "let's begin with x-ray diagnosis."

But outside the classroom, the world was shifting faster than any lesson could keep up with.

Soon after, the military government called on Nagai. Because of his experience in the field, they asked him to help prepare civil defenses in the Urakami district. He didn't hesitate.

His first task was to bring together the women from the neighborhood associations—eighteen groups in all. Many of them still believed what the newspapers told them: the war was far away, and Nagasaki was safe. But Nagai knew better.

He spoke plainly, his words stripped of false hope.

"Air raids could strike us anytime," he said. "You need to be ready—not just with your hands, but with your hearts. You must know how to treat the wounded. You must know how to carry people to safety. And when everything is falling apart around you, you must remain calm. But more than anything, you must love each other. Enough to act, enough to risk your life for someone else."

And he didn't stop there.

He started designing something few thought possible—an underground surgical center, complete with an x-ray unit. His colleagues raised their eyebrows. Some even laughed.

But Nagai wasn't joking.

He had done it before—built makeshift hospitals in tunnels, operated in the dark with only a miner's lamp strapped to his head. He had seen what war demanded. And now, he was trying to prepare his home, his people, for what he feared was coming.

Amid the encroaching darkness of war, something beautiful entered Dr. Nagai's life—a flicker of light in uncertain times. He and Midori welcomed a baby girl into the world. They named her **Kayano**, a name that whispered of nature and simplicity. It meant "of the miscanthus reed," a humble plant swaying in Japan's countryside, used for generations to thatch the roofs of small homes. But to Nagai, the name meant so much more. It was a tribute to the land he loved, the quiet places of his childhood, and the life of simplicity he cherished deep in his soul.

Each summer, he would find moments of peace in the layered green of rice fields stepping gently down the hills like waves. In autumn, when the mist crept down the mountains, it wrapped the earth in a soft, white silence. These were the scenes that lived in his heart—homes with thatched miscanthus roofs, skies painted with spring blossoms, autumn leaves burning gold and crimson, and the hush of snowfall in winter. They weren't just memories—they were anchors. Reminders of beauty, of love, of home.

He often reflected on how names in Roman letters couldn't capture that kind of soul. Written in English, names like "Kayano" or "Nagai" seemed cold—just marks on a page, no more expressive than "John" or "Mary." But in Japanese, in their original brushstrokes, they pulsed with life. "Kayano" brought to mind the gentle sway of reeds in the wind. And "Nagai"—with characters meaning something enduring and deep—evoked the quiet strength of a well, ancient and steadfast, offering water through the ages.

Back when Japan was still drunk on its early victories, Nagai's warnings seemed out of place—almost foolish. Newspapers shouted about triumphs. The people celebrated. But beneath the surface, the war was beginning to shift. The Americans had cracked Japan's naval codes. In June 1942, the Battle of Midway struck a devastating blow. Four of Japan's elite aircraft carriers were sunk, silencing the once-proud roar of Japanese dominance at sea. The public didn't know—censorship saw to that—but men like Nagai, who lived close to the pulse of war, felt the tremor.

Soon, U.S. Marines stormed ashore on Guadalcanal. Japan's momentum began to crumble. The Allies, armed with superior air power, were tearing apart Japan's supply lines. One by one, islands fell—Gilbert, the Marshalls, the Marianas. And then came **Saipan** in July 1944, a brutal battle that claimed the lives of **30,000 Japanese troops and more**

than 20,000 civilians. American forces lost over **14,000** of their own, but they emerged with a key prize: airbases from which bombers could now reach Japan's cities. Hiroshima. Nagasaki. Home.

Long before these storms gathered, Nagai had asked a simple, aching question: **What does the Church say about war?** He posed it to Father Moriyama while preparing to become Catholic. The priest spoke of *just war*—a difficult and ancient idea. But Nagai never found peace in that answer. He didn't believe Japan's war was just, but he also didn't see the Allies as purely righteous. All he knew for sure was this: **healing the wounded, no matter who they were, was a sacred duty.** A duty worth his life.

So he prepared. Relentlessly. He ran air-raid drills. Stocked supplies. Helped plan underground surgeries, just in case the worst came. Nagasaki, shielded by mountains and wrapped around its bay, had always felt safe. But that illusion shattered in **August 1944**, when the bombers started coming.

They came often. And loud. The skies over Nagasaki were no longer peaceful.

On **April 26, 1945**, after one particularly vicious raid, Nagai wrote in his journal about what he had seen. Moments after the bombs stopped falling, a military truck arrived at the hospital gates, packed with the injured. Nagai rushed to meet them. He carried the wounded inside, scrubbed blood from his hands, ordered x-rays, and moved from one broken body to the next. When it was over, there were bodies to prepare for grieving families. No one wanted that job. But Nagai didn't hesitate. Quietly, respectfully, he washed and readied the dead. His staff, moved by his calm and care, joined him— one by one.

But it wasn't just the bombs.

Hunger stalked the city. Tuberculosis was spreading.
Nagai screened thousands of patients, sometimes until he could barely stand. He pushed past exhaustion. As a radiologist, he knew he was absorbing lethal levels of radiation—far beyond the safe limit of 0.2 roentgens. But when a colleague begged him to slow down, Nagai simply shook his head.

"There's too much to do," he said.
"I can't stop. I won't."

He had students to train. Lives to save. A family to protect. And through it all, he held fast to the quiet strength of his name—the deep, enduring well that kept giving, even when everything else was running dry.

But his body was beginning to fail him. His hands started shaking, and he became so tired that even climbing stairs was hard. He hardly slept at night, acting as an air-raid warden, walking around the city while everyone waited for the sirens to scream. In his journal, he wrote about sitting alone in his office, holding a rosary and staring at a small statue of the Virgin Mary, trying to find peace in the middle of his worries. His nurses noticed him falling asleep during work. But whenever he woke up, he continued working without complaining.

His co-workers finally convinced him to get an x-ray. In his book *Horobinu Mono Wo*, he wrote about how strange it felt to be the patient instead of the doctor. Holding the cold metal x-ray plate in his hands, sitting quietly in the room—it all felt unreal. He had spent years looking at other people's scans. But now, as he faced his own, he felt fear building up inside. The results were bad: there was a shadow on the right side of his stomach, his spleen was swollen, and his liver had grown so big it pushed his heart out of place. The radiologist just stared at the images in silence.

Trying to ease the tension, Nagai joked, "Shall we call in a student to take a look?" Just then, the door opened.

A young nurse stepped in with a cheerful voice. "Professor Nagai, the fourth-year students are ready for class!" she said. She didn't see the sadness in the room. Nagai smiled calmly and said, "Thank you, Nurse Oyanagi. I'll be right there."

After the class, more tests were done. The news was heartbreaking. His white blood cells were ten times higher than normal. His red blood cells had dropped to half of what they should be. He looked at the paper and read the words softly, without fear: **advanced leukemia**. He had only two to three years left to live. The illness would get worse slowly—and painfully. His friends sat in silence. Nagai gave a small smile and said quietly, "This is our profession. Every doctor becomes a patient someday. And in the end, we all face death." Then he kindly told them to leave the room.

Alone, Nagai let his calm mask fall. His hands shook as emotions poured over him. In a soft whisper, he began to pray: "God, You know I am weak. I don't know if I can do this. Why now? Why so soon? What will happen to Midori and our children? There's still so much left for me to do." He thought of the Garden of Gethsemane, where Jesus prayed in sorrow before His suffering. Nagai felt close to that moment—alone and crushed by a heavy burden. "You said we each have a cross to carry... but this one feels too heavy, Lord. I'm so tired."

His eyes wandered and rested on the x-ray machine. For years, it had been like a part of his own body, helping him in his work. Now, it stood like a silent messenger, bringing him bad news. But instead of anger, he felt something like love. That machine had helped him heal people, discover sicknesses, and give hope. If it had a heart, would it feel sorry for him now? It had grown old with him—its shiny parts now scratched and faded. He saw himself in that machine. This is what it means to serve others, he thought. To give everything, even your strength, until there's nothing left but quiet dignity. A gentle peace settled in his heart—not giving up, but accepting. He had lived fully, even if his time was almost gone.

A soft knock came at the door. The university president stepped in, his face kind and full of care. Nagai bowed slightly and said sorry for letting his feelings show. But the president shook his head and said, "No need for that, Nagai-kun. You've done more than anyone could. You cared for so many without rest, without help. No one else could have done what you did."

And in that quiet room, with the soft hum of machines around him and the weight of truth in the air, Nagai realized—he was not alone.

Chapter 17

Midori-A Woman who never faltered

The hardest moment in Nagai's life had arrived—telling Midori the truth.

As he walked home, his steps were slow, almost dragging. His heart felt heavier with each block. The summer sun poured its golden light across Nagasaki, painting the city in warm, living color—but Nagai didn't notice any of it. Everything around him seemed distant and blurred, like a world he was slowly drifting away from.

Marrying him had never promised Midori a comfortable life. While other professors opened private clinics to earn extra money, Nagai had spent all his time buried in research. He stayed late at the university, night after night, while Midori waited quietly at home. She never complained—not once. She had a gentle way about her. Just a few days ago, she'd smiled and said, almost teasing, *"When things get better, we'll finally go to those restaurants and theaters we keep dreaming about."*

But now... because of his illness—because of his choices—there might be no "better." Only pain. Only goodbye.

The sliding door creaked as he stepped inside, and the sound brought him back to the present. He heard her light footsteps padding across the tatami mat. She appeared around the corner, beaming. "You're home early! What a nice surprise!" Her smile was warm, her joy real—or was it her way of keeping fear at bay?

She helped him out of his coat and into his kimono, humming softly, chatting about the dinner she was planning—raw tuna and clams. Her hands moved gracefully, doing what they'd done a thousand times before. Did she already know something was wrong? Was her cheerfulness her way of holding back the worry that was quietly building in her chest?

Nagai sat down and watched her for a moment, guilt pressing against his ribs.

Why had he buried himself so completely in work? Why had he let life pass by unnoticed?

He remembered the countless nights he had disappeared into books and papers, shutting out the world—shutting her out. There was that one day he'd walked right past her on the street and hadn't even seen her. She'd laughed about it later, brushing it off like it was nothing. But he had never forgotten. It haunted him.

He looked at her now—really looked. The lines near her eyes, the gentle wear of years on her hands. Signs of quiet strength. Signs of love. She had carried so much, so silently.

Then her eyes met his—calm, deep, and full of tenderness. She knew something was coming.

And so, he told her. Everything.

She didn't say a word. She just listened. Her face was still, not out of shock, but out of deep strength. Behind her silence was love. Behind her stillness, heartbreak she was trying to hold in.

And in that moment, surrounded by soft evening light and quiet domestic sounds, Nagai realized something: this woman—his Midori—had always been stronger than he ever gave her credit for.

Without a word, Midori stood and quietly walked to the family altar. Her movements were calm and familiar, like a ritual repeated countless times before. She lit the candles one by one, her hands steady, her face still. Then she knelt, her head bowed low beneath the crucifix that had watched over her family for generations—a silent witness to both joy and suffering.

Nagai followed her, his heart heavy. He knelt behind her, not daring to speak, his eyes fixed on her small, trembling shoulders. She didn't move. She just knelt there, silently weathering the storm of emotion that passed through her like a wave. And all he could do was watch.

Guilt rose in his chest like a tide.

He had chased his work with such blind devotion, never stopping to think about what it had cost her. Midori had never asked for anything. She had stayed quietly by his side, holding everything together, asking nothing in return. He had seen her love, but only now did he understand the depth of it.

Then she turned to him, slowly. Her voice, when she spoke, was steady and clear. "We made a promise before we married," she said softly. "And again before you went to China the second time. If our lives are lived for God's glory, then both life—and death—have meaning. You gave your whole self to your work, and that work was for Him."

Her words cut through him—not like a knife, but like light breaking into darkness. He couldn't speak. His throat tightened, and tears welled up, not from pain, but from the deep, aching gratitude swelling inside him.

She had stood by him through everything. And now, as he faced his most painful truth, she was still there—unshaken, full of grace.

In that quiet moment, surrounded by flickering candlelight and the scent of burning wax, Nagai felt he was in the presence of something sacred. Midori wasn't just his wife—she was a living reflection of the deep, unbreakable faith of the Urakami Christians, whose ancestors had suffered centuries of persecution and yet never gave up their hope.

That night, he returned home with despair sitting heavily on his shoulders. But the next morning, something was different.

When he stepped into the x-ray department, it was as if something inside him had shifted. He no longer felt crushed by exhaustion. Midori's acceptance—her quiet refusal to blame or despair—had lifted a burden from his heart. For the first time in months, he felt light. The fatigue that had haunted him was gone, replaced by a strange calm, a peace that made him want to cry.

Even the hardships of the past—long nights in the lab, years of war, the toll of his illness—now felt like they had meaning. They had been part of something bigger, something beautiful.

He remembered how Midori had said, almost casually, "Maybe one of our children will continue your research someday." That simple hope, so full of love, had planted something new in his heart.

There was no bitterness in her. Only faith.

And that gave him strength.

He looked at the x-ray machine and felt an unexpected wave of affection. He could have hugged it. It wasn't just a tool anymore—it was part of his offering to God. Maybe this was what Pascal had meant—the joy that comes when you surrender everything to the will of God.

But the outside world wasn't so calm.

The war continued to close in. Okinawa had fallen. Everyone feared that Kyushu—home to Nagasaki—would be next. The city's port had made it a target, and the military presence grew by the day. The kenpeitai—the military police—tightened their grip.

One day, the parish priest of Urakami was summoned to the police station. They questioned him about the church's "prayers for peace."

"Are you praying for Japan's defeat?" the chief demanded.

The priest stayed calm. "No," he said. "Christians everywhere pray for peace. Everyone knows war destroys everything. I'm sure you understand that."

The officer's face hardened. "The war will end when Japan wins. You may continue your prayers—but only if you include *Tenno Heika*—the Emperor—in place of Almighty God."

The priest didn't flinch. "Sir," he replied carefully, "even our Emperor Meiji said he was not the Creator of the universe. In his own rescript, he wrote, 'I, in obedience to the grace of heaven.' That Heaven—the one the Emperor himself acknowledges—is what we call Almighty God."

There was a tense silence.

Then, the officer nodded, and the priest was allowed to leave.

But outside that small room, chaos loomed. The invasion seemed inevitable. Japan could not be surrounded like an island—it was a fortress of mountains, and its people would fight to the end.

The Americans believed it might take years to break the spirit of Japan. But in that moment, Nagai knew that the true strength of his people—of people like Midori—could not be broken by war.

By the middle of July 1945, a group of Catholic laypeople in Nagasaki, including Dr. Nagai, were called to army headquarters. The atmosphere was tense. They were threatened and labeled as possible traitors. They were told that if the Americans landed, they must report immediately to the police. Fear began to spread through the Christian community. Families quietly began to prepare themselves for the worst.

As Nagai walked home, he passed by the spot where twenty-six Christians had been killed for their faith in 1597. He paused, his heart heavy, and silently prayed to Saint Paul Miki—the saint whose name he had taken at baptism. He asked for strength to stay faithful if death ever came for him too.

The next day, while working at the hospital, he took a moment to write about the pain he saw daily, especially in his cancer patients. Yet even in that sadness, he added with deep love, "At least Midori will be there. She'll pray with me, hold the crucifix to my forehead, and I'll die in her arms. She'll close my eyes and take me to the grave. My selfless Midori, thank you."

Japanese authorities had been dropping warning leaflets from the sky for months. At first, they were clumsy and easy to ignore. But now they were more serious. One recent leaflet in Nagasaki carried a chilling poem:

**"In April Nagasaki was all flowers.
In August it will be flame showers."**

Now it *was* August—and the weight of those words hung in the air like a storm cloud.

On the night of August 6, word spread about a terrible new bomb that had destroyed Hiroshima. Nagai and Midori immediately thought about their children, Kayano and Makoto. They had earlier tried to send them to their grandmother in the countryside, but the kids didn't want to go. After hearing the news about Hiroshima, they knew they had to insist.

The next morning, Midori and Grandma packed small bags and started walking with the children toward a safe home in Koba, a quiet valley surrounded by mountains and filled with the sound of cicadas and rushing water. It gave a small sense of peace. Midori returned to the city early the next morning.

Soon after, the air-raid alarm rang again. Nagai, weak and struggling because of his swollen spleen, needed help to walk. Midori, always by his side, gently placed his arm over her shoulder and wrapped her arm around his waist. They made their way slowly to the shelter. As they walked, Nagai began to laugh—and Midori laughed too.

Inside the shelter, it was like time paused. They spoke about the upcoming Feast of the Assumption on August 15, which was a special day for Christians in Nagasaki. It also marked the anniversary of Saint Francis Xavier's arrival in Japan. Midori smiled and said she might make sweet bean-jam cakes for the feast. Nagai laughed, remembering how many their son Makoto had eaten the year before.

As they sat close, Nagai asked, "When is confession this week?"
Midori replied gently, "I'll go tomorrow morning."
"Afternoon would be better for me," he said, smiling.

The siren sounded again, this time signaling the danger had passed. They walked home slowly. Nagai noticed something unusual—Midori's mood. She seemed filled with joy. Her laughter rang in the house as she told stories about the children and Grandma's struggles keeping up with them in the mountains.

She sat with him during breakfast, her eyes bright, her smile warm. As he got ready to leave for work, she knelt on the soft tatami mat and helped him slip into his white shoes. With a loving voice, she said, "Itte irasshai mase," the traditional goodbye.
He bowed slightly and replied, "Itte mairimasu," and stepped out the door.

His heart was full. *This is truly beautiful,* he thought. *She's so cheerful, even now.*

But just a few steps away, he suddenly remembered—he had forgotten his lunch. He turned back toward the house. And what he saw froze him in place.

There, in the entranceway, Midori was on the floor, crying like a child. Her body shook as she sobbed, her quiet strength now broken by emotion she had held in for so long.

Later that evening, Nagai was assigned to air-raid duty for August 8. Though he was offered a chance to rest because of his health, he refused. "Look at those young student wardens," he said firmly. "Some have given their lives. If they can do it without asking for anything special, so can I." His heart ached for the students who had died, but he was determined to lead by example.

August 9 began with another air-raid alarm. It seemed routine—just a single plane in the sky—and the all-clear siren came by 10 a.m. "What a waste of time," someone joked. "That plane wasn't even interested in Nagasaki."

But they were wrong. That lone plane was no random flyer. It had come to gather precise data.

The B-29 bomber named *Bock's Car* was already in the sky, heading toward Nagasaki, carrying a weapon that would change history forever.

After the air-raid sirens stopped and the all-clear was given, **Midori** stepped out of the shelter with her two relatives, **Tatsue** and **Grandma Urata**. The warm summer air surrounded them as they sat on the **veranda**, talking softly.

"Your children must be missing you," Grandma said gently.

With a smile, Midori replied, "**Kayano** probably is, but **Makoto** is happy like a fish in the river. I wouldn't be surprised if he starts growing webbed fingers!"

They laughed, but then Grandma's face turned serious. "And your husband—how is he doing, Midori?"

Midori's smile slowly disappeared. "He's not well. Someone as sick as he is, working so hard… it's really wearing him down. He was on air-raid duty last night. I haven't seen him since breakfast yesterday, and I'm very worried. Please pray for him."

Grandma nodded deeply. She silently wished she were younger. If she had more strength, she would walk with Midori to the **Lourdes Grotto**, behind the monastery on the edge of the city. That grotto had been built by **Father Maximilian Kolbe** when he visited in **1931**.

Just then, another young cousin came into the yard, full of life and joy. "Good morning!" she said cheerfully. "Who wants to go for a walk to **Topposui Mill**? It's the perfect weather for a walk down a beautiful country road."

Tatsue smiled, happy for a break. "I'll go," she said.

Then the young cousin, **Kikue**, turned to Midori with a teasing smile. "Well, our great leader of all the Women's Associations of **Urakami**, do you remember what you once said? 'Children should learn to move freely and gracefully, and grow a sense of beauty.' So of course, you must join us! Let's swing our arms and legs and enjoy the breeze as we walk to the mill."

Midori laughed at the joke. "I'd love to, but I have to grind some wheat and take lunch to my husband at the hospital. I'll visit the mill later."

The moment of parting came too soon. **Tatsue Urata**, in her book *We of Nagasaki*, later wrote with deep feeling:

"And so we split into two groups, one that would walk away safely, and one that would never return."

Chapter 18

Fat Man, the 4.5-ton atomic bomb

Major "Chuck" Sweeney sat in the cockpit of *Bockscar* long before the sun rose, the weight of the mission pressing heavily on his shoulders. Outside, the world was still dark, but inside the massive **B-29 bomber**, every man aboard knew that today, they weren't just flying another mission—they were carrying history in their hands. And that history weighed over four tons: the atomic bomb named **Fat Man**.

Their primary target was **Kokura**, but as they neared the city, they were met with a wall of thick smoke and cloud—likely from fires burning in nearby factories. Three times, Sweeney circled above, searching for a clear view. Three times, the smoke refused to part. Without visual confirmation, the bomb couldn't be dropped. Time was slipping through their fingers. Fuel was burning fast.

Then came another blow—**the backup fuel pump failed**. The reserve fuel they were depending on for their return was now trapped, unreachable. Every second they stayed in the air made getting home alive less likely. And yet, turning back meant carrying a live atomic bomb across the Pacific, back to their base.

Sweeney was trapped between two terrible choices. He chose to go forward.

With hope thinning and fuel almost gone, *Bockscar* turned toward the secondary target: **Nagasaki**. The minutes crawled. The silence inside the bomber was thick—no one spoke. Every man was thinking the same thing: *Will we make it back? And what are we about to do?*

By 11 a.m., they reached **Shimabara**, near Nagasaki. On the ground, a local radio announcer saw the bomber slicing through the sky and quickly warned the city. **People ran for their lives**, diving into shelters, praying, crying, clutching loved ones. But for many, it was already too late.

Just as *Bockscar* approached, a break in the clouds revealed the landscape below. The crew spotted the **Urakami River**, the **Matsuyama Sports Ground**—familiar landmarks, but they were nearly **two miles off target**. Time was up. There was no chance to correct course.

With a breath and a nod, Bombardier **Kermit Beahan** opened the bomb bay. At **11:02 a.m.**, the second atomic bomb ever used in war dropped from the sky, falling toward a city of nearly **200,000 souls**.

In the heart of Nagasaki, **Urakami Cathedral** stood like a symbol of hope. Inside, **Fathers Nishida and Tamaya** were hearing confessions. The all-clear siren had sounded minutes before, and the faithful had returned to pray. The cathedral, just **a third of a mile** from ground zero, vanished in a single, blinding flash. No one would ever know how many were inside.

A few miles away, **Chimoto-san** worked quietly in his **rice field on Mount Kawabira**. He looked up, saw a silver plane cutting through the sky—and then, a dark shape dropped. Something in him knew. Without thinking, he threw himself to the ground.

A second later, the world exploded.

There was a flash of light, so bright it seemed to tear through the sky, and then an eerie, **suffocating silence**. Chimoto lifted his head just as a **giant mushroom cloud** rose before him, thick and terrible, filling the heavens.

Then it came—the **blast wave**. The air shifted violently. Trees, buildings, the very earth seemed to heave. Chimoto was flung like a ragdoll, slammed into a stone wall over **sixteen feet away**. Dazed, aching, and stunned, he opened his eyes.

Everything around him was gone.

The towering **pines**, the blooming **chestnuts**, even the thick **camphor laurels**—all had been torn apart, ripped from the ground as if by an angry hand. The grass had vanished. The silence that followed was haunting. A silence filled not with peace, but with **loss**.

Elsewhere in the city, nineteen-year-old Sadako Moriyama had just found her younger brothers chasing dragonflies in the schoolyard—a rare moment of innocence in a world clouded by war. She gently called them over, saying their mother needed them. They turned to follow, but before they could take more than a few steps, the sound of a plane tore through the air. They ran for the school's air-raid shelter, but they didn't make it. A blinding flash, a roar like the sky itself was splitting apart—and then darkness.

Sadako was thrown hard against the wall, and everything went black.

When she came to, her head throbbing, she found the two boys crumpled at her feet, their whimpers the only sound in the suffocating silence. Dust hung thick in the air. The shelter was pitch dark. But then, slowly, light began to filter in—and with it came the horror.

At the entrance, two shapes were crawling in. They didn't look human. They made strange croaking noises, dragging their ruined bodies forward. Sadako froze, her heart pounding. As the dim light fell on their faces, she saw the truth: they *were* human—what was left of them. Their flesh was shredded, their skin hanging off in black, charred ribbons. They had been outside when the bomb exploded.

Sadako stumbled out into the early morning light, but the world no longer felt real. It was quiet, eerie, as if sound itself had been burned away. Near the sandbox, she saw them— four children. Or what remained. Their skin was gone, their bodies raw and red. Their small hands had been torn apart, the flesh hanging like empty gloves. She couldn't look away. The images burned into her memory.

Trembling, she turned back toward the shelter, her hands brushing against one of the burned bodies still crawling at the entrance. Its skin was soft and spongy, like rotting fruit. The strange, hoarse noises started again, then became words. A whisper, then a plea:

"Mizu… mizu…"
Water… water…

That broken voice, so full of pain, would echo in her mind forever.

Ten-year-old Michiko Ogino had been enjoying the last days of summer, her world still small and full of warmth. But at 11 a.m., a blinding flash split the sky—and in a heartbeat, everything changed. The blast hurled her beneath the wreckage of her home. Pinned, terrified, she screamed for help. A stranger—his face smeared with ash—found her, pulled her free.

Outside, the world was unrecognizable. The sky was blackened by a monstrous, twisting cloud, writhing like a living thing. The ground was littered with debris, bodies, and screams. She stood there, paralyzed, when a tiny voice pulled her back: her baby sister was trapped under a heavy beam.

She turned for help—and saw her mother stumbling toward them.

But something was wrong.

Her mother's skin was a deep purple, her hair singed and disheveled. She looked like someone who had walked through fire and somehow kept going. Without a word, Michiko pointed to her sister. Her mother, frantic, didn't hesitate. With a scream, she lifted the beam off her child. Michiko saw her shoulder, where the wood had pressed—it was stripped to muscle and bone. But she didn't stop. She scooped up her baby and held her close.

Then, quietly, she collapsed.

Right there, in front of her daughters, on scorched and broken ground, Michiko's mother took her last breath.

In the Aburagi air-raid shelter, a boy named Sakue Kawasaki sat numb with disbelief. Outside, it was hell. People wandered past in silence, their bodies bloated, their faces unrecognizable. They looked like shadows, or ghosts—lurching, groaning, dying.

One by one, they crawled toward a filthy puddle near the shelter. **"Mizu… mizu…"** came the cries. Water.

A man dipped his face into the murky pool, gulping it down with desperate speed. And then he collapsed, never moving again. Another followed. Then another. The act of drinking—so simple, so human—was now the final thing they would do before death.

Sakue watched, his young mind struggling to grasp the nightmare playing out before him. What kind of thirst could make people crawl like this? What kind of fire could turn people into husks with voices like animals?

He would never forget it. None of them would.

Not those who lived.
Not those who died.
Not those who carried their memories into the silence that followed.

The bomb that fell over Nagasaki on August 9, 1945, wasn't just an instrument of war—it was a force that forever changed the very meaning of devastation. Powered by plutonium-239, Fat Man unleashed an explosion the size of 22,000 tons of TNT. But its true horror wasn't in the sheer power it unleashed—it was in how it reshaped the world in the span of seconds.

At ground zero, the heat became unimaginable—millions of degrees Celsius, hot enough to turn flesh to vapor and melt steel. In an instant, buildings that had stood for generations crumbled to nothingness. The first flash of light was so bright, it seemed to burn away the very concept of day, turning morning into an otherworldly hell. The brightness was so intense, it seared the eyes of those miles away, and skin began to blister in an instant. The shockwave that followed shattered rooftops half a mile away. Winds, faster than the fiercest storms, tore through the air at more than a mile per second, pushing everything in their path before pulling back with a violent vacuum that sucked the very breath from the land.

Within two miles, whole neighborhoods were reduced to smoldering ruins. The trees, utility poles, and even the people stood frozen in place, their bodies burnt black and deformed, as if caught in the final moments of an eternal stare into the abyss. Fires erupted instantly, spiraling debris high into the air, feeding a monstrous column of smoke and ash that reached toward the heavens.

Five miles away, in the hills near Oyama, young Kato-san was with his cow when he saw the impossible. A flash—so white and so fierce that it burned itself into his vision—split the sky. Moments later, a towering column of fire and cloud rose into the heavens. It seemed alive, writhing and twisting, each pulse pushing it higher and higher, flashing red, yellow, and violet deep within, while its base churned black with soot and a deep, sorrowful darkness. It grew, taking the shape of the infamous mushroom cloud, but to Kato, it looked more like a beast rising from the earth, full of fury and hunger.

Then came the shockwave. Not the first—no, this was another. A thunderous, invisible fist that slammed into the land, knocking Kato backward, his body tossed like a ragdoll. The earth beneath him trembled as though the very mountain was groaning in agony. The sky above had changed. The light was gone. The sun had not set, yet under the weight of that monstrous cloud, the world had become darkness.

Chapter 19

I'm seeing hell! Hell!

At 10 a.m. on August 9, when the all-clear signal echoed across the air, Dr. Nagai stepped cautiously out of the hospital's air-raid shelter. For the first time that day, the heavy weight of his helmet and the suffocating pressure of the warden's gear were lifted. A rush of relief washed over him as he breathed in the cool, crisp air. The outside world, untouched by the horrors of war for a fleeting moment, seemed to pause with him. He stood still, absorbing the beauty around him—vibrant red oleanders and canna flowers swayed gently in the breeze, their petals like delicate brushstrokes on a canvas. Below, the rooftops of Nagasaki stretched across the landscape in a patchwork of dark purple tiles. Beyond that, Nagasaki Bay glimmered serenely between the rolling green hills of Mount Inasa, while soft white clouds drifted lazily across the clear blue sky. It was a rare moment of peace, so sharply at odds with the tension of war that seemed to hang in the air like an invisible weight.

A line from an ancient Chinese poet, Toho, flashed through his mind: "Kuni yaburete sanga ari."—"Though the nation be destroyed, the mountains and rivers remain." For a heartbeat, Dr. Nagai clung to the thought, finding solace in the idea that nature, unchanging and eternal, would endure long after the bloodshed of war had passed. But duty soon called him back. The weight of responsibility pressed against him, and with a sigh, he turned away from the beauty that surrounded him. Lives depended on him. He couldn't afford to linger in the calm; there was work to be done. The moment of peace, though fleeting, stayed with him as he returned to the hospital to face the next challenge.

Just an hour later, seated at his desk and preparing for a lecture, the stillness was shattered. At 11:02 a.m., a blinding flash split the sky, and before he could react, the window exploded inward with a deafening crack. It felt like the very earth had been ripped from beneath him, lifting him off his feet and throwing him across the room. Glass shards flew through the air, swirling around him like leaves caught in a violent storm. For a brief, surreal moment, he saw the outside world—wood, beams, and scraps of clothing suspended in mid-air as if defying gravity. Everything in the room was caught in the same chaotic whirlpool, and for an instant, Dr. Nagai thought it was the end. Blood from a deep gash on his temple poured into his eyes, blurring his vision. The world around him spun into oblivion. Low, rumbling sounds echoed through the building, as if the mountains themselves were shifting beneath his feet. And then, all was darkness.

Though his body felt strangely numb, fear gripped his heart as he heard the crackling of flames and smelled the sharp, acrid scent of smoke filling the air. In his panic, his thoughts turned inward, his guilt overwhelming him—three sins he had planned to confess that afternoon. He prayed silently, seeking forgiveness. "Midori," he whispered hoarsely, his voice trembling. "It's the end. I'm dying." But even as the darkness closed in, the hospital, as if awakening from a nightmare, groaned and shuddered. Through the haze of blood and confusion, Dr. Nagai could barely make out the world through his left eye. His right eye was completely obscured by the blood pouring from his temple. Trapped beneath the rubble, unable to move, he felt the cold sting of panic. Was he buried alive? The thought made his skin crawl, but he refused to give in. Fighting against the weight of debris, he called weakly, "Help, help!"

In the next room, Nurse Hashimoto, having been thrown against the wall by the blast, staggered to a window, her body shielded only by an anchored bookcase. As the chaos subsided, she looked out to see a scene beyond belief. The sea of houses that once filled her view had vanished, replaced by a barren, red wasteland. Mount Inasa, once lush with greenery, now lay dull and lifeless, its surface scorched and scarred. The world, once vibrant and full of life, had been stripped bare, as if the earth itself had been erased. Her gaze fell to the ground below, and her breath caught in her throat as she saw the mangled bodies of the dead, tangled in debris, scattered across the wreckage. The silence that followed was deafening. Was this the end? Was the world silent because it had already been destroyed?

Desperation clawed at her. "I'm seeing hell! Hell!" she cried out, unable to comprehend the horrors around her. When she opened her eyes again, the nightmare had not gone away. A sea of fire and destruction stretched before her, the air thick with smoke and death. Darkness descended, smothering what little hope remained. Trembling, the 17-year-old nurse couldn't shake the feeling that her life, too, was coming to an end. Her sobs, raw and uncontrollable, echoed in the empty space, a helpless child's cry in the face of overwhelming chaos.

Then, through the suffocating darkness, she heard it—a voice, sharp and desperate, cutting through the horror. "Help, help!" It was Dr. Nagai's voice, unmistakable. Her heart skipped a beat, and panic surged within her as she tried to reach his room. But the path was blocked—rubble, broken furniture, and shattered glass lay in her way. She couldn't do this alone. With no time to lose, she moved cautiously down the dark corridor, her hands brushing against something soft. She knelt down, fingers trembling as they touched something wet. A lifeless arm. Her heart sank. She felt for a pulse, but there was nothing. A quick prayer escaped her lips, and she moved on, the weight of sorrow heavy in her chest.

The darkness that surrounded her was suddenly pierced by the eerie red glow of flames. The crackling sound of fire filled the air, urging her to move faster. The hospital, though only half a mile from the bomb's epicenter, had somehow withstood the blast. The reinforced concrete walls held strong. But the cost was unimaginable—80 percent of the patients and staff had not survived. The x-ray department, at the far end of the building, had fared better, and it was here that Nurse Hashimoto found five of her colleagues, bloodied and broken, yet still alive. Determined, she rallied them together, forming a human chain, and together, they made their way through a broken window to reach Dr. Nagai. His calm, forged through years of hardship in China during the war, steadied them as they made their way toward him. But when they reached the others, the sight was more horrific than anything they could have imagined. Many were dead, their bodies grotesquely swollen, their skin peeling away like overripe fruit. Some were still alive, their screams of agony cutting through the chaos: "Mizu, mizu! I'm burning. Please, water! Mizu!"

The chaos around Nagai's students was equally devastating. The roof over the first-year students had caved in, trapping them under a crushing mountain of rubble. Fujimoto, the head student, strained with every ounce of strength to shift the heavy debris pressing down on him, but it was futile. His hands were bloodied, his breath short, and in the dim, suffocating space, desperation slowly seeped into his mind. The air was thick with a sense of helplessness as several of his classmates, too stunned to fully comprehend their fate, spoke in strange, detached voices, as if the world outside no longer made sense. The conversation faded, overshadowed by the encroaching fire. Then, one of them, resigned to their fate, screamed, "Sayonara!" before breaking into an eerie, sorrowful song:

"Whether we perish as bloated corpses in the sea,
Or fall and rot in grass on the mountainside,
If we die for you, O Emperor, we die without regret."

The haunting melody lingered, the words heavy with the tragic weight of young lives cut short. Fujimoto, shaking with terror, pushed with all his might, feeling the floorboards give slightly beneath him. Finally, with a final desperate effort, he freed himself—his body trembling, covered in dust and blood—but he was the only one to survive. His classmates were lost, swallowed by the rubble, and he was left alone in the silence that followed.

Meanwhile, within the hospital, Dr. Nagai's mind raced with a single thought: survival. He gathered his team urgently, the gravity of their situation pulling him into sharp focus. "The x-ray department has no patients. We need to check the equipment. If we can move it to safety, we should," he ordered, his voice steady despite the growing chaos. He knew time was slipping away. The war, now felt so much more real, so much closer. The Americans were expected to land within the week, and the incoming tide of casualties would be unlike anything they'd seen before. There would be no time for recovery if they didn't act swiftly.

His team scrambled to assess the damage, their faces pale as they came back with grim news. The x-ray equipment, a vital part of their work, was irreparably damaged. Valves were shattered, wires tangled and snapped, and the transformer lay buried under a mountain of debris. Nagai stood motionless for a moment, staring at the destruction. His mind, usually so sharp, felt paralyzed, overwhelmed by the sheer scope of the damage. It was a blow so brutal that for a moment, he couldn't fathom how to respond.

In that frozen moment, an odd, nervous laugh escaped from Nagai. It was an absurd sound—almost hollow—but it broke the silence in a way that was both surreal and real at the same time. His team, caught off guard by the strange sound, joined in, an awkward, uncomfortable laughter filling the room. It was a momentary escape from the crushing weight of despair. The absurdity of the situation—standing amidst ruins, laughing in the face of utter devastation—was their brief release from the helplessness that threatened to swallow them whole.

Outside, the destruction was unimaginable. The streets were littered with the broken bodies of the fallen. Some were so mangled that recognition was impossible, while others hung lifeless, caught on walls and fences like broken dolls. A mother, her face twisted in shock and grief, ran past, clutching the decapitated body of her child in her arms. Nearby, two children struggled to carry their father, their tiny hands pulling him up a hill, trying desperately to escape the hellish inferno consuming their city. On a rooftop in the distance, a man danced wildly, his voice rising in a jarring, erratic song. He had lost all touch with reality, drowning in the madness that followed the explosion, caught in the madness of a world that no longer made sense.

In the wake of such destruction, all Nagai and his team could do was move forward, the weight of their responsibility pressing down on them as they faced a reality that was beyond their worst nightmares.

Amidst the unrelenting chaos, there was an elderly couple, walking hand in hand up the hill, their faces serene and composed, untouched by the madness unfolding around them. It was as if the world had crumbled, but they remained steadfast, walking calmly toward an uncertain future.

For Nagai and his team, however, there was little to do but stand in stunned silence, their hearts heavy as the flames inched ever closer, creeping toward the hospital with terrifying speed. The firestorm was coming, and the reality of their situation was inescapable. The odds of survival seemed bleak, and yet they pressed on, knowing there was no time left to waste.

As more members of the x-ray staff gathered around, one of them posed a desperate question, "Should we try to move the equipment out?" It was a suggestion born of desperation, an attempt to salvage something in the face of impending disaster. But Nagai's response was firm, unwavering in its finality.

"No," he said, his voice slicing through the thick smoke that filled the room. "Forget it. There are patients in the wards who will burn alive if we don't get to them first. Go now!"

Without waiting for further discussion, Nagai turned and rushed toward the underground emergency theater. What he found there was even worse than he had feared. Burst pipes had flooded the area, leaving the floor covered in water that presented a deadly hazard. Medical supplies, instruments, and stretchers were scattered and broken, the space reduced to a chaotic mess. As Nagai surveyed the damage, a bitter thought crossed his mind: *I felt like a mosquito whose legs had been ripped off.* He realized, in that grim moment, that they had reached rock bottom. They had nothing left but their knowledge, their love for their patients, and their bare hands.

Returning upstairs, Nagai's eyes were immediately drawn to the mushroom cloud rising ominously over Nagasaki. The dark, towering mass was a harbinger of the destruction they had just witnessed and the devastation that still lay ahead. The fires were closing in, and his nurses had tied wet towels around their faces to shield themselves from the smoke. Yet, despite the suffocating air and the searing heat, they pressed on, diving into the smoke-filled wards, pulling patients from their beds, and doing what they could to save lives.

It was already afternoon, and the firestorms were drawing near. Dr. Okura, a young physician, hurried toward Nagai, urgency in his voice. "There's still an arthritis patient in that ward. He refuses to leave unless I get a stretcher, but there are no stretchers left."

Nagai glanced at the raging flames, now towering thirty-three feet high, their ferocity amplified by the fierce winds from the west. The hospital, situated on the east side of Mount Konpira, was dangerously close to the inferno. The decision was clear: returning to that ward would be a death sentence.

"Leave the patient," Nagai said quietly, his voice heavy with the burden of responsibility. "I take responsibility." It was the only choice that made sense in the face of imminent destruction. Yet, even as he spoke, a deep guilt began to gnaw at him. As the dust of the disaster settled, he and the other survivors would be left to question whether they could have done more, whether they could have saved more lives. The faces of those they left behind would haunt them forever.

As Nagai continued to assess the situation, the sharp sting of flying glass struck his temporal artery, and blood began to spill from the wound, spurting out in thick, steady jets, as though from a water pistol. His team rushed to stop the bleeding, quickly packing the wound and wrapping it tightly. But the blood continued to flow, and soon Nagai was walking with a red turban of blood on his head, his strength rapidly waning.

"The flames are getting closer!" Nagai shouted. "Hurry, get them further up the hill!" He carried two of the patients himself, but his strength soon faltered. Hisamatsu, the matron, caught his arm and felt his pulse, her face going pale. She gasped in shock—his blood loss, compounded by the effects of leukemia, was taking its toll. Reluctantly, his team forced him to sit down while they continued evacuating the patients.

Once he was seated, Nagai's breath slowly steadied, and as he looked around, he saw the fragile structure of their organization unraveling. More people, desperate for safety, flooded in from the city below, believing the hospital would offer refuge. But in truth, the hospital was no sanctuary. The staff was overwhelmed, unable to care for the patients they already had, and panic was beginning to spread. "It suddenly felt like everything was slipping beyond our control," said Matron Hisamatsu, who still lives in Nagasaki. "We began to lose our nerve."

In a desperate attempt to restore some order, Nagai shouted, "Quick, find a Hi no Maru!"—the Japanese flag. Dr. Okura, stunned by the absurdity of the request in such a moment, hesitated, disbelief in his eyes. He searched frantically in the few areas still not consumed by fire and soon returned, his voice flat and resigned. "It's impossible to find one."

Nagai scanned the scene, his eyes searching for something—anything—that could bring a sense of structure. Then, something caught his eye. A piece of white sheet was blowing toward him in the wind. Without hesitation, he rushed over, grabbed it, and tore it into a square. He then pulled the blood-soaked bandage from his head and pressed it into the center of the fabric, smearing the red blood into a rough circle. Others, including Matron Hisamatsu, followed suit, adding their own blood to the makeshift flag. Amid the horror and chaos, they had created a symbol of resilience—a symbol of survival in the face of overwhelming odds—the Japanese flag.

During his time in China, Nagai had learned that in moments of shock and chaos, sometimes a single bold action or a powerful symbol could bring order. For the Japanese people in 1945, no symbol was more powerful than the Hi no Maru, the national flag. For the past fifteen years, it had been proudly displayed at military bases, public buildings, and national events. After the bombing, Nagai decided to use this symbol to bring some structure to the chaos. He asked Dr. Okura to tie the makeshift flag to a bamboo pole and plant it into the ground a little uphill.

Matron Hisamatsu, remembering this moment 42 years later, described it clearly: "In that moment, we had a 'headquarters,' a place to focus that helped bring some order to the madness." Dr. Okura, who later became a priest and expert on Saint John of the Cross, agreed: "It was a simple act, yet the psychological impact was huge."

In the past, Nagai had always found peace in nature, but now he was struck by the devastation the bomb had caused—nature itself seemed broken. Black rain began to fall, its drops heavy and dark, leaving stains wherever they landed. The air was thick with smoke and the smell of burning materials. The fires, desperate for oxygen, were raging through the city, so much so that Nagai and his team struggled to breathe. It was 4 P.M., five hours after the explosion, and the fires were still raging. The hospital was overwhelmed. All they could do for the patients was remove shards of glass and debris, apply iodine to wounds, and bandage what they could. Water was in short supply, and the desperate cries for "Mizu, mizu!" (water) echoed through the chaos.

Nagai's heart sank when he found the university president lying in a field, his white coat soaked with black rain. After giving the president a quick report, Nagai moved on to tend to other patients. He saw X-ray technician Umezusan collapsed on the ground, exhausted and soaked. Without hesitation, Nagai took off his own coat and placed it over him. Since noon, when Nagai had realized that the entire suburb of Urakami was on fire, he had been overwhelmed with the need to find Midori. But he knew he couldn't abandon his responsibilities. He couldn't stop glancing at the refugees, hoping to spot her among them.

As the clock struck 4 P.M., he had to face the painful truth: Midori was not there. His mind and body, already at their breaking point, gave way. The certainty of her death hit him hard, and he collapsed to the ground. As he fell, a colleague heard him whispering, "She would have come by now. She's dead... she's dead. Midori!" He grabbed a handful of dirt, as if trying to hold on to something, but then lost consciousness.

When he came to, he heard Professor Fuse's anxious voice: "Thread. Forceps. Gauze, gauze. Press down... the end of the artery has slipped behind the bone!" Nagai passed out again, but when he woke, the bleeding had stopped. As his eyes opened, he saw the faint light of the moon above the destroyed landscape of Mount Inasa. The nurses had been resourceful, collecting pumpkins from nearby fields and cooking them in air-raid helmets, while the men worked on makeshift shelters for the patients.

Nagai watched the two nurses, "Little Bean" and "Little Barrel," as they moved steadily through the chaos, their faces covered in dust and sweat, but determined to keep working. Even though everything around them was falling apart, they stayed focused, driven by their strong commitment to their patients. But as Nagai watched, he couldn't help but feel sadness. Their trio had once been complete—"Little Octopus," the third nurse in their close team, had been lost in the explosion. The memory of her cheerful personality, her quick humor, and her ability to make even the darkest moments brighter now reminded him of the empty space her absence left behind.

Another memory that weighed on Nagai was Nurse Hamazaki, one of his best and most capable nurses. She had been with him at the hospital during the explosion, offering comfort even as the ground shook. But she, too, was lost. Her last moments were spent beside him, her voice urging him to keep going, to do whatever he could to save others.

Nagai's hand moved without thinking into his pocket, where he kept a lock of Hamazaki's hair. It was a small, fragile piece of her—something he could give to her family one day, a token of her love and service that they could place on their family altar in memory of her.

But as he thought of the families of those who had died, his sorrow grew. He imagined the many families who would never have a piece of their loved ones to hold onto, who would never have ashes to carry or a place to visit in remembrance. The devastation had left behind a silence that felt unbearable—a silence that would last for generations. There would be no final goodbyes, no ceremonies to bring closure, only the painful reality of lives taken without warning.

In that moment, Nagai understood the depth of the loss—not just for the individuals who had died, but for the entire city, mourning together. For the families who lost everything, their loved ones would simply be gone, their memories scattered like ashes. In the silence that followed, there would be no comfort, no way to fill the emptiness left behind. Only the constant, painful knowledge that they were lost to history.

Nagai's heart grew heavy with this realization, and for a moment, everything else—the noise of the hospital and the chaos outside—faded away. All that remained was the unbearable silence that came with such loss, a silence that seemed to echo deep inside his soul.

Chapter 20

When night fell on August 10

As night's darkness clung to the scorched earth, the fires below continued to burn fiercely, their red glow lighting up the sky like a nightmare. The destruction stretched endlessly, a cruel reminder of the devastation unleashed by the bomb. Despite their exhaustion, the medical team pressed on, moving through the smoke and chaos with a quiet determination. They searched the fields, every step an act of courage, hoping to find anyone who might have managed to crawl their way toward safety. But many had fallen, unable to reach the hill, their bodies scattered among the wreckage, lost to the unforgiving destruction.

The night was thick with danger. Every step was uncertain as rescuers stumbled over shards of glass or fell into hidden ditches, their feet torn and bleeding from the nails and broken debris beneath them. Yet, there was no time to stop, no time to rest. The drive to save whatever lives they could kept them going, even as the flames raged and the air grew thicker with smoke.

By midnight, the fires began to burn out, but the silence that followed only deepened the sorrow. The hospital, once a place of healing, now stood as a hollow shell, surrounded by the charred remains of the city. It was a fragile beacon of hope, fighting to stand tall amid the darkness.

Then, in the midst of it all, Matron Hisamatsu ran toward Nagai, her face pale and trembling. She held out a leaflet that had fluttered down from a U.S. plane, and with shaking hands, she handed it to him. Her voice was barely a whisper as she said, "Doctor, the cathedral is burning."

Nagai's eyes followed her gaze to the hilltop, where the cathedral had once stood—a symbol of faith and strength. Now, it was nothing but a pillar of fire, the flames licking at the wooden structure as it crumbled to the ground. He stood frozen, unable to look away as the fire twisted and curled, consuming everything in its path. The crackling sound of burning timber and collapsing stone filled the air, and in that moment, Nagai realized that the cathedral was no longer just a building. It was a symbol of everything they had lost—of faith, of hope, of a community now torn apart.

As he watched the flames dance higher, Nagai felt a chill run down his spine. It was as if the horrors from the Book of Revelation had come to life—the fire, the destruction, the endless suffering. The bomb, a creation of science and progress, had unleashed a terror unlike anything the world had ever seen. Nagai's mind, always analytical and logical, found itself struggling to grasp the unimaginable force that had been released. This wasn't just an explosion; it was something far more terrifying, something that defied understanding. What kind of power was this? What kind of darkness had turned their world upside down?

The night wore on, and as dawn's first light began to filter through the haze, a new, heartbreaking reality set in. The hospital, once a place of safety, was now a ruin. Its walls were blackened and broken, and the familiar surroundings had been replaced by a landscape that seemed completely unrecognizable. There was no life, no sound, no signs of the vibrant city that had once been. The streets of Nagasaki, once filled with life and laughter, were now silent, smothered under the weight of smoke and death. The city was gone, swallowed by the flames, and all that remained was a vast, empty wasteland.

Nagai lowered his gaze, his heart heavy with sorrow, and whispered a prayer for the lives that had been lost. He knew there was no way to count the dead—too many had perished in the firestorm, too many had vanished without a trace. All that remained were the memories, fading like the smoke in the air, of lives once filled with love and hope, now reduced to ash.

As they moved through the ruins, a cold wind stirred, and Matron Hisamatsu approached once again, holding up the leaflet from the plane. Nagai took it, his hands trembling as he scanned the words. His heart sank as he read the confirmation. The destruction had not come from a conventional bomb; it had been the atomic bomb.

"It was the atom bomb," he muttered, his voice breaking the heavy silence. The devastation around him—the total annihilation of Nagasaki—matched everything he had heard about atomic fission. What had once been an idea for scientific progress had now become an instrument of unimaginable destruction. The world would never be the same.

As Nagai stood there, lost in his thoughts, his eyes fell upon a bamboo spear, lying abandoned among the wreckage. It was one of the weapons women had been trained to use, a symbol of the futile resistance that had been prepared in case of an American invasion. These women, armed with bamboo spears, had been ready to defend their homes. But what good was a spear against the power of an atom bomb? The sight of the weapon filled Nagai with a bitter rage and helplessness.

The Japanese people, he thought, had been driven to this point—forced to witness their own destruction, with no chance of fighting back. What could they do now? What could anyone do against such overwhelming power?

Nagai made his way down to the makeshift air-raid shelter, where Professor Seiki lay stretched out on the cold, bare earth. The shelter was little more than a fleeting refuge, yet in the chaos of the aftermath, it was the only sanctuary they had. As Nagai handed Seiki the leaflet, the professor scanned it with weary eyes, and then, with a deep, guttural groan, he stared blankly at the sky above—his gaze lost in the devastation surrounding them. He remained motionless for what felt like an eternity, before finally breaking the silence, discussing the situation with the physicists around him. His words, though heavy with the weight of their circumstances, still carried the brilliance that had earned him the respect of his peers.

"Odd, isn't it?" Nagai later recalled. "We all became so absorbed in the conversation that nothing else seemed to matter anymore." The Japanese scientists had long been researching uranium-235, yet military officials had shut down the costly project. Now, amidst the ruin, the question lingered: who had cracked the code in the West? Their minds drifted to possible names—Einstein, Dohr, Fermi, Chadwick, the Joliot-Curies, Madame Meitner, Hahn—scientists whose work might have laid the groundwork for the bomb. But the conversation, as dark and surreal as it was, eventually shifted to the aftermath of atomic fission—the deadly radiation that followed the splitting of the atom.

Nagai, always a seeker of knowledge, had long been fascinated by the mysteries of the universe. As a child, he had felt an inexplicable bond with the stars, staring up at the Great Bear constellation or the North Star, overwhelmed by a sense of wonder. Now, sitting on the cold, hard ground beside Seiki, he found himself animatedly discussing radiation as though it were just another fascinating topic to explore, even as the world around them had crumbled. For him, this moment was not a disaster—it was an extraordinary opportunity to witness a groundbreaking scientific phenomenon. The hillside, once home to life, had become a laboratory, a place where they could study how humans, plants, and insects were affected by the destructive power of atomic fission.

But even as their minds swirled with thoughts of science and discovery, the horrors of the previous day still loomed over them, the grief they felt for their people yet to fully sink in. Still, something new had begun to stir within them—a desire to understand, to uncover the secrets buried within the chaos. They were beginning to view the wasteland as a fertile ground for new knowledge, a twisted new beginning where destruction had given birth to a different kind of energy—one that felt both terrifying and exhilarating.

Reluctantly, Nagai tore himself away from the conversation, drawn to the victims lying scattered across the earth. As daylight crept in, the full scope of the destruction became clearer. The wind from the bomb's detonation had been so violent it had decapitated some victims, their heads sliced clean off, as if by an invisible blade. The intense heat had burned others beyond recognition, leaving only charred remains. The effects of gamma radiation were becoming painfully visible—more and more people were showing signs of sickness, their bodies wracked with pain. Some described it as inhaling poisonous gas; others likened it to the feeling of a terrible hangover or seasickness. Even those who had thought themselves unscathed soon found themselves too weak to continue, collapsing in whatever shade they could find.

Nagai, too, could feel the radiation taking its toll on him. The double exposure to gamma rays was wearing him down, but it also gave him a rare and painful vantage point—he was now experiencing the full, devastating effects of the bomb firsthand. On August 10, the skies above were filled with the sound of U.S. planes, a constant reminder that more destruction could be on its way. The sight of each plane was a trigger for fear, a symbol of the anxiety that slowly took hold of them. Every plane, every sound, every vibration sent tremors through their already shattered nerves. The weight of hopelessness began to crush them, and it felt as though they were drowning in the endless waves of despair.

When night fell on August 10, the shelter provided little comfort. It felt more like a tomb than a sanctuary, its walls heavy with the groaning, restless bodies of those too weak to move. In the darkness, some of the wounded died, their bodies left where they fell. There was no energy to move them, no will to do anything but endure. And then, around midnight, a frantic figure shook Nagai from his fitful sleep. The figure gripped his shoulders tightly, their panicked voice breaking the silence, calling out the name of Oyanagi-san, a nurse who had died the previous day. The nightmare was far from over.

In that moment, the world felt as if it had collapsed entirely.

Chapter 21

But Midori—what had become of her?

The sun rose slowly on August 11, casting a harsh, unforgiving light over the devastation. The air, thick with the stench of death, seemed to weigh down on everyone. The medical team, exhausted to the bone, faced a task no one could have ever prepared for. Moving the injured, the dead, and the dying to designated areas for the military doctors and nurses was not just physically draining—it was an emotional and psychological toll that felt unbearable. The relentless summer heat clung to them, but it was the searing presence of loss that truly consumed their spirits.

The fields were scattered with broken wood and debris from destroyed buildings, remnants of a world that had been torn apart. In the midst of it all, makeshift cremation pyres were hastily constructed—makeshift because nothing felt permanent in a place that had just been reduced to rubble. For those few who could still be identified, a small wooden slat was driven into the ground, bearing their name. It was the last gesture of recognition, a final, fleeting acknowledgment of lives that had been extinguished too soon. And then, the pyres were set ablaze, their smoke rising into the sky in mournful plumes. The sight was surreal—a funeral for a lost world.

All around them, families desperately searched for their loved ones, combing through the wreckage with no regard for ceremony or proper mourning. Time had been swallowed up by chaos, and there was only one goal: to find someone—anyone—who might still be alive. In the madness, humanity seemed to blur. There was no time for compassion or care, just a hurried, frantic search. Wounded individuals were dismissed with a sharp, "No, not this one," as if the very sight of their suffering was too much to bear.

When the military doctors and nurses finally arrived, they took control of the scene. For a brief moment, Nagai felt a flicker of relief. His children and Gran were safe, hidden away in the mountains, far from the devastation. But Midori—what had become of her? The guilt surged through him like a storm, fierce and unrelenting. Why hadn't he gone to her immediately? Why had he hesitated? The area around their home was saturated with radiation, and yet he had not rushed to her side when he had the chance. Every thought felt like a jagged wound.

With a heart weighed down by guilt, Nagai made his way down the slope, his eyes scanning the barren wasteland that had once been Urakami. His heartbeat thundered in his chest as he moved through the ruins. What was once his sanctuary, the place where love and laughter had echoed through the walls, now lay in pieces—a pile of charred remains, broken tiles, and burned fragments.

Then, through the haze of ash and destruction, a shape caught his eye. It was almost too hard to believe, but there, among the ruins, lay the unrecognizable remains of Midori. The flames had taken everything from her—her beauty, her warmth, the life they had shared. What remained was just a pile of scorched bones, her skull, spine, and hips all that was left of the woman he had loved. His knees buckled beneath him as grief consumed him. His hands, shaking uncontrollably, reached out to gather the fragments of her bones, as though somehow, he could piece together the life they had lost.

As his hands sifted through the ashes, something caught his eye—a small, melted, misshapen object, deformed by the intense heat. It was unmistakable. It was the Rosary she had always held so close, its beads fused together but still bearing the cross. A wave of emotion washed over him—grief, sorrow, and an overwhelming sense of gratitude. He whispered a prayer, his voice breaking, "Dear God, thank you for letting her die with prayer on her lips. Mother of Sorrows, thank you for being with her in her final moments."

With great care, he placed her remains in the bucket, the weight of the loss too much to bear. His voice was barely a whisper as he prayed, "Jesus, our Savior, you who sweat blood and carried the Cross to your death—now, you have revealed the mysteries of suffering, of Midori's death, and my own." In that moment, Nagai understood that his grief was not just for her. It was for all those who had been stolen by this war—those whose lives had been ripped apart in an instant. The bomb, this unimaginable weapon, had obliterated so much. Lives, homes, dreams—all reduced to ash. Yet, even in the depths of despair, Nagai felt a flicker of something greater—a quiet understanding that pain, no matter how overwhelming, could one day lead to a deeper understanding of love and sacrifice.

With Midori's remains carefully gathered, he stood in the midst of the ruin, his heart breaking under the weight of sorrow but also filled with a quiet resolve. He would carry on. He would honor the memory of those lost and, in some way, seek redemption amidst this profound tragedy. The world had been shattered, but somehow, there was still a way forward.

As Nagai slowly began his walk toward Akagi Cemetery, an unexpected wave of emotion gripped him. He stopped, his feet heavy, his heart even heavier. He stared down at the bucket in his hands—the bones inside, a silent reminder of everything he had lost. "Midori," he whispered, his voice trembling, "those early morning pilgrimages you made to Hongochi Monastery, praying for me—they're over now. Thank you, for everything. For your prayers, for your kindness, for your selflessness. I'm sorry, so sorry. Forgive me for taking you for granted all those years."

The words came spilling out, raw and unfiltered, the pain and regret flooding him. He walked on, but as he did, his foot caught on some debris, and the bones rattled in the bucket. A fleeting, irrational thought crossed his mind—a momentary illusion—that the clattering sound had formed words: "No, forgive me. I am the one who should seek forgiveness." It wasn't real, of course. It was only his grief and guilt speaking. Yet, in that moment, it felt as if Midori had answered him, her voice somehow still alive in his heart.

The unfolding of the next chapter in Nagai's memoir, *Horobinu Mono Wo*, was a somber one. After he had gently laid Midori's bones to rest in their family plot at Akagi Bochi, beneath the shade of the red tree, he whispered a quiet prayer—one last act of devotion. His heart, though heavy, yearned to find some solace. But his feet, led by a mind weighed down with grief, turned back to the ruins of the home he had lost.

His hands trembled as he sifted through the charred remnants, the stick in his hand sweeping across the scorched earth. And then, through the blackened landscape, something caught his eye. A gleam—a twisted, metallic lump. It was his medals, the ones Midori had always cherished so deeply. He could almost see her now, carefully polishing them, lovingly placing them in the cedar box where she stored them with pride. The Order of the Rising Sun—her favorite—had once gleamed proudly in its delicate splendor. But now, all that remained was a shapeless, blackened mass, barely recognizable. The intricate beauty of the cloisonné had been swallowed by the fire.

A bitter thought flashed through his mind like a cold wind: *Is this the future of the Land of the Rising Sun?*

The flames, destructive and unforgiving, had consumed so much more than his medals. His scientific textbooks, the precious notes, and x-rays from his work at the hospital—all turned to ash. Even the classical literature that had brought him comfort, the books that had once filled the shelves of his home, had been swallowed by the inferno. He stared at the pile of soot-covered volumes, the sadness in his chest pressing down like an iron weight. But then, something glimmered faintly in the soot—a metallic print on a page, barely visible.

He leaned closer, his heart catching in his throat as recognition settled upon him. It was a poem by Kakinomoto, a revered poet from the seventh century—one whose words had soothed him through the years. The poem, written by a court official exiled in Shimane Prefecture, spoke of longing for his home and, above all, his wife.

"The whole hillside stirs with the rustling of bamboo grass... But my thoughts are with the one I left behind, my little sister."

The phrase *little sister*, a tender term for his wife, brought a wave of emotion that nearly knocked him to his knees. It was as if the poet's words had crossed time to speak directly to his heart.

A sudden, sharp realization struck Nagai like a blow. In this moment, he understood the depth of his loss. Everything had been taken from him—his books, his research, his cherished sanctuary, his friends, and most painfully, Midori. His dear, dependable Midori. The weight of it all pressed down on him like a mountain, and the dam he had fought so hard to keep sealed broke.

Tears, long held back, surged forward as he sobbed uncontrollably, his body fragile from leukemia, radiation, and exhaustion. The grief, all-consuming and raw, left him vulnerable. His knees gave way, and he collapsed into the ashes of his home, surrounded by the remnants of everything that had once held meaning. And there, amidst the silence of the ruin, he drifted into unconsciousness, overwhelmed by the enormity of his sorrow.

The next morning, the first rays of dawn slowly nudged him awake. The cool breeze from the bay kissed his face, stirring him from the depths of his despair. At first, disoriented, he blinked against the blinding light, unsure of what he was seeing. A streetlamp, perhaps? He squinted, and then, in the early morning glow, he realized with awe that it was Venus—the Morning Star, shining brightly above him.

"Morning Star, pray for us," he whispered instinctively, the words flowing from him as though guided by a force beyond his own. They were words from one of his favorite prayers, the Litany of Loreto, where Mary is honored as the "Morning Star."

A quiet, deep urge to pray stirred in his soul, and he rose unsteadily to his knees. The pain in his body, the ache of his spirit—he set them aside as he began the Rosary. Each bead brought a quiet sense of peace, a moment of connection to something far greater than the ashes that surrounded him. With each prayer, the weight on his heart seemed to lift, bit by bit. And when he finished, a deep sense of renewal washed over him—like a quiet, holy strength filling the spaces of his soul.

Whatever was to come, he was ready. Whatever God had in store for him, whatever path lay ahead, he would face it with faith. He would carry on, seeking redemption in the face of this profound tragedy. And one day—one day, he believed—he would be reunited with Midori. The world around him had shattered, but through the ashes, a path forward remained.

The soft light of morning spilled gently over the Urakami valley as he began his journey toward Koba, where Gran and the children waited. Behind him, the shattered city of Nagasaki receded, swallowed by distance and grief, its ruins slowly disappearing as he climbed the narrow mountain road. Beside him, a clear stream bubbled and flowed, its gentle voice the only sound in a world hushed by sorrow.

He paused by the stream, kneeling to wash his face and hands. The water was cold and pure. He cupped it in his palms and drank deeply, the chill running down his throat, clearing the heaviness from his chest—if only for a moment. As he rose to continue, his thoughts drifted to the task ahead. How could he tell his children that their world—their home, their mother—was gone?

The mountains ahead, touched by the soft gold of dawn, stood silent and strong. They looked eternal, unshaken by the fury that had consumed the valley below. A line from a Chinese poet echoed in his mind: *Though the nation may fall, the mountains and streams remain.* Yes, even if man releases the wrath of atom bombs, the sun will still rise. The world turns.

But his mind, ever rooted in science, quickly offered its correction. *The sun's energy is finite. One day it, too, will burn out. The mountains will erode and vanish. Nothing lasts—not Midori, not the medals, not the books. All turned to dust.*

Even his beloved New Testament had been reduced to ash in the flames. Yet, as his feet kept moving along the mountain path, one verse lingered in his heart—quiet, steady, unshaken by fire or logic: *Heaven and earth will pass away, but my words will never pass away.*

And there it was. Truth. Clearer than the stream, firmer than the mountain, more enduring than the sun itself. That verse—simple and eternal—cut through his sorrow like light in a dark room. He began to repeat it, silently at first, then in rhythm with his steps. The words became a steady march, just as they had when he wandered through distant fields in China, clinging to Scripture to carry him through.

Heaven and earth will pass away, but my words will never pass away. With each repetition, it filled his mind, then his heart, and finally his entire being. Peace settled over him—not the kind that erases grief, but the kind that stands in the middle of it, unmoved. Everything would be all right. Midori had simply reached the end of her journey first. She had gone to God.

As for him, the road ahead was unclear. Death might come suddenly. The war could sweep him away before the year's end. Or perhaps peace would return. If it did, there would be work to do—raising his children, caring for Gran, rebuilding the shattered university and the cathedral that once stood as a beacon of faith and hope.

He knew his time was short. Two, maybe three years—leukemia had already begun to weaken his body. But he did not fear what lay ahead. With Christ's word burning bright within him, he would continue, step by step, toward the end of his own journey. Toward God. Toward Midori. The same way this narrow mountain road led him now—toward what was left of his family.

As he walked, a quiet gratitude welled up from within. Each step became a prayer. The verse still echoed with every breath. The strength he felt wasn't loud or triumphant—it was quiet, sure, and steady. Like the road beneath his feet. Like the promise in that verse. Like hope, alive in the ruins.

Chapter 22

The Potsdam Proclamation.

The morning after the atomic bomb turned Nagasaki into ashes, Grandma Moriyama made the heartbreaking journey to what was left of Urakami. When she returned, her hands clutched a small metal container—nothing more than a tin, really—but what it held inside was sacred: the charred fragments of Midori's bones. Her eyes, swollen from endless crying, met Makoto's, and with a voice heavy with sorrow, she told him not to open it.

But he saw how she treated it. She moved with such care, almost reverence, as if every motion might disturb Midori's soul. And the way her tears silently fell whenever her hands brushed the lid... it stirred something deep inside him. Curiosity mixed with grief. When she left the room, just for a moment, he couldn't stop himself. His hands trembled as he reached for it, his heart already aching with what he knew he would find. Slowly, he opened the lid. The truth didn't surprise him—but it still shattered him. He didn't need anyone to explain. These were his mother's bones.

Days passed like dreams you can't wake from. One quiet afternoon, as they sat at the table—Makoto, Kayano, and Grandma—no one speaking, only the weight of absence sitting with them, the sliding door creaked open. A figure stood there. Thin, tattered, wrapped in blood-stained bandages. For a second, they all stared in silence, unable to place the stranger. Then he stepped forward, and when he reached for little Kayano, she screamed and ran behind her grandmother.

It was a homecoming, but not the kind you dream of. It was Nagai. Alive, but unrecognizable.

In the days that followed, Nagai began to understand what the bomb had done—not just to the city, but to the people. Survivors, burnt and broken, had wandered into the mountains, drawn to whispers of healing water from a local spring said to soothe burns. The valley had become a refuge. The farmers opened their homes. One neighbor, Takami-san, had taken in over a hundred people, turning his land into a sanctuary.

The wounded came in all forms. Some were swollen beyond recognition, barely clinging to life. Others carried splinters of glass, bits of buildings, and pieces of their homes inside their flesh. Yet they could still walk. Still hope. Still cry for help.

The few who remained from the hospital's X-ray department gathered, quiet but determined. They had little more than torn clothes and tired hands, but they formed a mobile medical team. Each morning, they set out through the valley—no proper equipment, no sterile bandages, just compassion and resolve. They dug glass from open wounds, cleaned burns with spring water, held dying hands. They came home each night covered in dirt and blood, too tired to speak, and then rose again with the sun to do it all over.

And yet, amid the pain, something unexpected bloomed.

There were moments—brief, gentle moments—that felt almost like grace. Nagai would find himself walking a mountain trail, letting the scent of summer grasses drift around him, the soft breeze brushing his face. Sometimes he'd stop by a stream to wash his hands, letting the cold water steal away the fatigue. These walks began to heal something inside him, something words couldn't touch.

He started to see meaning in what surrounded him. The mountains, solid and unmoved by wind or storm, became a symbol of God's quiet strength. On clear nights, he would look up at the stars—endless, brilliant, unwavering. They reminded him of something eternal. Of hope, maybe. Or faith. Or just the aching beauty of being alive in a world that still turned, even after so much had been lost.

And for the first time since August 9, he felt that perhaps even in ashes, life could still grow.

One quiet night, as the mountains slept and the world around him was steeped in stillness, Dr. Nagai lifted his weary eyes to the sky. There, shining gently above the wreckage of his world, was the constellation Virgo. Something about it caught his breath. He remembered the ancient Greek tale—how Virgo, the maiden of purity and justice, had once walked the earth, only to flee in sorrow when humankind lost its way. She had escaped to the heavens, heartbroken by the cruelty she witnessed.

As Nagai stood there, the story no longer felt like myth. It felt real—painfully so. In Virgo, he saw the faces of women he had known and loved—nurses like Hamazaki, bright-eyed and full of promise; young women from his hospital, whose lives had been stolen by bombs and brutality; daughters, sisters, and wives who never had the chance to laugh freely, to fall in love, or to cradle their own children. Their dreams had been cut short not by choice, but by war. Nagai's chest tightened with grief. The purity Virgo once symbolized was still here—in these women—but now it was scattered in ashes.

By August, Japan had become a shell of its former self. The mighty military that once roared across oceans was now broken. The navy was sunk. The air force crippled. Cities had turned to rubble. Fields lay empty. What remained was a wounded nation, limping through the final days of a war it could no longer win. Even those in power began to see it—this wasn't a matter of "if" they would fall, but "when."

Desperate to save what was left, Prime Minister Suzuki sent Foreign Minister Togo to Moscow, praying that the Soviets might help negotiate peace. But the Soviets, sensing an opportunity, chose silence. They were waiting for Japan to grow weaker, to crumble completely, so they could strike without resistance.

Across the ocean, a different debate raged. In Washington, some officials believed Japan would never surrender unless one thing was protected—the Emperor. To the Japanese, the Emperor wasn't just a man. He was a symbol, a living thread tying generations together. Joseph Grew, who had once served as U.S. ambassador to Japan and had come to understand its soul, pleaded with his government. He argued that Emperor Hirohito had quietly tried to stop the war, and punishing him now would only prolong the suffering. He wasn't alone—men like Dooman, Ballantine, Professor Blakeslee, and Assistant Secretary of War McCloy echoed the same. They believed that if the Emperor could be spared, peace might finally come.

But their voices were drowned out. The Allies, determined to crush all resistance, issued the Potsdam Proclamation on July 27, demanding Japan's unconditional surrender. The very next day, Suzuki responded with one word—*mokusatsu*—a term that translated, chillingly, as "to ignore" or "to treat with silent contempt." Whether he meant rejection or simply hesitation, the result was the same: the Allies took it as defiance. And Japan braced itself for what everyone now feared—the final blow.

The press said nothing of Hiroshima. The public remained in the dark. But on August 9, as Japan's leaders gathered once more to debate surrender, the news of Nagasaki's annihilation arrived like a thunderclap. In that moment, something shifted inside the Emperor.

For years, he had remained silent, a symbol above politics, untouched by decisions of war. But now, as he listened to his people cry out in agony, he began to ask himself: If I do nothing, am I not also guilty?

That night, while the world outside burned and trembled, Emperor Hirohito made his decision. He summoned the highest officials to his air raid shelter—no formal greetings, no rituals, just urgency. And there, standing in the dim light of a nation's darkest hour, he broke centuries of silence.

He told them Japan would surrender.

His voice, quiet yet unmistakable, cut through the room like a blade. It was as if history itself had stopped to listen. Grown men wept. Ministers bowed their heads. Some clutched their chests, overwhelmed by the weight of what they had just heard. For the first time, the voice of the Emperor would not be wrapped in myth or filtered through palace halls. It would speak directly to the people. And with it, the war that had shattered millions of lives began its slow, sorrowful end.

On August 15, 1945, people all across Japan sat tensely by their radios at noon. Most thought they'd hear a call to fight, a final cry to defend their land like their ancestors had done against the Mongols long ago. But instead, something entirely unexpected came: the voice of the Emperor. His message stunned the nation. He told them they "must bear the unbearable and suffer the insufferable." With those few words, he announced Japan's unconditional surrender.

The message hit like a thunderclap. People broke down in tears, some collapsing to the floor, pressing their heads low in sorrow. The pain was too much to carry. For many, it felt as if everything that gave their lives meaning had suddenly vanished.

For Nagai, the news felt like the end of Japan itself. He thought of Mount Fuji, rising proudly each morning to meet the sun—and now, even that symbol of Japan's spirit seemed silent and defeated. "Our Japan was dead! Our race was plunging into a bottomless pit!" he wrote in despair. Rumors began to swirl wildly. People said the Americans would kill all Japanese men, and use the women to create a new, mixed race. Panic grew. Nagai and his fellow doctors felt helpless. Would Japan become just a forgotten colony, stripped of its pride, its culture, its soul?

That night, their hearts were heavy. They sat still, unable to eat or speak. Even the small comforts of food and company meant nothing. The next morning brought no relief. Still numb, they faced the day like sleepwalkers—until a knock came at the door. A man stood outside. His friend was sick and needed a doctor.

Nagai snapped, "One sick person doesn't matter when a whole nation is doomed." His words were sharp and full of grief. The man turned away slowly, shoulders heavy with disappointment, walking back across the fields.

But then, something broke through the darkness in Nagai's heart. He paused, then called out to Little Bean. "Go get him. Bring him back." Nagai's voice was firm again—tired, but determined. Slowly, the team went back to work. Their bodies were weak, but their purpose began to return.

Yet the radiation was now claiming them, too. Strange fevers, bleeding gums, and hair falling out—signs of something terrible growing inside them. Then, on September 8, Nagai himself collapsed. His fever shot up to 104°F and refused to come down. His body swelled painfully, his face puffing up like a ball. The old wound on his temple reopened, bleeding and rotting. He was dying.

Dr. Tomita and Nurse Morita rushed to help him. They pressed his artery, trying to stop the bleeding. His heartbeat was faint. His pulse barely there. Someone gave him an injection—probably nikethamide. Nagai recognized the sting. In that moment, facing death, he asked for Father Tagawa. He made a final confession, and received the Eucharist. A deep peace settled over him. "I was ready to die," he later said.

Then, Nagai asked for a brush and ink. He wanted to write his *jisei no uta*—a farewell poem. Just like the samurai of old, he wanted to face death with honor and leave behind his last words. In that quiet, sacred act, he showed the soul of a warrior.

He drifted in and out of consciousness. His body was heavy. His mind clouded with fever. But still, he heard voices. One was his son—gentle, worried. Another was soft and loving. A woman's voice. It was his grandmother. "This is water from our Lady's grotto at Hongochi Monastery," she whispered. At her words, his mind lit up with memories. He saw Lourdes, the holy grotto, and in his heart, the calm, loving face of the Virgin Mary.

Then something even deeper happened. A voice—not quite his, not quite someone else's—cut through the fog. It gave him one clear message: call on Father Maximilian Kolbe. Nagai obeyed, crying out in his heart for Kolbe's prayers. And in that sacred silence, he turned fully to Christ. No fear. No resistance. Just a quiet surrender:

"Lord, I place myself in your hands."

Nurse Morita had been working without rest, trying to stop the bleeding from Nagai's wound. Then, she suddenly looked up in shock. Turning to Dr. Tomita, she said with disbelief in her voice, "The bleeding has stopped." The large, stubborn wound—one that had refused to heal for so long—was now closing by itself. No medicine had been used.

Later, Nagai would speak about the moment. He admitted that people can always doubt miracles, but he and the medical team truly believed his healing couldn't be explained by science. Still, Nagai was careful to say that a miraculous healing doesn't mean a person is holy. He pointed out that even at Lourdes, where many healings have taken place, sometimes people with little or no faith were cured. Doctors often called these healings "medically unexplainable."

For Nagai, the answer was clear. He believed it was the prayers of Father Kolbe that had saved him. Father Maximilian Kolbe was a Polish Franciscan priest who came to Japan in 1930. He started a monastery in Nagasaki and built a small shrine behind it, like the one in Lourdes. Over time, the shrine became a popular place for pilgrims, and the Catholic magazine Kolbe started became the most-read in Japan.

Nagai had known Kolbe personally. He even treated him once for tuberculosis. In 1936, Kolbe returned to Poland, where he became the head of a large monastery. He helped launch Catholic newspapers, which became very popular.

But Kolbe's work caught the attention of the Nazis. In May 1941, they arrested him and sent him to Auschwitz. There, he was given the prisoner number 16670. In July that year, a prisoner escaped. As punishment, the camp's leader chose ten men to be killed. One of them, Sergeant Francis Gajowniczek, cried for his wife and children. Kolbe stepped forward and said he would take the sergeant's place because he had no family.

Thanks to Kolbe's brave choice, Gajowniczek lived. But Kolbe and the others were locked in a dark cell with no food or water. By August 14, they had all died—except Kolbe and three others who were still alive but unconscious. The next day, a worker was sent to give them an injection of poison to finish the job.

At the time Nagai recovered, his family didn't know all these details about Kolbe. But Midori, Nagai's wife, often visited the shrine Kolbe had built and sometimes thought about him. She remembered his kindness and the peace of that place, not knowing how important it would one day become in their lives.

When Gran gave Nagai water from the shrine to soothe his lips, she never mentioned Kolbe. No one else in the room did either. But in Nagai's heart, he was sure it was Kolbe's prayers that helped him heal. Kolbe was not yet a saint, but Nagai deeply believed in his power to pray for others.

Today, people who visit Nagasaki often go to two places: Father Kolbe's shrine and Nagai's home. The two spots are different in their stories, but they shine with the same light— one that rose from the pain of Auschwitz and Nagasaki. Both were places of terrible suffering, yet they became symbols of hope, faith, and courage because of two men whose lives still inspire all who come to remember them.

Chapter 23

I see something of God's greater plan.

By October 5, something remarkable happened—Dr. Nagai began to recover. After weeks of clinging to life, his strength slowly returned. Government relief teams had started arriving in Nagasaki, finally taking over the tireless work he and his small band of companions had shouldered since the day of the blast. With help now on the ground, those who had served alongside him were able to return to whatever was left of their homes—if they had any left at all.

As his body began to heal, Nagai's heart entered a time of deep mourning. Every day, he prayed—sometimes in silence, sometimes through tears—for Midori, the woman he had loved with all his soul, and for the countless others lost at the university hospital. In keeping with an ancient Eastern tradition, he let his hair and beard grow long, refusing to trim them as a sign of sorrow and repentance. But his grief didn't make him withdraw from the world. Instead, it gave him a new sense of direction—one rooted in the ashes of Urakami, the community he once called home.

Returning to the desolate land, he faced a haunting question: Was it still dangerous to live there? The invisible threat of radiation lingered in everyone's minds. Nagai had no scientific tools—no Geiger counter, no lab. But he trusted nature. When he saw ants crawling across the burnt ground, and earthworms moving slowly through the blackened soil, he took it as a sign. Life, however fragile, was stirring again. He believed the heavy rains of autumn had helped cleanse the land, washing away much of the fallout. Those terrifying rumors—that nothing would grow in Nagasaki for seventy years—were wrong. Life was already coming back.

With help from a few loyal friends, Nagai built a simple shelter. He gathered scorched wood and leaned it against the old stone foundation of his former home. They covered it with warped sheets of tin salvaged from the ruins. It wasn't much, but it was something. His children, still young and aching with loss, insisted on staying by his side. So together with their grandmother, they moved into that tiny hut—four people living amid what had once been a thriving community.

Urakami had been the heart of Catholic life in Nagasaki. Nearly 8,000 believers died when the bomb fell. But some survived—soldiers away on duty, travelers out of town, and those spared by chance. When Nagai reached out, calling on the survivors to return and rebuild, many did. One by one, other huts sprang up beside his, and a new village quietly took shape—born from ashes, but rooted in faith and hope.

Even the university, reduced to rubble, began to stir. Former professors, staff, and students gathered to dream of a new beginning. Nagai, still weak in body but alive with purpose, offered his ideas and energy freely. The bomb had shattered his health, but not his spirit.

He had chosen to live again on sacred ground—the very soil where Midori had perished. When asked why, he simply said, *"I needed to be here… to understand what all of this meant."* But not everyone shared his faith in the future. Whispers spread among some that the bombing was **tenbatsu**—divine punishment.

Still, Nagai didn't turn away. He stood in the ruins with his heart wide open, searching not for vengeance or answers, but for meaning. In the silence of Urakami, surrounded by death and loss, he chose life—and through that choice, he gave others the courage to begin again.

It was around this time that the local bishop made an announcement—there would be a public Mass to honor those who had died. He asked Dr. Nagai to speak on behalf of the laypeople. It was a simple invitation, but for Nagai, it reopened the deepest questions of his soul. What was the meaning behind such overwhelming loss? What was he supposed to say in the face of such destruction?

He didn't search for explanations—there were none. But he began to look for signs. Not answers, exactly… more like moments. Little glimmers of something greater than the horror they had endured.

One story wouldn't leave his mind. It was something almost ghostly, something sacred. Nurse Kosasa, along with a few of Nagai's colleagues from the radiology department, had told him what they heard just after midnight on the night of the bombing. Singing—soft and strange, carried on the still air. Latin hymns, they said. They were so exhausted, so shaken, they didn't know if what they heard was real.

But the next morning, they walked past the area where the voices had seemed to come from. Near a stream, they found them—the lifeless bodies of twenty-seven nuns from the Josei Convent. The bomb had obliterated their convent. Some had died instantly. Others had been fatally wounded. But before they passed, they gathered together by the water. And they sang.

That image stayed with Nagai: women dying in agony, their bodies broken—but their voices, strong and sure, lifting up a hymn. It wasn't a song of fear or despair. It was a song of faith. For Nagai, that was the beginning of something—a thread of meaning pulled from the rubble.

Another memory gripped him just as tightly. Junshin Girls' School—where his beloved Midori had once taught. The school was run by nuns who had been close to his family. As the war dragged on and air raids became a terrifying routine, the headmistress, Sister Ezumi, started a new daily ritual.

Every morning, the students would gather and sing a hymn of surrender to the Blessed Virgin Mary: *"Mary, Mother! I offer myself to you, body, soul, and spirit."*

As 1945 pressed on and hope grew thin, the girls sang louder, with more feeling. They didn't know what would happen, but they kept singing.

On August 9, the day the bomb fell, many of those same girls were working in factories outside the city—in Tokitsu and Michino. Some died instantly. Others were left with deep, gruesome wounds—glass embedded in their skin, limbs scorched by fire, their mouths dry with an unbearable thirst.

In the days that followed, Nagai heard reports. Injured Junshin girls, gathered in small groups wherever they could—beneath broken trees, under pieces of cloth, beside the river. They were dying, but they still sang. Whispering, gasping, struggling to breathe. Still singing their hymn to Mary.

That memory broke something open in him.

And so, when the day of the Mass came, and Nagai stood before the survivors in the ruins of Urakami Cathedral, he paused. The silence stretched long, heavy with grief. The people waited.

Then he began to speak—not with polished words, but with the quiet weight of a man who had lost everything and still chose to hope.

"Maybe it feels impossible to believe that anything meaningful can come from this," he said gently. "How are we—those left behind—supposed to look at this wasteland and see anything but suffering and sorrow? And yet… standing here, among the ashes, I see something else."

He looked out at the people, at their wounded faces, their tired eyes. Some had no homes, no families, no future they could imagine. But they had come.

"I think of the twenty-seven sisters from the Josei Convent," he said, his voice steadying. "They could have died in silence. But they didn't. They sang. I think of the girls from Junshin—brave, faithful, still clinging to that one simple hymn, even as they slipped away. That is not just death. That is a kind of offering. A sacrifice. A song."

He turned to look at what was left of the altar—once so beautiful, now just shattered stone and memory.

"Our cathedral was a place of peace," he said. "It stood for everything we believed in. Now it's broken. But even in ruins, it stands as proof of something greater—our faith has not died. It lives on. Not in safety, not in comfort, but in fire. And fire does not destroy faith. It refines it."

He paused again, his eyes wet, his voice soft but strong.

"This is what I believe," he said. "That in our darkest hour, when all light seems gone, there is still one flame that refuses to go out. And that flame—it lives in you, in all of us. This is the heart of Christianity. Not that we are spared from suffering… but that we are never alone in it."

Nagai's gaze swept across the crowd of survivors—some still wrapped in bandages, others leaning on crutches. But all stood, present and listening.

"It is not by accident," he began, "that Nagasaki, with its long history of martyrdom and suffering, was chosen to bear the weight of this tragedy. In the darkness of destruction, we've been given a new understanding of life, of suffering. And in that understanding, we find Christ—the Lamb who was slain. His sacrifice was not in vain. And now, we join His song."

He glanced down at the poem he had written earlier. Now, it felt less like a reflection and more like an offering. Slowly, clearly, he recited it:

Hansai no hono no naka ni utai tsutsu
Shira yuri otome moe ni keru kamo.
White lily maidens, singing as they were consumed in sacred fire—
a living sacrifice, pure, they gave their final song.

"I pray that we, too, may give our song," he continued, "a song of faith, a song of hope, a song of peace. And when the dust of Nagasaki's destruction finally settles, may we not see it as an end, but a beginning. A new beginning—where God's love shines through every dark moment, and we rise from the ashes, united, stronger than before."

He drew a breath, his chest rising with the weight of the moment.

"Today, we gather not just to remember, but to offer our lives to God as living sacrifices. And in doing so, we join the song of the martyrs—those who came before us, those who have fallen, and those who still rise from the ashes of this world. May we find, in our own suffering, the same grace that carried them through."

Nagai paused once more. Silence stretched over the cathedral ruins. Then, with a solemn nod, he concluded:

"May God grant us peace."

The crowd stood still, motionless. For a long moment, no one moved. Then a low murmur of whispered prayers stirred in the air, a quiet response from hearts too burdened for words. In the ruins of the cathedral, amidst loss and grief, the people of Nagasaki found a shared song—one of peace that could not be silenced.

Then came the deeper question, the one Nagai voiced with trembling sincerity:

"Could there be a sacred link between Nagasaki's destruction and the ending of the war? Was our city chosen—like a spotless lamb—to be offered in sacrifice for a wounded world, so that the bloodshed might finally end?"

He used the word *hansai*—a biblical term for a burnt offering, wholly consumed, completely given.

Not everyone welcomed his words. Some in the crowd stood up in protest, voices breaking with anguish, eyes burning with sorrow. Among them were parents who had lost children, widows left with only memories, and orphans whose world had collapsed in a moment. They could not bear to see this horror described with religious meaning.

Director Keisuke Kinoshita later captured this moment in *Children of Nagasaki*, a film based on Nagai's life. The grief in the crowd was raw, real, and wholly justified.

But Nagai did not flinch.

His expression remained calm, even gentle. He understood their pain—because he lived in it too. He had walked through that same valley of mourning.

In a steady, unwavering voice, he continued:

"We carry within us the ancient guilt of humanity—Adam's fall, Cain's violence. Again and again, brother has turned against brother. We have forgotten our Maker and chased after lesser things. We have allowed hatred to replace love. We have killed—and even rejoiced in the killing. This war was the end result of that long forgetting.

"And when it finally ended, it wasn't because we suddenly felt regret. Peace required more than that. It required something immense—something that could break the chain.

"Bombed cities alone did not bring that peace. It was only here, in Nagasaki, that a sacrifice deep enough was made. Only this act of *hansai*—this complete offering—was enough. And at that very moment, the Emperor declared peace.

"For more than 300 years, our Christian community in Nagasaki has remained faithful, even through terrible persecution. During the war, we prayed unceasingly for peace. In the end, it was this very community—devoted, enduring, pure—that became the offering on the altar. Not in vain, but so that millions of others might live."

Nagai often drew strength from his faith, especially its quiet rituals. One that remained close to his heart was the Easter Vigil. Every year, just before sunrise, they gathered in the cathedral, where a single tall Paschal Candle would be lit in the darkness. It was a silent, powerful moment. Thinking back to August 9, Nagai spoke of the fire that had engulfed the cathedral—not just as a loss, but as a sign.
"That blaze, rising at midnight, lit up the sky and broke through the darkness," he said. "Though our hearts were broken, in the midst of the loss, we saw a light pointing to something sacred—something pure and full of hope."

He ended his words by guiding people's thoughts to the places where Jesus once walked: to the mountain where He taught about blessings, and to the hill where He carried His Cross.
"Blessed are those who mourn, for they shall be comforted,"

he reminded them. "We are called to walk the path of justice, even when we are mocked, beaten, or bleeding. But we can lift our eyes and picture Christ on His way to Calvary. 'The Lord gave, and the Lord has taken away. Blessed be His name.' Let us not curse what has happened. Let us be thankful that Nagasaki became an offering. And because of that offering, peace came—not only to us, but to the world. With peace came freedom of worship for our country."

When he finished, the room fell silent. His way of seeing God's hand even in the suffering of August 9 touched everyone deeply. Later, when these reflections were published, they moved not only Christians, but many across Nagasaki and Japan.

Back at what now passed for a home, Nagai was starting a new chapter. It was just a rough hut—unable to keep out the wind, rain, or snow, as the coming winter would show. Doctors had given him only two or three years to live. But what worried him most was his children—a ten-year-old boy and a four-year-old girl. He was determined to use whatever time he had left to teach them how to stand on their own. Japan was broken, and only those with strength inside could survive. This simple shelter, bare as it was, would become their classroom.

He spoke of his plan to Gran. Still buried in grief, she didn't object.

Their first kitchen was an open fire. They had one iron pot—missing its handle—and a cracked clay jar. Two relatives who had lost everything joined them in the tiny space. At night, all six of them squeezed into the room, sleeping head-to-foot, sharing just a few thin blankets. The bomb had taken nearly everything, even most of their clothes and bedding. When winter came, wind and snow crept through every crack, yet strangely, no one fell ill. Nagai quietly wondered if the radiation had made their bodies tougher.

He noticed strange changes in the plants around them too. Wheat was growing fast and strong, but corn stalks rose up empty, without ears. Morning glories bloomed, but their petals were twisted and small. Green vegetables were doing well, but sweet potatoes, though quick to sprout, never gave a harvest.

One day, Professor Suetsugu—now leading the radiology department at Kyoto University—came to visit. He and Nagai had known each other for years, and since Nagai had taken over his old post in Nagasaki, they had much to talk about. But there was no proper place to welcome him. In traditional Japanese homes, a guest is shown to the room with the *tokonoma*—a quiet corner with a scroll and a sense of grace. Nagai's hut had no such place. It didn't even have a real floor.

Still, Suetsugu understood. He pulled out a brush and wrote a Chinese verse on a scrap of paper: "Not a single possession, yet infinite wealth dwells here."
Nagai smiled as he read it. The words matched the lessons he'd been teaching his children. Carefully, he pasted the paper to the wall. To him, it meant more than any scroll that had ever hung in their old home.

On another day, as Nagai and his son Makoto walked near a well, they saw an old man struggling to draw water. The well was still full of debris from the blast, and the man had to lower his bucket deep and pull with all his strength.
"You see, son?" Nagai said softly. "That's how life is for us now. We're scraping from the very bottom. But this is where we begin again—with faith and steady hands. God is walking this road with us."

Not long after, Nagai saw a young man standing alone, staring at the ruins of Urakami. He recognized him—a former member of the St. Vincent de Paul Society. The war had drafted him into the marines when he was just a teenager. He had survived brutal battles in the South Pacific, cut off from supplies, surviving malaria and near starvation. What kept him alive was the thought of coming home to care for his parents.

But now that he was back, all he found was ashes. His parents had been lost in the August 9 blast. He sat on a blackened rock where his house used to be and cried, like a child.

Nagai, watching nearby, walked over and gently placed his arm around him. He said nothing. After a while, the young man's sobs slowed.
"I survived hell in the jungle because I thought my parents needed me," he finally said. "But they're gone. Everything I went through… it feels like it was for nothing. I just want to leave this place. Forget it all."

"I understand," Nagai said gently. "It makes sense to want to run away. But if you do, their deaths and your pain will feel meaningless. If you stay—if you build something here, like we have—you'll keep their memory alive. Your suffering will have meaning."

The young man took those words to heart. He stayed. He built a small hut where his home had once stood. A year later, he came to Nagai, bowed deeply, and introduced the woman he was going to marry.

Getting pen and ink was nearly impossible, so Nagai began his first book with just a pencil. It wasn't a novel or memoir, but a medical record—a hundred-page account of what he had seen and done in the month after the bombing. His goal was simple: to help doctors in Nagasaki and Hiroshima treat the wounded. What made his writing different was that he wasn't just a radiologist—he was also a survivor. He had felt the blast, breathed the fallout, and received a double dose of radiation.

The book became the first medical report on the effects of the atomic bomb. It added real knowledge to the world of medicine.

While he worked, some friends encouraged him to remarry. There were many good widows, they said, who could help raise his children. Nagai considered it seriously, but in the end, he refused.
"The pain of losing a mother is heavier for a child than losing a father," he wrote. "My son and daughter still carry the warmth of their mother, Midori, in their hearts. Bringing another woman into their lives now would only make things harder."

There was another reason that touched his heart deeply. Both children looked like Midori, especially little Kayano. Every time he looked at them, he was reminded of her. Because of that, he knew he could never forget her or try to find someone else.

Even so, he believed Japan needed a book—something ordinary people could understand—that would explain the bomb and what followed. The idea came to him on Christmas Eve, in December 1945, while sitting with his friend Ichitaro Yamada.

Before the bomb, Urakami Cathedral stood tall with two towers. Each tower had a rounded top and a big bell inside. The northern dome had been blown far away by the explosion and landed deep in a nearby hill. Its bell was broken and couldn't ring anymore. The southern dome had fallen straight down. Its bell lay buried under piles of bricks, iron, and ashes.

Yamada had been stationed as a soldier on a nearby island when the bomb dropped. He hurried back to Nagasaki and found that his whole family—his wife, five children, and his parents—were all gone. No one survived. In deep sorrow, he went to see Nagai, unsure how to handle the pain. He let out his grief, speaking in anger. Nagai listened silently. Then, when Yamada had said all he could, Nagai replied. He, too, had lost the person he loved most. But instead of becoming bitter, he asked Yamada to see this tragedy through the eyes of faith. He believed God could still bring something good from all the pain.

With a gentle smile, Nagai reminded Yamada of his name, which meant "mountain field," and said, "Let's climb the Mount of the Beatitudes together." From that moment, Yamada was no longer just a friend. He became Nagai's companion and follower.

Later that same month, the two came up with an idea. They wanted to find the bell buried under the ruins of the cathedral. Maybe finding it would give people hope—a sign that something still remained. On December 24, Yamada gathered some young men and started digging through the rubble. By late morning, they could see the top of the bell. They stopped for a simple lunch, and Nagai led them in praying the Rosary. Afterward, they returned to digging. Bit by bit, they pulled the bell out. To their surprise, it wasn't broken. There were no cracks.

Using logs and ropes, they made a simple frame to lift the bell. It was dark by the time they raised it off the ground. As the sky began to brighten, they rang it—for the first time since the bombing. The sound of the Angelus rang out across Nagasaki on Christmas morning.

Nagai, Yamada, and the others hadn't told anyone about the bell. They weren't sure if it would work after being buried for so long. So they kept it a secret, not wanting to give false hope to the Christian community. That night, the people of Urakami were preparing for a very sad Christmas Eve. They were cold in temporary shelters, eating small meals, and waiting for a quiet midnight Mass in the burned-down Saint Francis Hospital.

Then something unexpected happened—something that changed everything. Out of the silence came the sound of a bell.

It rang clearly and beautifully. Because most of the tall buildings were gone, the sound traveled far. It cut through the night like a light in darkness. It was the Angelus, the same prayer they used to hear. For many, it felt like the old cathedral was alive again, telling the world that Christ was born. It touched people's hearts, like the shepherds who once heard angels in Bethlehem. That bell became the reason for the title of Nagai's new book: *The Bells of Nagasaki*.

His message was simple and strong—no power, not even an atomic bomb, could silence faith or the voice of God.

Even though he had very little paper and no proper place to write, Nagai started working on the book slowly. As he wrote, he realized it wasn't just his own story. He was speaking for the 72,000 people who had died and those who were still living—the widows, the orphans, the ones with broken hearts.

In *The Bells of Nagasaki*, Nagai's words are quiet but full of feeling. His writing shows the sadness, but also the deep hope that rose from the ruins. He didn't focus only on facts. He showed the pain and the strength of the people who lived through it. His book turns a terrible event into something deeply personal and emotional.

One moment in the book, with his daughter Kayano, is especially touching. It's simple, but it shows the sadness of a child who lost her mother. Many readers can relate to this—losing something important and wanting it back, only to realize it's gone forever. Nagai wrote in a way that speaks to all people. He helped readers feel that Nagasaki's pain was not just Japan's, but the world's.

Nagai also asked a question that still matters today: Now that we have this great power—atomic energy—how will we use it? Will we use it to heal or to destroy? He believed only real faith could guide people to make the right choice. Faith, to him, wasn't just a belief—it was a power that could shape lives, communities, and even decisions.

At the end of the book, Nagai kneels with his children and prays the Angelus. This simple act brings the story full circle. It's not about big ideas or deep philosophy. It's about love, prayer, and family—the small things that give people strength during hard times. Nagai believed that suffering had meaning and that God's love was always there. Through this, readers could see the strength of the human heart.

He wrote that without hope, people fade away. But hope isn't just a nice idea. It shows itself in real actions—in prayer, in love, in helping each other. For Nagai, prayer was like a light guiding people through the darkness. It helped them keep going, keep loving, and find meaning even in loss.

In a world filled with fear and uncertainty, Nagai's message stands firm: keep going, keep loving, and keep praying. Through true faith, people can move forward, together, with purpose.

Chapter 24

Nyokodo

Nagai's character truly comes to life in the decisions he made during the aftermath of the bombing. Amidst the wreckage and unimaginable suffering, he showed a strength and compassion that spoke volumes about his spirit. Despite facing his own severe health challenges, Nagai never wavered in his commitment to his community. He tirelessly worked to rebuild not just the physical structures, but the very heart of his people. His actions—selfless, enduring, and quietly powerful—are a testament to his faith and the deep love he had for those around him.

The effort to rebuild the church, beginning with a modest wooden structure, is so much more than just reconstruction—it's a symbol of Nagai's vision for his people. His focus on restoring the church first reflects his belief that faith is the foundation of everything, even in the face of total destruction. As he once said, "Our first task should be to restore our place of worship." These words aren't just about bricks and mortar—they're a reminder that spiritual healing and renewal are just as vital as physical recovery. The community's collective efforts, working together to haul logs and shape wood, became an act of shared healing, of finding strength together in the face of despair.

But Nagai's compassion went beyond just the physical. His involvement with Junshin Girls' School showed a deeply personal side to his character. Even as the scars of war lingered, Nagai dedicated himself to nurturing the young minds that would shape the future. Through his work there, he gave them more than just an education—he gave them hope. His ability to introduce humor, even in the darkest times, was a testament to his resilience. It wasn't just about lifting spirits; it was about showing people that there could still be light, even in the most tragic of circumstances. His unwavering optimism, fueled by faith in humanity's strength, inspired those around him to hold on to hope, even when the weight of sorrow seemed unbearable.

In Nagai's journey, we see not just a man enduring unimaginable hardship, but a leader who believed, deeply, in the power of faith, community, and the human spirit to overcome even the most devastating challenges. His life was a quiet but powerful testament to the strength that can emerge from even the deepest suffering.

Even as his health continued to fail him, Nagai's resolve remained unshaken. In the face of overwhelming physical pain, he refused to surrender to despair. His decision to keep writing, despite the severity of his illness, speaks volumes about his unyielding spirit. Nagai even devised a device to help him write while lying flat on his back, a testament to his relentless determination to contribute to the world. It was a quiet act of defiance against suffering, showing that even in the darkest personal struggles, one can still create, still offer something valuable to others.

His humility was equally profound. After receiving a financial award, Nagai could have built a comfortable home for himself, yet he chose not to. He never lost sight of the broader suffering of his community, always prioritizing their needs over his own. Instead of indulging in comfort, he planted cherry trees around Urakami—a simple, beautiful gesture that symbolized renewal, even in a community scarred by the ravages of war. It was an act of faith in the power of beauty to heal and inspire, reminding everyone that hope could still blossom amidst destruction. This seemingly impractical gesture was a powerful reflection of Nagai's belief that symbols of hope and renewal could rise even in the most impossible circumstances.

The community, recognizing his extraordinary selflessness, proposed to build him a proper home through the Saint Vincent de Paul Society. But Nagai's request for a tiny house, influenced by the ancient Eastern tradition of simplicity, revealed a deeper, personal philosophy rooted in spiritual humility. He didn't want grandeur. He wanted a modest, peaceful space where he could continue his life of service and reflection. His desire for a humble dwelling—despite all he had given—spoke volumes about his character: unpretentious, humble, and ever devoted to others.

Nagai's life after the bombing is a powerful story of resilience and faith. It's a testament to the unwavering belief that, even in the face of profound suffering, there is always something worth rebuilding. His actions—whether it was restoring his community, continuing his work despite illness, or planting symbolic seeds of hope—were guided by the same core principles: love, faith, and hope. These were the lifeblood of his existence, the forces that kept him moving forward even when the world seemed broken beyond repair.

The idea of retreating to a simple hut, a quiet space for solitude and reflection, had deep roots in Japanese culture, especially in Buddhist and Zen traditions. Nagai's vision of such a hut was shaped by these traditions. One of his greatest inspirations was Kamono Chomei, the 13th-century hermit and author of *The Ten Foot Square Hut*, a beloved work that celebrated simplicity, solitude, and spiritual growth. Like Chomei, Nagai cherished the idea of living simply, focusing on his spiritual journey, and being available to guide others in need.

When he asked the Urakami carpenters to build his hut, he knew exactly what he wanted: a modest space that reflected his values of simplicity and spiritual depth. The hut would be small—only two tatami mats, one for him and one for the children who would visit. It would have minimal furnishings:

just a single electric light, shelves for his Bible and writing materials, a crucifix, and a statue of Mary. There would be a narrow ledge for visitors to sit and talk with him, a space for shared wisdom and conversation. Though the physical structure was modest, the meaning behind it was profound—a quiet testament to Nagai's commitment to living out his faith and traditions in the humblest of ways.

Named *Nyokodo*, the hut's title carried deep significance. The word "nyo" means "just as," "ko" means "yourself," and "do" means "shrine"—a beautiful combination that evoked simplicity and reverence. For Nagai's Christian friends, the name immediately called to mind the Gospel's command to love one's neighbor "just as yourself." Nagai chose this name as a tribute to the selfless carpenters who had built his hut, seeing in their work the very spirit of Gospel love. Their craftsmanship, like Nagai's life, was grounded in faith, humility, and a deep care for others.

The hut was never intended to be a place of comfort. In the sweltering heat of Nagasaki, there was no fan to offer relief, and in the summer, the air buzzed with swarms of mosquitoes. Winter brought icy Siberian winds that slipped through the gaps in the sliding doors, chilling the space to its core. Yet, despite these harsh conditions, Nagai rarely spoke of these discomforts. Instead, he focused on the blessings of his humble refuge, finding peace in the smallest of details. He marveled at the beauty of the roses in the garden designed by Professor Kataoka, writing, "Even a garden designed by Professor Kataoka, look at those roses!" To him, roses weren't just flowers—they were a symbol of love, deeply embedded in Christian tradition. Despite the harshness of his circumstances, Nagai found joy in discovering new varieties, taking pleasure in the simple beauty of nature. Even in the most difficult moments, it was these small wonders that nourished his spirit.

In the spring of 1948, despite being weakened by his frail health and the swelling in his abdomen, Nagai moved into Nyokodo—a modest dwelling that would be his home for the rest of his life. His body, ravaged by the ravages of radiation sickness, stood in stark contrast to the strength of his spirit, which remained unbroken. It was in this isolated, simple space that Nagai truly embraced the life of simplicity and service he had always believed in. Surrounded by the quiet of his small hut, he continued to live a life of devotion, untouched by the demands of the world outside.

At this time, Mohandas Gandhi had become a revered figure across Japan. His philosophy of non-violence, simplicity, and self-sacrifice resonated deeply with the Japanese people. His commitment to living for others, his decision to forgo comforts and dedicate himself to serving the poor in New Delhi, made him a symbol of selflessness—a living example of love in action. There was a deep connection between the lives of Gandhi and Nagai: both had chosen paths of simplicity, rejecting material wealth in favor of lives driven by love, faith, and the service of others.

When Gandhi was tragically assassinated in January 1948, the Japanese media made a poignant comparison between the two men, dubbing Nagai "the Gandhi of Nyokodo." While some may have dismissed this comparison as sensational, it held deep significance for many. Gandhi had become a moral icon, a figure whose life embodied truth, compassion, and sacrifice. And even in his frail, diminished state, Nagai reflected those same qualities. Though his life was quieter, more secluded than Gandhi's, his unwavering devotion to others and to a higher purpose made him a symbol of the same selfless ideals. Nagai's life, though lived in the shadows of hardship and illness, shone brightly with the same light that had guided Gandhi.

Nyokodo, the small hut where Nagai had taken refuge, was more than just a place to live—it was a symbol of everything he believed in. Stripped of excess and luxury, this humble dwelling was deeply rooted in both the Japanese tea hut tradition and Indian Buddhist philosophy. One particular concept that resonated with Nagai was the idea of the "bare hut" found in the Yuima Sutra, a Buddhist text. This text speaks of the hut as a metaphor for shedding all that is unnecessary, creating a space that is open and receptive to the divine. For Nagai, Nyokodo wasn't just a shelter from the outside world—it was a sanctuary for his soul, a place where he could open his heart to God, seeking meaning and purpose even in his suffering.

His choice to live in such a simple, solitary space reflected his deep understanding of life—not as a quest for comfort or wealth, but as a journey of spiritual depth. In Nyokodo, despite the constant physical pain caused by his illness, Nagai embraced the wisdom found in both Buddhist teachings and the life of Gandhi: clarity and purpose come not from material abundance, but from simplicity and a commitment to serve others. Nagai's daily existence in his modest hut was a living testament to these values, as he found solace not in ease but in the quiet pursuit of faith, devotion, and selflessness.

The nickname "the Gandhi of Nyokodo" wasn't just a tribute to Nagai's lifestyle—it was a recognition of the spiritual power he found in his suffering. It was through his unwavering devotion to his community, his deep faith, and his simple, solitary life that Nagai became a beacon of hope for those around him. Just as Gandhi dedicated his life to serving the poor, Nagai gave everything he had to help rebuild his community, sharing his spiritual wisdom even as his own health continued to decline.

In the quiet of his humble hut, Nagai found profound truths: that it is in simplicity, faith, and love that we find enduring strength in a world broken by pain. His time in Nyokodo was not just a physical retreat; it was a deeply transformative spiritual journey—one that continues to inspire all who come to know his story.

Chapter 25

The Little Girl Kayano

Nagai's young daughter, Kayano, was a lively and affectionate child, instinctively trying to fill the void left by her mother's absence. Her deep love for her father, however, became a concern for his fragile health. One day, his doctor warned him, "If she runs to you and leaps into your arms, the pressure could cause your spleen to rupture, and that could be fatal. You need to stop her from being so affectionate." With a heavy heart, Nagai put up a small barrier next to his bed in Nyokodo. One afternoon, while he was resting, Kayano silently crept over to him, bent down, and pressed her cheek to his. Nagai, pretending to be asleep, listened as she whispered, "Ah! The lovely smell of my daddy."

His emotions surged. "You might think that a man with leukemia would be cold-hearted," he later reflected, "but when I heard those words, my blood rushed through my body as if alive. I knew my time was near, and I imagined Kayano, alone and grieving after my funeral, returning home, motherless and fatherless. I could almost hear her, years from now, burying her face in my empty mattress, trying to catch one last 'smell of my daddy.'"

Though his health was failing, Nagai found himself busier than ever. His writings, and the articles written about him, attracted visitors from all over Japan. Many sought his guidance, including some who were not Christians. Despite the increasing demands on his time, his sleepless nights were filled with anxiety about his children's future. The doctors had predicted he had only a couple more years to live, and he wondered how his death would affect Kayano and her younger brother. In his troubled state, he began writing letters to them, hoping to offer wisdom for their future. These writings would later form the foundation of two books, which would become bestsellers.

In these letters, Nagai shared his thoughts with a sincerity that reflected his deep love and care. He wrote, "You are young, and you've already lost your mother. There is no replacing that loss. While my death will leave you orphans, it is not the same as losing a mother. You will mourn, yes, and it's okay to cry, even to cry until your heart aches. But when you cry, cry before your Father in heaven, because we know from Jesus himself that those who mourn will be comforted. He promised us that. That is the message of the Sermon on the Mount, a place of answers and solace. Life can feel hard, like climbing a mountain in fog and rain, but when the clouds clear, you'll see a vast and beautiful landscape of peace, love, and meaning—things that endure and give purpose to our struggles."

Nagai continued, "Right now, I have little to leave you. This hut, Nyokodo, is all I can give you. But Jesus tells us to value our eternal selves more than anything material. We are children of the heavenly Father, and that gives us immense worth. Do you understand? You are more valuable in God's eyes than the sun, that star that sustains life on Earth. You are His children, and so are all those around you. Love them and trust in God's providence, and you will find peace. I've lived this, and I can tell you it's true."

"I must be honest with you, though," he went on. "You will face a difficult path as orphans. There will be times when you feel resentment toward your friends who still have both parents. You might also feel the pull of resignation, like you've accepted some cold, unfeeling fate. But don't fall into that trap. Life isn't about blindly accepting a fate that feels heavy and meaningless. It's about living with purpose and love, trusting that God's plan for you is full of care and grace. He has asked us to drink from a bitter cup. This is our path to peace, a way to be part of the great plan Jesus spoke of when he talked about the lilies of the field and the sparrows, who are so precious in the eyes of God."

"As a doctor, I had to give bitter medicine to my patients sometimes. I never thought, 'Poor thing, suffering so! Let's give him something sweet instead.' You understand this, don't you? We believe in a mighty God, one who doesn't offer us cheap comforts but gives us the pure, healing waters of life. Sometimes they seem bitter because our hearts are sick, but if you persevere, you'll see that He is preparing us for eternal life with Him and those we love."

Nagai concluded, "I'm sure you remember the fairy tale about the bluebird of happiness. When your mother passed away, your bluebird flew away with her. You won't find it again on this Earth, but in heaven, you will."

In his later work *Rozario No Kusari* (The Chain of the Rosary), Nagai painted a picture of Urakami as the day turned to dusk. Once a bustling neighborhood, it now lay in ruins, its landscape marked by the devastation of the atomic bomb. As the sun sank beneath the horizon, faint lights flickered from the small homes, and smoke rose lazily from makeshift stoves. During these quiet moments, Nagai's thoughts often turned to Midori. A deep sadness would descend on him, so overwhelming it nearly brought tears to his eyes. But Kayano, his daughter, never cried. Instead, she would sit silently as darkness enveloped their shattered world, her little face fixed on the bleak surroundings. She would bite her lip, lost in thought, as though the loss of her mother had carved a silence into her soul.

One afternoon, his brother Hajime's young daughter woke from a nap, still dazed, and asked where her mother was. Kayano, with innocent simplicity, answered, "In heaven." Just then, Hajime's wife entered the room, and the little girl, seeing her, rushed into her arms, calling out for her mother. Nagai watched as Kayano's expression shifted, her face clouded with confusion. She wandered over to the sliding paper door, stood there for a moment, and absentmindedly traced a line along its frame. This small, seemingly insignificant act spoke volumes to Nagai. Around them, the world was still in ruins, a constant reminder of the devastation. Kayano stumbled, scraping her knees as she fell, yet she never cried. When a dog chased her playfully, she ran into Nagai's room, her face contorted with fear, but not a single sound escaped her lips. This quiet resilience troubled him. How could his daughter not cry?

His hatred for the war and the bomb that had stolen so much deepened with every moment he watched her endure in silence. It led him to reflect on the nature of childhood, and in his writing, he shared these thoughts, hoping that one day Kayano would understand. "Our childhood is full of joy because we have the freedom to cry," he wrote. "When we cry, our mother is there to comfort us. Since your mother passed away, Kayano, I've often longed to weep. But as an adult, I can't cry the way a child does. A child with a mother can cry freely. I've worked in an orphanage, and I've seen how children who cry are often ridiculed. They learn to hold their tears back." He continued, quoting the words of Jesus: "Blessed are those who mourn, for they will be comforted." He reassured her, "You can always bring your tears to Him, and He will listen."

Nagai held great admiration for scientists—men like Pascal, Copernicus, Mendel, Pasteur, and Marconi—whom he saw as free spirits, humble and enlightened in their pursuit of knowledge. He found it infuriating when people claimed that science and faith were at odds. "If you read what the great scientists actually said," he wrote, "you'll see that's not the case. It's the critics who have never worked with test tubes, who use words but not experience, that create that false narrative." For Nagai, science was a sacred endeavor, one that deserved respect and purity. He believed that a scientist in a lab was no different from a monk in his cell. "Science is prayer," he declared. "In my own work, I've always approached it with a deep respect, a kind of chastity. The study of the atom and radiation, for me, was more than just work—it was a devotion."

He loved science not for the sake of progress, but because of the purity it represented. His departure from the university and laboratory was not marked by bitterness. He left them, and even Midori, without resentment—toward the Americans, or even toward God. His books and the people who knew him best speak of a man who loved deeply, yet harbored no anger, no bitterness. He "cared and did not care," they would say, embodying a paradox that defined his life.

Throughout his writing, Nagai often found solace in the stars and the constellations. Their constant presence in the night sky reminded him of the order and reliability that had guided travelers across the earth for centuries. The mountains, too, held a special place in his heart—whether it was the autumn storms, the winter snow, or the summer heat, the mountains stood firm, unwavering. These were the sacred places of his people, the locations of profound spiritual discoveries—mountains like Fuji, Yakumo, Hiei, and Koya. But there was one mountain that began to take on even greater significance in his later works: the Mount of Beatitudes. In one of his books, he wrote to his children: "Being poor in spirit and pure in heart may not lead to riches, but it will bring you something far more valuable—peace of heart." He repeated this message often, especially as gifts from his readers poured in, and he shared them with the impoverished community around him.

One of the moments that brought Nagai the most comfort during those difficult years came from his six-year-old daughter, Kayano. She had just started at Yamazato Primary School, a short walk from their home. One afternoon, when she hadn't come home even though school had ended more than thirty minutes ago, he began to worry. Then, he heard the soft shuffle of her little feet. She appeared at the door, carefully cradling a cup as if it held something sacred, something delicate, something worth protecting at all costs.

She quietly removed her shoes, stepping onto the tatami mat with the care of someone holding the world in their hands. Her eyes were fixed on the cup as if it were the most important thing in the room. Only when she had safely placed it on the shelf did she let out a sigh of relief.

Nagai, with a mixture of curiosity and concern, asked what she was carrying so carefully. A bright smile spread across her face as she explained, "Today at school, everyone got pineapple juice. It tasted so good, I thought it would help Daddy feel better, so I kept it safe until I could bring it to you." Her voice was full of sincerity, and as she told him how a boy had bumped into her earlier, causing a small spill, but how she had guarded every drop since, Nagai's heart swelled with emotion. This simple, childlike act of love struck him to his core. His eyes filled with tears at the pure kindness she had shown.

Life in their little hut was far from easy. The rainy season brought leaks that dripped down onto their floor, and cooking outside, exposed to the elements, was a constant challenge. As the year wore on, the biting cold of winter joined their struggles, and hunger became a familiar companion at their makeshift table. One evening, in desperation, Nagai caught a rat, cleaned it, and cooked it. It was a harsh lesson in the old Japanese saying: to an empty stomach, all food tastes good. But through all the hardship, there were signs of progress. When the carpenters built them a new home, Nyokodo, their lives began to improve.

Meanwhile, General MacArthur's leadership of the American occupation slowly began to transform Japan. His efforts to root democracy in the country and dismantle its military were met with a certain hope from the people. Yet, the Americans were wary of how the atomic bomb's story would be told. When a publisher sought permission to print *The Bells of Nagasaki*, MacArthur's office initially rejected it, fearing how the bomb's portrayal might affect the public. But by early 1949, a compromise was reached. The book would be published with a section detailing Japanese atrocities in the Philippines, a condition set by the U.S. military. Nagai reluctantly accepted, and the book was released on April 1, 1949, to immediate success. A year later, the film adaptation of the story, *The Bells of Nagasaki*, became a powerful cinematic moment for the Japanese people.

Japan, a country still reeling from the devastation of war that had claimed 2.5 million lives, found solace in Nagai's story of survival, faith, and resilience. As families across the nation mourned their losses, *The Bells of Nagasaki* resonated deeply, its themes of pain, hope, and the longing for peace striking a chord in the hearts of its viewers. The accompanying song became a massive hit, reflecting the raw emotions of a nation in mourning, yet yearning for healing.

Between 1945 and 1951, Nagai poured his soul into his writing, producing twenty books, several of which became bestsellers. One, *Reflections from Nyokodo*, delved into themes of peace and the fragile nature of the world's peace, particularly after the outbreak of the Korean War. His writing on atomic energy was especially poignant. Even though he died in 1951, just months before the explosion of the hydrogen bomb, his words about the future of nuclear energy continue to echo.

Nagai did not see atomic energy as an inevitable disaster but as part of the unfolding of the universe. He likened it to fire or electricity: powerful forces that could be used for both good and ill. He believed atomic energy could solve Japan's energy problems, a key concern that had played a part in leading the country to war. After having witnessed the horrors of war and the devastation wrought by the atomic bomb, Nagai hoped that nuclear energy could be a force for good, used responsibly by humanity. He envisioned a future where the world would live in harmony with the powerful forces of science, understanding their potential and the dangers they carried.

Though Nagai didn't live to see the full development of nuclear power, Japan began to harness its energy in the years that followed. The nation, still recovering from the scars of war, realized that nuclear power, despite its risks, offered a chance for a future beyond their dependence on imported oil. The Japanese understood the dangers but also recognized the need for innovation and progress in a world where old ways no longer sufficed.

Before the outbreak of the Korean War in 1950, Nagai had clung to a fragile hope that the sheer horror of nuclear weapons would prevent further conflicts. But the eruption of war in Korea shattered that hope, leaving him devastated. Despite his failing health—his body ravaged by leukemia, with a swollen spleen that pushed his heart out of place, high fevers, and bone-deep pain—he began work on a new book.

In this work, Nagai reflected on the global power struggle between the West and Communism. He set the stage by explaining how, in territories controlled by the Soviet Union and China, opponents of Communism were labeled "enemies of mankind," often imprisoned or sent to labor camps. In stark contrast, Nagai pointed out that the Western Allies, led by General MacArthur, had treated Japan differently. After Japan's surrender, MacArthur had overseen efforts to rebuild the war-torn country, feeding the Japanese people during the harsh winters and supporting the rehabilitation of their economy. He also respected Japan's traditions, including the role of the Emperor.

Nagai's reflections were not just about the past; they were about a future that seemed ever more uncertain. But even in his weakening state, Nagai's belief in the power of compassion, resilience, and the need for humanity to find its way in a new world burned brightly within him.

In the final days of the war, as the atomic bomb fell on Hiroshima, the Soviet Union entered the fray. They rounded up Japanese soldiers in Manchuria and China, forcing them into brutal labor camps in the desolate cold of Siberia. One of those soldiers was Nagai's brother, Hajime, who spent thirty harrowing months in one of these camps. When he finally returned, he shared with Nagai the unimaginable horrors he had witnessed—the brutal conditions, the suffering, and the staggering death toll. It was a stark contrast to the treatment of Japanese soldiers by the Western Allies, who, with the exception of those accused of war crimes, allowed them to return to civilian life with legal representation, a far cry from the Soviet treatment.

Nagai, now deeply reflective, poured his thoughts into his new book, urging those who felt drawn to the ideals of Communism to take a hard look at history and judge the system by its results. Yet, he was careful not to fall into the trap of anti-Western sentiment that was becoming prevalent in some peace movements. He wasn't swayed by ideological slogans. To Nagai, peace was a noble goal, but one that demanded a deep, responsible commitment—not one born from anger or political agendas. He cautioned that such movements, though outwardly peaceful, often concealed hearts filled with violence.

Nagai's stance wasn't popular, and he faced much criticism. But undeterred, he boldly advocated for the Sermon on the

Mount as the guiding principle for world peace. To him, a true Christian wouldn't demand that a Communist lay down his weapon before seeking peace. Instead, a Christian would approach without a weapon, ready to embrace, even at the risk of being harmed. He knew how impractical such an approach seemed, but he believed in the transformative power of prayer. It wasn't about wishful thinking—it was about connecting with the loving force that created the universe, a force that could turn the most impossible ideals into real possibilities.

In one of his writings, Nagai described how even children, kneeling and praying before the crib on Christmas, could experience true contemplation. Contemplation, he believed, was not reserved for mystics or ascetics. It was for everyone. Drawing from the Gospel, he quoted, "I thank you, Father, for hiding these things from the clever and revealing them to little ones." In the midst of the devastation of Nagasaki, in the wreckage of Urakami, he felt the profound presence of God. This divine presence, even in the heart of disaster, led him toward a deep and enduring peace.

Walking through the desolate ruins of Nagasaki, Nagai reflected, "Walking with God through Urakami's nuclear wasteland has taught me the depths of his friendship." To many, the nuclear cloud was a symbol of despair, but for Nagai, it became something profoundly different. It reminded him of the cloud that guided the Israelites out of Egypt during the Exodus. To him, the devastation of Nagasaki could one day give way to peace and renewal, just as the destruction of Jerusalem eventually led to the beauty of Zion.

Nagai's reflections were deeply shaped by the work of William Johnston, a specialist in Zen Buddhism and Christian mysticism, who saw Nagai as a mystic of peace for modern times. Johnston believed that Nagai's suffering and transformation birthed a theology of love and reconciliation, making his message resonate deeply with both Christian and Buddhist teachings. In *The Bells of Nagasaki*, Johnston placed Nagai among the great prophets, recognizing his unique contribution to the dialogue between human suffering, faith, and the looming threat of nuclear war.

This belief in peace, despite the most horrific of circumstances, was powerfully expressed through two paintings Nagai created while bedridden in his Nyokodo hut. One painting depicted the Virgin Mary, inspired by Murillo's famous depiction of the Assumption. The other was of his beloved wife, Midori, who had perished in the atomic explosion. In this painting, she was not draped in the flowing robes of the Virgin but wore the simple, wartime attire she had on when the bomb fell. And instead of standing on a cloud, Midori was shown on a mushroom cloud—an image that combined Nagai's personal grief with his unwavering belief in the possibility of redemption and peace, even in the face of utter destruction.

Chapter 26

His death (Fall of the Iroko)

In February of 1950, Nagai's health took a heartbreaking turn for the worse. His doctors were stunned as his white blood cell count skyrocketed to a devastating 390,000 per cubic millimeter—a number that left them with little hope for his survival. The gravity of his condition settled over the room like a heavy fog, and his family, gathered at his bedside, could feel the crushing weight of the moment. His younger brother, Hajime, had called them all together, knowing that time was slipping away. The air was thick with unspoken fears, and the family could only wait for what seemed inevitable.

Yet, even as death seemed so close, Nagai's spirit refused to surrender. With an unshakeable resolve, he refused to let despair steal the final moments with his loved ones. Drawing on a well of strength and courage that had always been part of him, he began to share stories from his time in the army—tales of his youthful misadventures, moments of humor, and the lighthearted side of life. His voice, warm and filled with the laughter of old memories, cut through the heavy silence. His family, gathered around him in grief, found themselves smiling, then chuckling, and finally laughing. The once oppressive sorrow in the room began to melt away, replaced by the soothing sound of joy. For a fleeting moment, the weight of the world seemed to lift, and in that space, there was a rare, shared peace.

Kataoka, Nagai's biographer, later reflected on this poignant moment as a testament to Nagai's extraordinary ability to bring light into the darkest of times. This resilience wasn't just a matter of facing his own suffering—it was a deep, abiding faith that allowed him to transcend his pain and lift the spirits of everyone around him. It was this gift of joy in the midst of sorrow that truly defined Nagai. It wasn't just strength—it was a reflection of the profound peace he had found within himself, a peace that never wavered, even when death was knocking at the door.

Those who knew Nagai often spoke with deep admiration of a remarkable trait that set him apart—his ability to find humor and hope even in the darkest moments. In times of unimaginable hardship, when most would have been consumed by despair, Nagai became a beacon of light. His blend of humor, unshakable faith, and unwavering positivity inspired all who crossed his path. It was this rare quality—his gift of joy in the face of suffering—that drew people to him. Even as his body deteriorated, his spirit remained unbroken, and his laughter became a powerful reminder of the resilience of the human soul. Nagai's ability to bring light into the shadows of life remains one of the most profound and enduring aspects of his legacy.

In the broader cultural landscape of Buddhist Japan, there was a deep spiritual practice rooted in the Nenbutsu—the repetitive chanting of "Namu Amida Butsu," meaning "I entrust myself completely to you, Amida Buddha." This simple, rhythmic prayer was woven into the lives of many, offering solace and strength. During the seventeenth century, when Christians in Japan faced brutal persecution, some prisoners—subjected to unimaginable tortures—turned to a similar form of prayer. As they were tied to stakes, immersed in freezing waters, or scalded in hot springs, they whispered the names "Jesus, Mary, Joseph," as a quiet plea for divine strength in their suffering.

For Nagai, in the final stages of his illness, this kind of prayer became an essential part of his life. On the toughest days, when fever wracked his body and his temperature soared to 102 degrees, his family would find him in a state of peaceful contemplation. Quietly, he would sit before his altar, softly whispering "Jesus, Mary, Joseph" in a rhythm that soothed his pain and connected him to something greater than himself. Even in the midst of his immense suffering, this repetitive prayer offered him comfort—a steady rhythm of hope that transcended the physical anguish he endured.

By 1950, Nagai's leukemia had taken a devastating toll. His bones were swollen with pain, a constant ache for which there was no relief. Yet, despite the overwhelming exhaustion and the relentless march of illness, his doctor was astonished by what he saw. Nagai, driven by an indomitable will, continued to work—steadily and with great purpose—on what many would come to regard as his finest work: *Nyokodo Zuihitsu* (Reflections from Nyokodo). His nights were short; he rarely slept past three or four in the morning. When he awoke, he would sip his coffee and dive into his writing, as though every moment was precious, a gift to be seized before it slipped away.

As he wrote, Nagai's thoughts increasingly turned to the martyrs of Nagasaki—old friends whose stories he had once chronicled. But this time, his approach was different. In *Nyokodo Zuihitsu*, the chapter dedicated to them was long, detailed, and filled with a depth of emotion that set it apart from anything he had written before. It felt more like a personal pilgrimage—an intimate exploration of suffering, sacrifice, and the search for meaning in the face of unbearable pain. In vivid detail, he described their brutal deaths, the silence that followed, and the unimaginable courage they displayed. But more than just an account of their martyrdom, this chapter was Nagai's own reckoning with his impending death, a way of making sense of the suffering he had endured and would soon face.

In the quiet of his writing, he found solace. He reflected on his own pain, the future of his two children, and the larger question of why suffering existed at all. And through these reflections, he found a way to believe—truly believe—that the martyrdom of the twenty-six in Nagasaki was not in vain. Their sacrifice, he wrote, was beautiful and meaningful, a testament to the strength of the human spirit, and to the power of faith in the face of death.

Nagai's deep reflection on the final moments of Paul Miki, one of the twenty-six martyrs crucified in Nagasaki, reveals a profound connection between his own suffering and the tragic beauty of sacrifice. Paul Miki's death, so rich in courage and faith, echoed the ideals of the samurai code—a code that values loyalty and honor, even unto death. This code, symbolized by the cherry blossom, reminded Nagai of life's fleeting nature, much like the petals of the flower that fall soon after blooming. While he recognized the dangers of such an ideal, he also saw its inherent beauty—a sentiment shared by early missionaries like Francis Xavier and Valignano, who understood the noble aspects of sacrifice.

Moved by Paul Miki's final song, Nagai felt inspired to compose his own farewell. But rather than drawing inspiration from the cherry blossom, he found solace in the white rose, a symbol of purity and quiet grace. The words of his poem, simple yet poignant, captured the essence of his spirit: "Goodbye, my flesh. I must now journey beyond, as the fragrance must leave the rose." It was a gentle acceptance, a surrender to the inevitable, wrapped in the quiet beauty of nature's own impermanence.

In early 1951, a spark of hope rekindled in Nagai's heart. He learned that the Jesuits were building a pilgrimage shrine at Otome Tooge, a sacred place for him, one that held memories of unimaginable suffering and resilience. This was the very site where Jinzaburo Moriyama, the father of the priest who had baptized Nagai, endured cruel tortures—burned by fire and frozen by ice—and where Nagai's own brother, Yujiro, along with thirty-five others, perished for their faith. For years, Nagai had discussed this "exile in

Babylon" with Jinzaburo and other survivors, knowing that someday he would write about it. Now, with this new development, he realized the time had finally come to share their story.

On April 1, 1951, Nagai began his work on *Otome Tooge* (The Virgin Pass), a book that would forever immortalize the place where Christians had suffered and died for their beliefs. In just three weeks, Nagai completed the 81-page book—a remarkable achievement considering the state of his health. By April 22, just three days before a massive hemorrhage paralyzed his right arm, the book was finished. Less than a week later, he passed away.

Otome Tooge would go on to play a key role in establishing Tsuwano as a significant destination for Christian pilgrims in modern Japan. Despite his failing body and mind, Nagai's determination to complete the book left those who witnessed it in awe. His lifelong passion for Chinese characters, once flawless in his writing, had now been marred by errors—errors that his friends understood as a result of the immense physical toll he had endured. Nagai, however, accepted this final suffering with a sense of peace, feeling it was fitting for someone who had written about martyrs.

The last words he wrote before his death were taken from Tertullian, an early Christian writer: "The blood of martyrs is the seed of Christians." These words, a final reflection of his life's work, would echo through the generations, reminding all who read them of the enduring power of sacrifice. As his own death drew near, Nagai made one final request: that his alma mater, Nagasaki University Hospital, observe the final stages of his illness, so that students could learn from his experience. But there was one final matter he wanted to settle before leaving his home at Nyokodo.

The statue of Our Lady of Peace, sculpted from flawless white Carrara marble, was a tribute to Nagai's unwavering commitment to peace. Its creation was inspired by his passionate writings, which called for global peace and the prevention of nuclear war. Before it was sent to Japan, the statue had been taken to Rome, where it was blessed by Pope Pius XII in December of 1950. The statue was meant to stand as a beacon of hope and prayer for all who passed by Nagasaki Cathedral. The cathedral administrator visited Nagai at Nyokodo, and together, they decided that it should be placed at the southwestern entrance of the cathedral, with plans for stonemasons to build a sturdy base to support it.

However, when the ship carrying the statue arrived in Kobe in March, it was discovered that the statue was missing. No explanation was given as to where it had gone. The loss of the statue was another mystery that weighed heavily on Nagai, adding to the many struggles he already faced. Despite the uncertainty surrounding its whereabouts, he remained focused on his mission for peace. Even as his health continued to decline, his mind remained clear, and he became increasingly vocal about the need for peace in the world. He often spoke with visitors, friends, and family, urging them to strive toward global peace, emphasizing the importance of justice, patience, and love. "A peace movement is crucial," he said, "built upon the foundation of justice, patience, and love, with individuals willing to sacrifice and undergo a change of heart. Without these qualities, we cannot overcome the selfishness that truly threatens peace."

As Nagai's body grew weaker under the relentless grip of leukemia, his thoughts increasingly turned to the suffering he had witnessed among the victims of the atomic bombing. He had once referred to them as "hansai"—sacrifices to be offered up to God with faith. Now, as he faced his own suffering, he saw himself as a living embodiment of hansai. His physical pain became an extension of his earlier reflections on the need for personal sacrifice in the pursuit of peace. Despite the severity of his pain, his spirit remained resolute.

Nagai's thoughts also turned to those who denied faith—atheists and agnostics. Having once been an unbeliever himself, he never lost his empathy for them. "We must keep praying for them," he said with a trace of sadness. "A scientist who believes we come from random mutations can never truly see the beauty of a rainbow. What a pity!"

By this time, Nagai's health had deteriorated significantly. His right arm was completely paralyzed, and he endured excruciating pain, the full extent of which only his doctor knew. Despite his suffering, Nagai's serene expression revealed none of the agony he was experiencing. He remained absorbed in prayer throughout the day, finding solace in his deep faith.

On the night of April 29, Nagai experienced a violent hemorrhage in his right thigh, which swelled massively. The pain was unbearable, and for the first time in days, he could no longer hide his suffering. His family, hearing his groans, knelt beside him, offering their love and support. They brought his bedridden sister to his side. She was horrified by his condition, and with tears in her eyes, she begged him, "Hold on, so many depend on you." Nagai, gasping with great effort, replied, "But it hurts so much. If only He would come quickly... Please, pray for me."

His doctor administered a dose of morphine, which allowed him to sleep for a few hours. Nurse Utako, who had become a constant presence by his side, stayed with him throughout the night. When he awoke in the early hours of the morning, his thirst became overwhelming. Nurse Utako offered him a drink, but Nagai, with great determination, refused. "No, I wish to receive the Eucharist today. I will wait until after that," he insisted.

"But Doctor, the sick are not required to fast," she gently reminded him.

"I know," he replied, his voice barely audible, "but I'll wait."

As time passed, Nagai kept asking what time it was. When Nurse Utako told him it was 5 A.M., he said, "Quickly, send my son Makoto to the cathedral. The priest must be awake by now. Tell him I want to receive the Eucharist." The priest came without delay. Even though he was weak, Nagai tried to bow in greeting. He listened carefully to the prayers and, with effort, bowed again before receiving the small Host. Then, he stayed still for fifteen minutes, silently giving thanks.

After the ceremony, Nurse Utako helped him drink a mixture of crushed strawberries, milk, and water to ease his pain. Soon, friends from the Society of Saint Vincent de Paul came with a wooden stretcher to take him to the hospital. As they lifted him, Matsuo-san, a close follower of Nagai, saw pain flash across his face with every small movement.

Nagai closed his eyes and pretended to sleep. But as the stretcher passed the window, he opened his eyes to look at Nyokodo—his home and place of prayer and peace. His eyes showed both gratitude and sorrow, just like Saint Francis of Assisi, who once looked lovingly at the city before he died.

That final look captured the deep love, sacrifice, and quiet strength that defined Nagai's life—a life fully given to peace, faith, and the belief that love could change the world.

The small group slowly made its way toward the cathedral hill. They stopped at the base where the missing statue had once stood. Nagai asked to pray there, looking at the empty pedestal with a painful expression. He spoke softly about the war in Korea, just across the Tsushima Straits, and asked everyone to pray for peace. After bowing toward the cathedral, he told them to continue. But the heat and emotion became too much for his weak body. Matsuo-san noticed something was wrong and asked how he was. "I've gone blind," Nagai answered. One man ran off and returned with a bottle of whiskey. Nagai gave a soft laugh, agreed to try it, took a sip—and his sight came back. They continued their journey.

When they reached the hospital, Nagai breathed in deeply and joked, "This place smells like a hospital." His friends laughed in relief. His old friend, Matron Hisamatsu, welcomed them and took them to his room. Matron Maeda came in next. When she saw Nagai's condition, she tried not to cry and covered her face with a handkerchief. Nagai smiled kindly and said, "Yes, this is our Matron Maeda—still as dignified as the empress!" Everyone laughed, even in that sad moment.

"Would you like us to sponge you down?" Hisamatsu asked gently. "Yes, my whole body, please," Nagai replied. He was asking to be bathed in the traditional way before death. His friends understood and washed him with great care and respect.

As evening came, more people arrived—doctors, professors, and family. They were glad to see Nagai looking better than before. The family stayed by his side and prayed together as night fell. The doctors said he was stable and encouraged them to rest. As they left, a small frown crossed Nagai's face, but he said nothing. His son Makoto and Nurse Utako chose to stay with him through the night.

At 9:40 PM, Nagai suddenly felt dizzy. He looked around the room, confused. "Where's everyone else?" he asked quietly as convulsions shook his body. In a low, strained voice, he said,

"Call the priest quickly." Utako told Makoto to run to the cathedral. She gave Nagai some Lourdes water, which he drank eagerly before falling unconscious.

A doctor quickly came in and gave him a stimulant. Nagai's eyes opened but were unfocused. He started to pray. "Jesus, Mary, Joseph…" His voice faded. He barely whispered the last words: "…Into your hands I commend my spirit." Utako handed a large crucifix to Makoto, who brought it to his father. Nagai's right hand, which had been limp, suddenly moved with strength. His left arm, which couldn't even hold a rosary before, lifted toward the crucifix. With surprising energy, he took it and said in a loud voice, "Inotte kudasai. Pray, please pray."

Then, everything became still. Matron Hisamatsu, who had seen many people die, said she had never seen a death like his—so intense, yet peaceful and quick. The priest from the cathedral rushed in, upset that he hadn't arrived in time for the last rites. The doctor, also shocked, said, "None of us expected this. There was no way to know it would happen so fast."

Hisamatsu spoke gently: "Dr. Nagai was worried that he might bleed badly at the end, like many patients with his illness. That would have upset his family. But it was a gift that he passed so quietly and peacefully." The priest, comforted, said, "Today is May 1st, the month of Mary. I don't think this is just a coincidence. I believe she came herself to bring him home to the Lord.".

Chapter 27

Funeral and Legacy

On the quiet afternoon of May 2, from 1:30 to 5:30, a team of doctors and professors gathered around the body of Dr. Takashi Nagai to conduct his autopsy. These weren't just any doctors—they were top experts: university professors, department heads, and officials from the Atomic Bomb Casualty Commission. Their mission was to understand how this extraordinary man had died. But what they found left them stunned. Dr. Nagai hadn't simply passed from old age or exhaustion—he had died of heart failure caused by the advanced stages of leukemia. His body had been carrying a burden far heavier than anyone could have imagined. His spleen alone weighed an astonishing 7.5 pounds, when a healthy one weighs just over 3 ounces. His liver was four and a half times its normal size.

And yet, through all of that, Nagai had still found the strength to write—*to finish two final books*. The doctors could only shake their heads in disbelief. How had he endured so much? How had he kept going?

After the autopsy, Nagai's friends gently placed his body into a simple pine coffin—modest, just as he would have wanted—and carried him back to Nyokodō, the tiny home where he had lived, prayed, and healed. As they neared the house, people began to gather. The crowd grew. Neighbors, friends, strangers—drawn to this humble hut by love, sorrow, and a deep sense of gratitude.

And there, at the foot of the coffin, collapsed young Makoto, his son. He had been strong throughout his father's illness, a quiet pillar. But now the wave of loss hit him full force. He threw himself onto the coffin and wept, crying out, "Look, Daddy, look! Look at how much everyone loved you!" His voice broke hearts.

Beside him stood Nagai's younger brother, Hajime, with his wife, Takako, and their children. They paused to take a photo—more than a keepsake, it was a silent vow. Hajime, who had walked beside his brother in life, now promised to walk beside Makoto in his place. He would be the father figure the boy had lost, a thread that would hold the family together.

The next day, May 3, the city of Nagasaki came to a halt. At Urakami Cathedral—the same place where Nagai's journey in faith had begun with a Christmas Eve Mass in 1932—his funeral was held. Twenty thousand people came. Twenty thousand hearts beat with grief and reverence. The church overflowed. The streets outside swelled with mourners.

At 9:00 a.m., Archbishop Yamaguchi began the Latin Requiem Mass that Nagai had always held dear. When the final absolution was read, the mayor of Nagasaki approached the coffin. With solemn grace, he bowed deeply to Nagai, then again to the archbishop, and finally to the sea of people around him. Then, with a heavy heart, he began reading aloud the messages of condolence—three hundred in total. One came from the Prime Minister. Each word, each message, was soaked in emotion. It took him ninety minutes.

Then came the holy water. The archbishop sprinkled it over the coffin, followed by Nagai's family and the mayor. Just as the sprinkler was returned to the altar, the cathedral bells began to chime—*12 noon*. It was as if all of Nagasaki had stopped to breathe with that moment. The Angelus bells rang, but they didn't ring alone.

From every corner of the city, other bells joined in. Church bells. Temple gongs. Factory whistles. Boat horns from Nagasaki Bay. Sirens. All rising together in a strange, beautiful harmony—a city singing its final goodbye.

And then, one full minute of silence.

No footsteps. No voices. Just stillness. A sacred pause. One breath held by an entire city in honor of a man who had become its symbol of peace, of suffering transformed into love.

At Yamazato Primary School, not far from the cathedral, where Nagai had once served as a friend and guardian, the children froze mid-lesson. When the bells fell silent, their sobs could be heard. Teachers wiped their eyes. They remembered him not just as a doctor or a writer, but as someone who had truly cared.

Nagai had lived humbly, served quietly, and loved fiercely. He was the "poor man of Nyokodō," but to Nagasaki, he was a giant. A man whose strength defied science, whose heart embraced a wounded city, and whose death stirred an entire nation. His final journey was not just a farewell—it was a legacy etched into the soul of Japan.

As the coffin was carried out of the cathedral to the slow, solemn music of *In Paradisum*, the funeral procession began its walk to the cemetery, about a mile south. From above, the archbishop watched the long line of mourners. He was deeply moved by what he saw—a sea of black kimonos, gently softened by the white veils worn by Catholic women. One person watching the scene was so struck by its beauty that he imagined the heavens might open and Beethoven himself would descend to lead the funeral march.

Dr. Nagai's body was buried beside Midori's in a small garden plot, cared for by the city. It was just a short walk from the Urakami train station and close to the western entrance of Gaijin Bochi, the "foreigners' cemetery."

Nagai had chosen the gravestones himself. Midori's stone carried Mary's words to the angel Gabriel from the Gospel of Luke: "I am the handmaid of the Lord. Let it be done unto me according to thy word." On his own gravestone, Nagai had selected another verse from Luke, chapter 17, verse 10: "We are unworthy servants; we have only done what was our duty."

Thirty-four years later, I found myself standing by those graves. I was with a man I had only met the day before. He had opened up to me quickly, eager to share his story. Though he had never met Nagai in person, he called him his *onshi*—his spiritual teacher. He told me, "After the war, I was full of anger. I felt betrayed by our leaders and everyone who had told us that Japan could never be defeated. The future looked dark. Then, one day, I found a book by Dr. Nagai in a library. Here was a man who had suffered more than most of us, yet he still spoke of hope. His writing made me question everything: Was life meaningless? Were human efforts and values pointless? Or was there a greater plan, a good God, even when life feels unbearable? Dr. Nagai's words pushed me to take Christianity seriously. I later became a Christian and was baptized."

The man, now a high school science teacher, often visited Nagasaki on pilgrimages—first to Nyokodo, then to the graves of Takashi and Midori. As we stood there, sunlight filtered through the trees. The light danced on the ground like gentle waves. A cool breeze from the harbor passed through, making the leaves sway, casting shifting shadows that looked like nature's own ballet.

Earlier that week, I had attended a seminar on nuclear war. One of the speakers said something that stuck with me: photosynthesis, the process triggered by sunlight in plants, is essential for all life. He added something strange: "The same process that produces sunlight is used to trigger the hydrogen bomb."

I asked my friend if this was really true. He nodded and said, "Yes, it is. At the center of the sun, hydrogen atoms fuse under extreme heat and pressure, turning into helium. This reaction gives off a massive amount of energy, including the sunlight we depend on. The sun uses about a hundred billion tons of hydrogen each day. It will keep burning for millions of years. But without the perfect distance between Earth and the sun—and the shield of our atmosphere—that sunlight would be deadly."

He went on to explain the science behind the hydrogen bomb. "The bomb works in a similar way. First, atoms like uranium or plutonium are split through fission. This creates the heat and pressure needed to trigger fusion. The result is a much bigger explosion. The bombs dropped on Hiroshima and Nagasaki used fission, which is less powerful than the fusion used in hydrogen bombs."

I had no technical knowledge to add, but I wanted to share something that had been on my mind. "Dr. Nagai often wrote about St. Francis of Assisi," I said. "I once visited Assisi and met a Franciscan there. He told me something I think also applies to Dr. Nagai. In his *Canticle of the Sun*, St. Francis calls the sun and wind his brothers, and the moon and water his sisters. Later, when he started going blind, doctors from Rome tried to help him. Their solution was to press red-hot iron plates to his head. After this painful treatment, Francis added a new line to his prayer. He praised Brother Fire, calling him 'beautiful and cheerful, strong and mighty.' It's easy to see God in soft sunshine or gentle rain.

But Francis—and Nagai—could see God even in fire, storms, cold, and pain. If St. Francis lived today, maybe he would've added a verse about Brother Nuclear Fusion, don't you think?"

My friend nodded. "Yes. Both St. Francis and Dr. Nagai could see the divine in nature—not just in its beauty, but even in its danger. Modern poets often struggle with life because they only see the physical world. But the Franciscan way sees more. It sees the universe as connected, meaningful. Dr. Nagai loved the old *Manyoshu* poems from Japan, especially their focus on romantic love. But as he studied and thought more deeply, he saw something was missing—a spiritual side to love. Without that higher love, even the most passionate relationships can lead to pain. Nagai understood the kind of love St. Francis had for St. Clare—a love beyond the physical. So when he found the burnt body of his beloved Midori, he did not fall into despair."

He continued: "That's why Dr. Nagai told the story of the hen and the egg. A hen finds an abandoned egg and, moved by compassion, sits on it through wind and rain. When the egg hatches, a duckling comes out. It waddles away to the pond without even a thank you. For Nagai, this story had a clear lesson: everything we have—our lives, our health, our families, our talents—is a gift from God. So we must never take others for granted. We should serve them joyfully. Nagai, like St. Francis, had a deep love for life and nature, but he was also ready to let go of them peacefully because he saw beyond them—to the One who gave them."

Then, after a quiet moment, my friend turned to me and asked, "We're standing by his grave here in Nagasaki. Would you mind if I sang *The Bells of Nagasaki*?" This song, written by Hachiro Sato and set to music by Yuji Koseki for the first film about Dr. Nagai, had become well-known in Japan. It was deeply emotional, much like the Irish song *Danny Boy*. I smiled and said, "I'd be honored."

He began to sing. His voice was strong and clear. Birds that had been perched nearby flew off at the sudden sound.

The first verse floated across the quiet graveyard:

"From a glorious blue sky,
Sorrow came that rent my heart.
This life of ours is as unstable as the waves,
As impermanent as wild flowers in the field!"

Then came the chorus, gentle and comforting:

"Ah yes, but they still ring out,
Comforting and encouraging,
The Bells of Nagasaki."

The song went on, full of feeling—about loss, memory, and beauty found even in sadness:

"She died alone, my wife, called to heaven before me,
Leaving me as keepsake her Rosary.
Now it glistens with my tears."

Another chorus followed, then more verses:

"That funeral Mass!
Under a sky that wept in mourning,
A moaning wind for our hymns.
I clutched the cross fashioned for her grave.
The sparkling sea was gray with grief."

In the final part of the song, the words turned inward—toward sin and grace:

"There I bared my soul in its sinfulness.
Night fell, its darkness softened by a clear moon
And the statue of the holy one, Mary,
Fixed to a wooden beam in my poor hut."

As the last notes faded, I thought of Nagai's life. He reminded me of Dag Hammarskjöld, the former UN Secretary-General, who died in 1961. Both men wrote deeply about peace. Both loved the simplicity of haiku. I imagined Hammarskjöld might have written a verse for the women of Nagasaki who sang as they died. And I imagined Nagai might have written something like Hammarskjöld's words in *Markings*: "For all that has been, thanks. For all that will be, yes."

Both men had walked a similar path—from doubt to faith, from questions to deep trust in the God of the Bible.

Printed in Dunstable, United Kingdom